TAMING THE MOUSE

How a Small Hong Kong Theme Park Came to Dominate Disney

10 Lessons That Will Turn Your Business into a Success

Tom Mehrmann
and
Michael Switow

National Library Board, Singapore Cataloguing in Publication Data

Name(s): Mehrmann, Tom, 1959- | Switow, Michael, 1967-, author.

Title: Taming the mouse: how a small Hong Kong theme park came to dominate Disney : 10 lessons that will turn your business into a success / Tom Mehrmann and Michael Switow.

Other title(s): Taming the mouse: how a small Hong Kong theme park came to dominate Disney : ten lessons that will turn your business into a success

Description: First edition. | Singapore : Switow Media : Themed Attractions, [2018]

Identifier(s): OCN 1054887199 | ISBN 978-981-11-9055-1 (hardcover) | ISBN 978-981-11-8981-4 (paperback) | ISBN 978-981-11-8982-1 (ebook)

Subject(s): LCSH: Success in business. | Entrepreneurship. | Small business--Management.

Classification: DDC 650.1--dc23

Cover design by Cover design by James Eric Jones, jamesericjones.com
Edited, in part, by Author Connections, LLC
Typesetting and e-book conversion by BookCoverCafe.com
Photo Credits: Photo of Michael Switow by Bernard Lim; photo of Tom Mehrmann by Michael Switow
Harry's View political cartoons are reprinted with permission from the artist, Harry Harrison

Taming the Mouse is dedicated to leaders seeking ways to transform their business when faced with seemingly overwhelming odds against them — new competition entering the market, declining revenue and profit, naysaying analysts and even sentiments from colleagues and others within the company that the business is doomed.

CONTENTS

Hong Kong's 'Mouse Killer'

by Allan Zeman

As I waited backstage for the media launch of a new attraction — the first to be designed and built since I had become chairman of Ocean Park Hong Kong's board two years earlier — I felt absolutely ridiculous. Beside me were four little schoolgirls, each dressed like a giant jellyfish. On their heads were bright over-sized bell-shaped hats with flowery warts and long tentacles extending to the ground. The full-body costumes were radiant — bright pinks and pastel blues — with 3D scaly patterns. They wore textured pink gloves. The only human part that you could see were their cute faces.

I was dressed exactly the same.

Looking into the mirror, I thought "I can't go out there like this!" But then I turned to my chief executive, Tom Mehrmann, and said, "Well, let's do it!"

I had hired Tom soon after joining the board, so this was his first Ocean Park opening too (we would have many more over the years to come), but at least he didn't look absurd.

As we emerged from behind the screen, there was a moment of silence and shock, before the press went wild. The media's gasps were quickly followed by uproarious laughter and the flashes of their cameras.

How did we get here? How did I end up dressed so outrageously, so vulnerably, in front of the world?

There's no short answer to these questions, but the most immediate is that about a week earlier, I met with Ocean Park's marketing team and asked how they planned to promote Sea Jelly Spectacular. We had designed this attraction to keep the company in the public eye, in the face of competition from one of the world's most-dynamic entertainment giants, The Walt Disney Company. Disney had opened Hong Kong Disneyland several months earlier, and the Sea Jelly Spectacular, which made innovative use of theatre lighting, mood music and visual effects, was a way of letting the public know what else we had in store.

In response to my question, the marketing team replied that they planned to dress up four little girls as sea jellies.

"If I was chairman of a bank, I would wear a suit and tie to the launch," I told them. "But we're a theme park, not a bank. I should dress for the occasion. Make me a sea jelly costume too."

They looked at me like I was out of my mind.

"Are you sure?" they asked.

I didn't hesitate, well, not until I looked into the mirror on the day of the event.

The next day, though, I was on the front page of every newspaper in Hong Kong. The story was carried in papers from Bangkok to Seattle. To this day, you don't have to look too hard to find the sea jelly photo, or another one of me dressed outrageously at the park.

You can't buy advertising that good, at least not on our budget.

❖

The Sea Jelly Spectacular debuted in April 2006, about six months after Hong Kong Disneyland opened its gates. Not quite three years earlier, Hong Kong's Chief Executive asked me to join Ocean Park's board, as its chairman. Disney had inked a deal with Hong Kong, and the future of the city's 26-year old marine park appeared bleak. I didn't know a thing about the theme park business, and I hadn't been to Ocean Park in years. When I finally visited it again, I found the paint peeling and the food inedible. Morale was low. It felt like the park was going under. But when I rode the cable car, I fell in love with the place. The sea views were amazing. No other theme park in the world has such a good view. We had to save it.

Since 1977, Ocean Park had been the only attraction in town. But faced with competition from the world's biggest and best theme park brand, Ocean Park had to become world-class if it were to have any chance of surviving. We didn't have Disney's money, though, so we needed to think differently. No problem there. What you need to understand about me is that I don't play by conventional rules. Disney, in my view, is stand-offish. They do things the normal way. I bring an unorthodox approach to business. In my world, there is only first-class. I won't accept business or economy.

My background is in fashion and entertainment. For Ocean Park to succeed, I knew we needed someone with a fluent understanding of the attractions industry. I needed a chief executive I could trust to transform the park, and who in turn could win back the trust and love of the Hong Kong people.

From the first moment I set eyes on Tom Mehrmann, I found him to be well-grounded. He had a world of experience, leading projects in the US and Europe. When the Board and I interviewed him, he answered every question in a thoughtful, intelligent manner that demonstrated great sensibilities and insight.

Over the years, as I've worked with Tom and watched him, I've learned that he's a truly excellent leader . . . and an excellent man. His staff love and respect him. They look up to him, as do his peers. He was able to heal divisions within the company, while executing the park's redevelopment flawlessly. He also adapted to my style quickly. We made a great duo. While I was often the public face of the park, in interactions with the media and government, Tom led it internally.

When he decided to step down as Ocean Park's CEO after twelve years in the role, and two years after my term as chairman came to an end, shockwaves rippled through the company.

"My staff asked 'What have we done to make Tom leave?' Was he pissed off and decided to go?' I told them 'No, this is absolutely not the case'. We really felt shocked and devastated," recalls Ocean Park's executive director for revenue, Joseph Leung, who worked with Tom for more than a decade.

"When the announcement about Tom not renewing his contract went out in October, the reactions were very very strong from my staff, including part timers who only come in at Halloween and have put makeup on alongside him," adds the company's chief of operations and entertainment, Todd Hougland. "On Facebook, there were people who don't even work here anymore expressing dismay. People were really emotional, just thinking about Tom not being a part of Ocean Park."

There's no better testament to Tom's leadership, perhaps, than listening to his direct reports describe Tom's impact on the company and their own professional development. Five members of his executive team, including Leung and Hougland, sat down for tea with a reporter[1] to discuss Tom's legacy. They met in Neptune's, a sustainable seafood restaurant with an awesome view into Ocean Park's Grand Aquarium. Here are some excerpts of their conversation:

"Tom is a calm, empowering leader," says Walter Kerr, a proud Scotsman who has overseen the successful on-time within-budget completion of the company's redevelopment projects.

---

1 That reporter, Michael Switow, is a co-author of this book.

"He is exceptionally patient and insightful. His leadership style is embracing. He expects the people he selects for a position to be capable of doing it. If I were being mischievous, I'd say he's selected us, even though most of the team was here before he arrived."

"I've worked for four different CEOs at Ocean Park. Compared with his predecessors, Tom really goes into the workforce and gets to know people," notes Matthias Li, Tom's deputy and successor. "He promotes a harmonious organization and looks after the welfare of the staff. That's why he's so well-liked. Not many CEOs can do this. He's very attentive to the staff needs."

I noticed that as well. When I first visited Ocean Park, the staff uniforms looked like they were from the 1950s, and not in a good retro-sort-of-way. Ocean Park needed to look like it was *in* business, not going out of business. Tom realised this right away. When he upgraded the uniforms, you could immediately see the change in people's disposition. They began to feel important and proud to work in Ocean Park. This is key. The staff needs to feel happy. If they're not, you can't expect guests to feel comfortable. Tom and I both understood that software drives the hardware, and in a corporate setting, software consists of your people. Back at Neptune's, Li observes that he had never seen Tom get angry:

"You might feel he is upset," he says, "but he never shows any anger, which for Chinese, is a very good virtue. I thought I have very good patience, but at certain points, there's a breaking point. He doesn't have that."

"Tom is like Superman," chimes in Leung. "I've never seen him sick. For me, he knows everything. He's generous. He always tells you what's on his mind. He starts with the end result, then gives you the latitude to achieve it. He's very supportive of the whole team. He's forgiving if you make mistakes, as long as you don't do it again. He always told me to 'put my shortcomings in my pocket, not on the table'. He really has a talent for pulling out the best in people."

"He really wanted us to be a learning organization," explains Vivian Lee, who has 17-years' experience in the park and currently leads the company's sales and marketing team. "He accepts risks and encourages innovative ideas. In my department, we always want to try new things. Tom has no hesitation for this. At the same time, he always reminds us to be culturally relevant. I've seen some Westerners who apply their own thinking from elsewhere. When Tom has an idea, even after all these years in Hong Kong, he still asks if it's relevant to the local Hong Kong culture."

"He has this look, and when you see it, you know he wants you to solve a problem," Kerr continues. "At the same time, he has a deep grasp of the details of my profession, project development, which is pretty unusual for the C-suite. The Tom-Allan duo has really underpinned Ocean Park's success. I consider myself lucky to have had him as a boss for eight years; he's probably a once-in-a-career boss."

"He's a team builder. He brings everyone into the fold. He doesn't lead from arm's length. We laugh and cry together. He's broken down silos that may have existed in the past. He's very supportive, driving, facilitating, encouraging," says Hougland, who worked with Tom on projects in California and Spain, before moving to Hong Kong. "Tom transformed Ocean Park, from an aspirational organization to an expectation-based organization. We expect to be delivering high standards; we don't just hope to do so. He and Allan really pushed this."

❖

After I hired Tom and he started work, I asked him to show me the world's best theme parks, particularly those with marine animals like Ocean Park. We visited aquariums in Okinawa, Osaka and Yokohama, as well as Tokyo DisneySea and Universal Studios Japan. In the US, we went to Atlanta to see what was at the time the world's largest aquarium, then to Monterey Bay to visit a marine attraction, which like Ocean Park, is situated on the coast.

On that trip, I saw that most aquariums are designed by engineers. They're flat cement boxes with acrylic windows. Efficient, but not exciting. Ocean Park was going to build a new aquarium, and we wanted it to stand out. Instead of a normal building, we took inspiration from Frank Gehry, and I'm proud of the end result in Ocean Park's Aqua City.

Tom helped me realise that Disney was not the competition. They're a totally different type of attraction. At Ocean Park, walk into an area called the Hong Kong Jockey Club Sichuan Treasures and one day you'll find the giant pandas cuddling. Another day, they might be fighting or lazing in a tree. You begin to expect the unexpected. At Disney, on the other hand, every day is the same. Their attractions are all mechanical.

While we focused on becoming world-class, Tom showed me that Ocean Park also needed to differentiate itself.

The media used to ask me, 'What's the difference between Ocean Park and Hong Kong Disneyland?'.

"Disney has the fake mouse. We have the real one," I would reply.

By 2007, it was clear that the reports of Ocean Park's demise were premature. In fact, we were routinely dominating Disney. Choose your metric — attendance, profitability, community engagement and impact — the little park that could was clearly on top. In February of that year, Forbes Magazine ran a piece dubbing me the 'Mouse Killer':

On a day last week when Mickey Mouse was looking increasingly lonely in Hong Kong, with Walt Disney reporting that attendance had dropped at Hong Kong Disneyland in the last quarter of 2006, Allan Zeman, chairman of competitor Ocean Park Hong Kong, was literally floating on air, arriving at his aquatic-themed amusement park in a giant helium balloon to launch its newest attraction. The famed Hong Kong entertainment tycoon had every reason to be ebullient after a year in which Ocean Park set records for attendance and profit[2].

Subsequently, Ocean Park was recognised by a panel of international judges to be one of the world's best theme parks, an honour yet to be bestowed on Hong Kong Disneyland.

Fast forward to 2017. Economic conditions in Hong Kong are challenging. Twenty years after the handover from Britain to China, the political atmosphere can be trying at times too. But Tom and I left Ocean Park in the best state imaginable:

- Fiscally sound (with nearly US$300 million in cash reserves in the bank, plus financing secured for capital developments)
- With a clear vision, and construction underway, to transform the park into a destination resort
- Easier to reach, with the opening of a new train line and
- Ingrained in people's hearts.

While I regularly meet folk who tell me that they prefer Ocean Park to Hong Kong Disneyland, the park's triumph over an international behemoth was far from guaranteed.

Tom's steady leadership — and a set of principles that any business can apply, regardless of its industry — made all the difference. He drove the company to aspire for success, based on well-defined objectives, values and metrics. Then, when these goals were met, success became an expectation.

---

2   Kwok, Vivian Wai-yin, "Allan Zeman: Hong Kong's Mouse Killer", Forbes Magazine, 13 February 2007.

I'm proud of the work that Tom Mehrmann and I did together. I'm even prouder to be able to call Tom my friend.

Allan Zeman
Chairman, Lan Kwai Fong Group
Former Chairman, Ocean Park Hong Kong (2003–2014)

INTRODUCTION

'Thrill Ride into Debt?'

Hope is Not a Management Concept

On 2 November 1999, Hong Kong Chief Executive Tung Chee-hwa announced that his government had signed a US$3.2 billion deal with The Walt Disney Company to create China's first Disney resort.

Not quite six years later, on 12 September 2005, Hong Kong Disneyland opened to the public.

Amidst the excitement of Disney coming to town, the impact on Hong Kong's homegrown theme park seemed an afterthought. Ocean Park was a popular family destination, though it had seen better days. Opened in 1977 with an aquarium and rides on the mountainous southwest coast of Hong Kong Island, Ocean Park expanded over the years, adding outdoor water slides and welcoming giant pandas from China. The marine park's high water mark coincided with its 20th anniversary, when it welcomed nearly 3.8 million people, alongside the euphoria and celebrations marking Hong Kong's return to China in 1997 after more than 150 years of British rule.

But then came Bird Flu and the Asian Financial Crisis. Tourists stopped crossing the border; Hong Kongers stayed home. In 1998, Ocean Park went from a HK$85 million surplus to a deficit of the same magnitude: a HK$170 million (US$22 million) swing. Three more years of losses followed. A rebound was cut short by the SARS epidemic. Now on top of that, Ocean Park faced the prospect of impending competition with Disney — a global giant with deep pockets, amazing intellectual property and the best brand name in theme parks. Ocean Park's prospects did not appear bright.

"Thrill Ride into Debt" screamed a 2001 headline in the *South China Morning Post (SCMP).*
"Hong Kong's Ocean Park May Shut Down in 4 Years' Time" added China's *People's Daily.*

"When it was opened, [Ocean Park] had an advantage of being the only amusement park of its kind in Asia," Ken Chang Kin-ming, the chairman of the Hong Kong Association of Travel Agents told the SCMP. "But now, most Asian countries and some mainland cities have similar places, so Ocean Park has lost its uniqueness. There are better marine parks and aquariums in other countries."

"Some expect tourists will just go to Disneyland, and some believe they will go to both [parks]," Chang added. "But we all believe Disneyland will be a must-see. Ocean Park will not only have to compete on price but also for time, as some tourists stay in Hong Kong for only two or three days."

Many observers — including part of Ocean Park's management team — believed Disney might divert a million visitors a year from Ocean Park.

"The thought was that Ocean Park would be destroyed," Ocean Park's chairman later told *The Wall Street Journal.* "The paint was peeling, the food was inedible . . . It looked like it was going out of business."

The Hong Kong government had indeed considered shuttering the government-owned attraction, or perhaps moving it to Lantau Island, where

Disneyland would be situated. But by 2003, even though it appeared to be in free-fall, with just three months cash reserves in the bank, the government and the company's directors were keen to give Ocean Park one more shot.

❖

In November 2003, my wife and I were living in Spain with our children, preparing to wrap up a four-year assignment at Warner Bros. Movie World Madrid, when I received an email from the executive search company Korn Ferry International about a job opening.

A major marine attraction in Hong Kong, faced with the prospect of new competition and challenging economic conditions, was looking to hire a chief executive who could meet these challenges and lead the company's transformation. The language in the email was vague, as headhunter correspondence tends to be, but I knew immediately that the position had to be at Ocean Park. It was the only attraction that fit the description.

The chance to lead Ocean Park was too good to pass up, but it almost passed me by. In fact, I almost didn't see Korn Ferry's email. The recruiter sent it to an old America Online account that I didn't check often. I was also busy preparing for a move to San Antonio to run Six Flags Fiesta Texas. My wife and I were even researching housing and schools there for the kids. Good thing, though, that I logged into AOL that day.

Even though I had never visited Hong Kong before, I actually knew a good bit about Ocean Park. It had been a reference point for me, during a previous role at Six Flags Marine World in California, because the Hong Kong park was a pioneer in offering rides and entertainment, alongside educational and more traditional animal attractions. At the time, we were aiming to do the same thing at Marine World. Ocean Park CEO Randy Guthrie offered advice, and we ended up collaborating to create a sister park relationship.

Now, Randy would be sitting across the table from me, as part of an interview committee, as I applied to take his place.

Korn Ferry had identified four candidates for the position and the interviews were staggered throughout the day. I was the last prospect to be interviewed. I was calm as I walked into the room in the recruiter's Ice House Street office in Hong Kong's Central district and took my place at the far end of a long wooden boardroom table. I had done my homework. I studied Ocean Park's annual report and toured the park. The visit solidified my views on what actions needed to be taken to improve the company's performance. I knew I had the experience and expertise to lead the effort. It just felt like a good fit. Plus, I entered the interview knowing that my family supported me and would be willing to make the move to Asia, should I get the job.

Across the room from me was Ocean Park's new chairman, Allan Zeman. He had joined the board just a few months earlier, at the behest of Hong Kong's Chief Executive Tung Chee-hwa. Allan was a successful developer and the creator of a popular nightlife district called Lan Kwai Fong, situated just a few minutes' walk from Korn Ferry's office. Along the sides of the table were Allan's deputy Kevin Westley — the chief executive of HSBC Investment Bank — and other board members, including Randy Guthrie and Hong Kong Deputy Secretary for Home Affairs Lolly Chiu.

As we talked, I realised there were three fundamental differences between my view and the Board's current thinking. One, the directors believed Ocean Park was running well, and that the focus could be placed entirely on redevelopment. Two, they thought the best way to address Disney's entry into the market was to redevelop with high-tech attractions and new intellectual property, then compete head-on. And three, they wanted to shutter the park until the redevelopment was complete.

"Closing Ocean Park would be the greatest mistake you could make," I told the board. "Even if you don't hire me, don't do it! If Ocean Park goes off the radar and allows Disney to get firmly established in the market, it may never recover."

"Ocean Park's single greatest value is that it's open, running and connected to the community," I continued. "Stay open and operate. What you need to do is redevelop the park at the same time."

"Can you do that?" several members of the board asked, astonished. "Can you continue operating and redevelop on the scale that we're considering?" They were bankers and property developers, no surprise given the importance of these sectors to the Hong Kong economy. They did not have theme park experience, though, and had never considered this option.

"Every park in the world does it. It's not easy. It's a bit like performing open heart surgery on a marathon runner, while he's still running," I added for emphasis. "But it's the only way to stay in the race."

As the Board asked me for more details, I explained that I had observed a number of opportunities to immediately address revenue generation and operational efficiencies. Ocean Park has a captive market. Once you arrived, there was nowhere else nearby to go for lunch or shopping. But the park's food offerings weren't great. There wasn't enough variety, the prices were too high and frankly, it didn't taste very good. As a result, visitors were leaving at mid-day or arriving after lunchtime. Ocean Park needed to lengthen visitor stay, and in the process increase per capita spending.

"Ocean Park needs to own every aspect of the guest experience," I explained. "Currently, though, the park is not fully in control of its own destiny. A third party vendor is handling the F & B. I would bring the food in-house, just as you did for retail four years ago. Ocean Park should also make it easier for visitors to buy food, drinks, fans, souvenirs and other retail items by bringing the items closer to them; to do this, it needs more roving carts. We need to go for the quick wins. Redeveloping will take time."

Most importantly, Ocean Park had to rethink the vision behind its redevelopment.

"You don't want to pick a fight with an 800-pound gorilla," I said. "Ocean Park should aspire to complement Disney, not compete directly with it. Yes, we are competing for consumers' discretionary time and income, but that's it. Instead of building simulators or developing new characters — things that Disney does phenomenally well —

Ocean Park should focus on its strengths and the ways that it stands apart from Disney."

Ocean Park — with its aquarium, pandas and beautiful mountainous topography — offers a reality experience. Walt Disney offers a fantasy experience and a piece of Americana. Ocean Park entertains, while also educating. It offers a culturally-relevant Hong Kong experience and a generational connection. People who visited as children bring their own kids to the park. These are not Disney's strong suit.

"We need to carve out a unique niche. These differential values should drive Ocean Park's redevelopment plans," I concluded. "We need to keep the Hong Kong spirit, while also adopting a more international approach to the business. Our job is to design a park with differential values that will complement Disney."

❖

As the meeting was drawing to a close, after about an hour of discussion, the Board's chairman intervened.

"I want him," Allan said. "That's it. Let's hire him."

I was still in the room.

"Dr. Zeman, sorry, you can't really do that right now," Andrew Tsui, the Korn Ferry recruiter said. "There's a process here."

"I don't care about process," Allan exclaimed. "This guy is going to get on a plane and go back to Spain and we'll never hear from him again. He's our best candidate. Let's sign him!"

"Excuse me," Andrew said, this time talking to me. "Do you mind stepping out of the room for a bit?"

His colleague led me down the hall to another room. About fifteen minutes later, Andrew returned. "Obviously there's no secret here. The Chairman would like you and we'd like to work out a deal as quickly as possible. When are you flying out?"

By the time I boarded a red-eye flight the next evening, we had ironed out the details and my journey was tied to Ocean Park's.

DISNEY OPENS ITS BOOKS...

Once upon a time, there was a magical theme park that wanted all the gold in the enchanted republic. But a wicked witch put a spell on the park and its losses were considerable. Then one day...

Dominating Disney: An Overview

When I started work at Ocean Park on 1 February 2004, we had less than twenty months to prepare for Hong Kong Disneyland's opening. We were determined to transform the park and avoid the fate that was being played out for it in the media. All the while, though, most people in the company still assumed that Ocean Park would play second fiddle to Disney.

After all, The Walt Disney Company was one of the most successful entertainment companies in the world, with hit movies, consumer products, home videos and tremendous marketing power. A Fortune 500 company, its annual turnover was 3000 times greater than Ocean Park's.[3]

Disney also had the full backing of the Hong Kong government, which covered 80% of Hong Kong Disneyland's initial costs in return for a 57% stake. The government invested more than US$3 billion in the resort and undertook major infrastructure projects to make it easier for visitors to reach the resort. No wonder people were writing off Ocean Park.

---

3   At the end of 2003, The Walt Disney Company ranked 61 on the Fortune 500 list, with annual turnover of US$25,329,000. Ocean Park's turnover was less than US$8 million.

The story did not play out as they planned, though.

The first year that Disney opened, after nearly six years of media buzz, Ocean Park did not suffer. On the contrary, the park's attendance actually rose more than 30 percent to 5.1 million people. It's hard to know exactly how many people visited Hong Kong Disneyland during this time, as the company wasn't required to publicly report its numbers until 2009, but industry analysts estimate that it welcomed 5.2 million people, just a hair more than Ocean Park. In 2007, Disney's attendance dropped more than twenty percent, while Ocean Park's generally continued to climb[4].

Table 1: Attendance (in millions of visitors)		
	Ocean Park	HK Disneyland
2006	5.1	5.2
2007	4.92	4.15
2008	5.03	4.5
2009	4.8	4.6
2010	5.1	5.2
2011	6.95	5.9
2012	7.44	6.7
2013	7.47	7.4
2014	7.79	7.5
2015	7.39	6.8
TOTAL	**62**	**58**

4 Since 2006, the Themed Entertainment Association (TEA), in collaboration with the engineering business AECOM, has published a Global Attractions Attendance Report. That first year, TEA/AECOM reported Ocean Park's 2005–2006 Fiscal Year attendance to be 4.38 million. However, since Ocean Park's fiscal year ends 30 June, we have calculated the 2006 calendar year attendance (5.1 million) to more correctly compare with Disney.

In subsequent years, TEA/AECOM (for the most part) used Ocean Park's calendar year numbers. Note that Ocean Park's attendance figures are a matter of public record. They are audited and reported to Hong Kong's Legislative Council. Hong Kong Disneyland (HKDL) provided (unaudited) estimates of its early year attendance numbers in testimony to Hong Kong's Legislative Council. HKDL released its first 'Annual Business Review' for Fiscal Year 2009, which is when it also published FY08 numbers.

By 2007, media headlines were beginning to portray a starkly different picture.

One of the first international publications to remark on Ocean Park's success and Disney's struggles was Forbes, which dubbed my chairman, Allan Zeman, 'Hong Kong's Mouse Killer'. The L.A. Times picked up on this theme, declaring "Hong Kong Theme Park Outsmarts the Mouse". TIME Magazine followed up in 2009, asking "Can Hong Kong Disneyland Get the Magic Back?".

Government officials were also growing nervous. "The first two years of Hong Kong Disneyland's operation were not satisfactory," Secretary for Commerce and Economic Development Frederick Ma told lawmakers in December 2007. The Hong Kong government had urged Disney, he added, to "critically review the operation of the park with a view to enhancing its operational efficiency and revamping its marketing and promotion strategies.[5]"

Disney's attendance during its first year of operations was 400,000 less than the company had projected. Still, it would take several years before Hong Kong Disneyland could attract as many people as it had in 2005–2006 for a second time. The resort would not top 5 million visitors again until 2010.

Over a ten year period, from Disney's launch through the end of 2015, Ocean Park attracted four million more visitors than Hong Kong Disneyland. It proved to be a more popular attraction with locals and overseas visitors alike in eight out of the ten years.

❖

Throughout this period, Hong Kong Disneyland was also bleeding money. It didn't report a profitable year until 2012. During its first six years of operation, the resort lost more than US$700 million. Following three years in the black, it lost money again in 2015.

---

5 Panel on Economic Development, Meeting Minutes, 21 Dec 2007, www.legco.gov.hk/yr07-08/english/panels/es/minutes/ev071221.pdf

Hong Kong Disneyland consistently has higher revenue that Ocean Park. Disney tickets cost about one-third to nearly twice as much, depending on the type of ticket. Hong Kong Disneyland has two hotels, whereas Ocean Park currently has none, and most products inside Disney are more expensive.

But all the while that Disney was in the red, Ocean Park was reporting surpluses. During Disney's first year in Hong Kong, when it lost an estimated US$46 million, Ocean Park reported a record budget surplus: more than US$20 million, up more than 30 percent from a year earlier.[6] Only twice during Hong Kong Disneyland's first decade did the resort record larger profits than Ocean Park, and even then, only once did it have a higher profit margin.

Table 2: Profit/Loss (in USD)[7]			Profit Margin	
	Ocean Park	HK Disneyland	Ocean Park	HK Disneyland[8]
2006	20,115,681	(46,000,000)	21.5%	Not available
2007	20,017,995	(162,000,000)	20.3%	Not available
2008	26,311,054	(202,313,625)	22.1%	-61.3%
2009	12,673,522	(169,023,136)	11.0%	-51.8%
2010	10,539,846	(92,287,918)	8.3%	-23.8%
2011	13,508,997	(30,462,725)	8.4%	-6.5%

6 As a non-profit entity, Ocean Park Hong Kong does not record 'profits'. It does however report a budget surplus or loss, which is comparable. In 2005–2006, Ocean Park recorded a surplus of HK$156.5 million, up from HK$119.5 million a year earlier. The Hong Kong Dollar is pegged to the US dollar at 7.78 HKD to 1 USD.

7 Ocean Park and Hong Kong Disneyland report financial results in Hong Kong dollars. We have used an exchange rate of 7.78 to convert to USD. 2006 and 2007 Disney losses are calculated by Euromonitor and reported by Bloomberg. Subsequent numbers were publicly reported.

8 Disney has not released total revenue numbers for Hong Kong Disneyland in 2006 or 2007, so it is not possible to calculate a profit/loss margin.

	Table 2: Profit/Loss (in USD)		Profit Margin	
	Ocean Park	HK Disneyland	Ocean Park	HK Disneyland
2012	13,277,635	(14,010,283)	6.5%	2.6%
2013	16,349,614	(31,362,468)	6.9%	5.0%
2014	12,339,332	(42,673,522)	4.9%	6.1%
2015	5,809,769	(19,023,136)	2.3%	-2.9%
TOTAL	152,943,445	(633,064,267)		

Some observers believe Hong Kong Disneyland would be profitable, though, if not for the terms of the deal signed between The Walt Disney Company (TWDC) and the Hong Kong government.

"'Unequal' Disney Deal Leaving Hongkongers to Foot the Bill," screams a 2017 South China Morning Post headline.[9]

Calling the deal 'unequal' harkens back to the treaties that the West imposed on China in the 19th and early 20th centuries, including the one that made Hong Kong a British colony.

Regardless of Hong Kong Disneyland's performance, it must pay a large chunk of its revenue to TWDC in the form of management fees and royalty payments for the use of Disney's intellectual property. While Disney has not disclosed the details, a Hong Kong lawmaker estimates that Hong Kong Disneyland pays its parent company HK$250 million (US$32 million) every year. Accounting losses, meanwhile, ensure that the park does not have to pay Hong Kong taxes.

"The American parent company receive(s) millions in potential profits while the city's taxpayers are left to foot most of the park's bills," writes the SCMP's Nikki Sun.

---

9   Nikki Sun, 'Unequal' Disney deal leaving Hongkongers to foot the bill," SCMP, 20 Feb 2017.

At the same time, each time HKDL records an annual loss, the Hong Kong government has to kick in additional money to cover the shortfall, and since it's the majority shareholder, it has to pay the most. Based on the numbers recorded in the table above, the Hong Kong government would have been required to pay HKDL more than US$410 million from 2006–2015, though about one-tenth of this would have been offset by US$46 million in profits from 2012–2014[10].

The Fantasy becomes a... REALITY!

As you look at Table 2 above, you'll notice that Ocean Park's surpluses and profit margin fell over the years. Ocean Park may be the only theme park in the world to come under pressure to make less money. In 2008, after reporting a new record surplus of more than HK$200 million (US$26

---

10 Initially, the Hong Kong government owned a 57% stake in Hong Kong Disneyland. This was reduced to 53% in 2009. So in 2006, when HKDL lost US$46 million, the government's share of this loss was US$26.2 million.

million), we were expecting accolades. But instead, key stakeholders in the government and on our board of directors instructed us to reduce the annual surplus; if not, we risked creating the wrong impression and stoking public discontent.

"You're a non-profit," we were told. "You're for the people of Hong Kong. The public will ask, 'Why are you making so much money? Why aren't your ticket prices lower?'" The criticism was a wake-up call for me, reflecting a big difference between running a private company and one that is publicly held. We had actually been contemplating raising ticket prices, because we had calculated the optimum level would be about 80% of Hong Kong Disneyland's price: too low, the park could be too crowded; too high, attendance, revenue and the park's 'rainy day fund' (reserves) would suffer. Faced with this reaction to the park's surplus, though, we delayed plans to adjust entrance fees. The following year, we also accelerated expenditure on programmes to enhance guest experience — such as a makeover of our children's play area, Whiskers Harbour — in order to report surpluses more in line with Ocean Park's not-for-profit status.

❖

During its first 28 years, Ocean Park never took out a loan. Even through the tough years, the park was able to survive on its own cash reserves, a testament to the management team.

When I arrived in 2004, though, there was just about US$13 million in the bank. Not only did we need to grow the bank account — to ensure that there would be at least two years' worth of operating expenses on hand in case of a market downturn — we would also need to borrow US$700 million to finance the park's ambitious redevelopment plans.

Half of this amount would be backed by the government, 25% as a subordinated loan (to be repaid last) and 25% from banks, but guaranteed by the public purse. For the remaining US$350 million, we needed to convince a consortium of financial institutions that Ocean Park's redevelopment made sense. We promised a 16% internal rate of return, which was definitely higher than anything else you could invest in at the time. Turns out that was a conservative projection, thanks to the higher-than-expected increase in Ocean Park's attendance.[11]

In 2013, Ocean Park took out a second government loan — this time for US$300 million — to build a new water park built on a series of terraced platforms overlooking the ocean. While significant, the two loans pale in comparison to the more than US$3 billion that Hong Kong invested in Disney. Unlike Ocean Park, Disney also has no requirement to repay the government. In fact, it's been able to pressure the government to convert debt to equity so that Hong Kong can maintain its majority stake in the venture.

Disney already has complete control of the management agreement and can largely do what it likes. The government's majority equity position provides it with some veto power, and as a result, it does not want to give this up. In late 2016, for example, Disney announced a US$1.3 billion investment in park improvements and was prepared to make the investment on its own. The Hong Kong government anted up US$750 million, though, in order to maintain its majority position. If this plays out like Disneyland Paris — which has been a great source of royalty fees for Disney, but a boondoggle for investors who have witnessed Euro Disney's share price drop 99% from a high of 152 euros in 1999 to barely more than 1 euro today — Disney could eventually push Hong Kong into selling its stake.

❖

Companies in our industry often devise plans for the attraction they want, rather than the attraction they can afford. Ocean Park takes a different

---

11 Ocean Park refinanced these loans in 2016 to get a better deal and consolidate the debt under one bank, rather than the original consortium of 24.

approach. From the beginning, even though the park is ultimately owned by the government, we wanted to ensure that it never becomes a burden to Hong Kong's taxpayers. Every cent is not only being paid back, it's being paid at above-market interest rates.[12] There's no question that the Hong Kong government is receiving a good return on its investment in Ocean Park. The same cannot be said for its much larger investment in Hong Kong Disneyland.

Ocean Park's Renaissance

My first task at Ocean Park was to oversee the design of a Master Redevelopment Plan that would transform the park, while enhancing its best characteristics and remaining true to the company's core values.

Due to mountainous terrain, Ocean Park is divided into two sections: an area that used to be called the Lowland (now the Waterfront) and another called the Headland (renamed the Summit). One of the first things that many visitors to Ocean Park used to do was queue up for the cable car to go to the Headland. The 12–15 minute cable car ride offers spectacular views of the surrounding hills and the South China Sea. However it was also a bottleneck, slowing down access to most of the park's attractions.

Before I arrived, there was some discussion about moving the park off the Summit and consolidating it in the Lowland area. Fortunately our chairman, Allan Zeman, vetoed this idea. He recognised that the topography was a gift, and that if Ocean Park moved everything to the Lowland area, it would resemble a generic theme park. It would no longer be 'Uniquely Hong Kong'.

Instead we would create a new level area for additional attractions at the Summit and build a funicular express that can transport 10,000 people per hour through the mountain, as a supplement to the cable car. In the process, we had to move a million cubic metres of dirt.

---

12 The loan will be paid off in full in 2022. Ocean Park could have actually repaid the government in seven years, but decided to stick to the original terms in order to maintain its cash reserves.

Despite our name, we also realised that visitors never saw the ocean until they were in the cable car, so we built a breathtaking new aquarium and a lovely lagoon in the Waterfront area.

Over the next seven years, we would more than double the number of attractions inside Ocean Park, adding climatic zones showcasing animals from the Earth's rainforests as well as its poles. We welcomed a second pair of giant pandas, plus four rare red pandas from Sichuan. The number of animals at Ocean Park climbed to nearly 11,000, cared for by a team of 200. We built on Ocean Park's history as a marine park offering entertainment alongside educational animal exhibits, by introducing more visceral rides, including Hong Kong's fastest and first floorless roller coaster, and a unique nightly outdoor animated show. Hardly a spot in the park was left untouched by the US$700 million redevelopment effort. Yet all the while, we managed to maintain Ocean Park's intrinsic charm, and we never lost sight of the park's founding values or its focus on education, conservation and entertainment.

Imitation: From A to Y

While Ocean Park was improving its brand and connection with the community, Hong Kong Disneyland's opening was characterised by missteps. To begin with, visitors from the mainland initially lacked a familiarity with Disney's characters. They hadn't grown up with Mickey, Minnie and Donald. At most, they might recognise their images from (pirated) bedsheets and consumer products. As a result, park-goers didn't fully appreciate Disney's ads, nor the five and six-foot high 'mice' roaming the resort and approaching their children. To address this issue, Disney created an immersion space near the main gate to educate Chinese tour groups about the Disney stories.

Hong Kong Disneyland was also initially plagued by long lines and a lack of things to do. They lost the plot when it came to designing the park and measuring its entertainment value. In addition, Disney began to realise that many Asian families — whether from Hong Kong or the mainland — wanted their theme park experience to not only be fun, but also to have some redeeming and educational value. Ocean Park was tailor-made for this; Disney had to improvise.

As it struggled to live up to expectations, and faced with sagging visitor numbers, Hong Kong Disneyland began looking to its 'smaller' attractions neighbour, just ten miles across the water, for answers. Actually, they did much more than look. In late 2006 and 2007, Disney actively copied our programmes and events, with varying degrees of success.

❖

"Imitation is the sincerest [form] of flattery," the English cleric Charles Caleb Colton famously wrote in 1824.

If Colton is correct, Disney must be enamoured with Ocean Park.

October is one of the most important — and most fun — times of the year to visit Ocean Park. Hundreds of monsters roam freely. We set up haunted houses and produce live shows. Three hundred and thirty thousand people celebrated Halloween with us in 2005. Now, more than a million visitors participate in the expanded six-week-long festivities.

In 2005, Ocean Park's Halloween diverted media attention — and visitors — from Hong Kong Disneyland, just a month after its launch. Disney then attempted to copy Ocean Park's Halloween in 2006. Not that Disney had never produced a Halloween event before, but in its other resorts, Halloween with Disney was always family-friendly, not scary. Now, for the first time, Disney attempted to produce a frightful Halloween. The park rolled out some of Disney's more famous villains — Captain Hook, Jafar (the antihero in *Aladdin*, who desired to be the world's most powerful sorcerer) and Cruella de Vil of *101 Dalmatians* fame. It also superimposed Mickey Mouse's smiling face onto a Jack-O-Lantern, and added two pumpkins for his ears.

The result was a dismal failure. For the next seven years, Hong Kong Disneyland continued to copy Ocean Park with a haunted house format and characters that came from outside Disney's fabled realm. To attract more visitors, they tried offering night-time discounts. But while Ocean Park's Halloween rapidly grew, Disney's did not. Finally, Hong Kong Disneyland stopped trying to compete with Ocean Park for the teen and young adult market and reverted to its roots, focusing on not-so-ghoulish entertainment with Mickey's Halloween Time Celebration.

❖

Conservation and education are not only founding principles and core values for Ocean Park; the two concepts are in the company's DNA. Without these foci, there would be no reason to build an aquarium or other animal facilities at all. Education and conservation are also ways in which Ocean Park has distinguished itself from Disney, rather than competing directly with the corporate giant. But Disney has tried encroaching on our space.

In 2004, we introduced the Ocean Park Academy to provide environmental education programmes that blend into the school curriculum. There are experiential classes in the park, teacher training seminars and resources that teachers can access for use at Ocean Park or in their own classrooms. In an average year, about 55,000 students from pre-kindergarten through secondary school attend Ocean Park Academy programmes. They learn how dolphins and other marine mammals adapted over time to live in the ocean, and how to spot the footprints of penguins in the arctic. They discuss environmental threats and suggest ways that humans can live in harmony with animals and the planet.

Ocean Park also runs seasonal academies — tied to Chinese New Year, Easter, summer holidays, Halloween and Christmas — for parents and young children. These are generally crafts and do-it-yourself activities with educational messaging, held in our Whiskers Harbour playground. A typical academy session might involve teaching children to make a hat out of recycled paper in the form of a rainforest animal. In the process, the children learn about the animal — why it's endangered and what they can do to help — and about recycling. Afterwards, they wear the hats throughout the park as a badge of honour. Parents love it because their children are thoroughly entertained and they learn something too. The seasonal academies are always fully subscribed.

I should note here that we consciously chose to call these educational initiatives 'academies' because, in this part of the world, the word 'academy' conveys a meaning of value and quality education.

In 2007, after poaching a senior Ocean Park education official, Hong Kong Disneyland launched its own academy — the Animation Academy, where guests learn to draw a Disney character. While Ocean Park doesn't own the seven letters starting with 'a' and ending with 'y', you can imagine our surprise when we learned of Disney's linguistic choice. No doubt they could argue that they came up with the name on their own — though it was already a common reference to our programmes — not to mention that similar activities in its Tokyo, Paris and Hollywood Studios parks were called the 'Disney Drawing Class', the 'Art of Disney Animation' and the 'Magic of Disney Animation' respectively.

The Hong Kong Disneyland Animation Academy is located in the same building on Main Street where Disney had been teaching mainland tour groups about the Disney storyline. They must have felt that after two years most visitors now had a basic understanding of the Disney universe. There's not much space there for a lot of participants to learn to draw, but it did give Disney one more thing to add to their relatively short list of entertainment offerings.

Disney has also introduced new courses for children from kindergarten through secondary school, including "Disney's Environmental Exploration" to "observe the unique natural environment" of the Disney park and "acquire an understanding of the importance of environment protection". Sound familiar? From Ocean Park's perspective, these botanic tours really appeared to be a desperate attempt to counter Ocean Park's success and to address three types of criticism, that: (a) there wasn't enough to do in

Hong Kong Disneyland, (b) Disney needed to be a better corporate citizen and (c) it should offer more redeeming content.

Disney's environmental push was not without missteps, though. Prior to opening, the resort placed shark's fin soup on the menu. Shark's fin has been considered a Chinese delicacy, one that used to be particularly popular at wedding banquets. But a growing awareness of the cruelty that is often involved with 'harvesting' fins, as well as its impact on endangered species, has shifted public opinion. Disney faced a backlash when its plans went public. It tried to backtrack by saying it would only serve the dish at weddings and other special events, if a client insisted. Environmental groups were understandably not satisfied and kept up the pressure, leading Disney to do a complete about-face, taking shark's fin off all menus, prior to the park's opening.

In contrast, Ocean Park, which stopped serving the dishes in 1995, has been a pioneer in Hong Kong shark fin campaigns. We actively engage visitors and the public in educational campaigns about the impact of eating shark's fin, and in 2014, we launched one of Asia's largest shark aquariums, drawing further awareness to the animal's beauty and diversity, and human impact on their species.

AFTER TOXIC MUD AND RUINED FISHING GROUNDS, THEY'VE FINALLY GOT CULTURAL CONSIDERATIONS

NO SPITTING

❖

In 1984, seven years after Ocean Park's debut, the company opened a popular seasonal attraction, right by the front gate, called Water World. Adults and kids alike loved to cool off on a hot summer day in the lazy river and race down the iconic 5-lane rainbow slides. Most years, Water World would open in May and close in mid-September when kids went back to school. But in 1999, as company officials were looking for a way to stem the financial losses that had begun a year earlier, Ocean Park shut down Water World for good. It was just too expensive to operate and maintain a seasonal park, and the market couldn't support a year-round facility.

In my first year at Ocean Park, we decided to bring back elements of the old water park. We knew Hong Kongers were looking for fun ways to cool off, and while reopening Water World wasn't an option, there were other solutions. We introduced an annual event called Summer Splash. There are live shows, where cast members turn water guns and sprays onto the guests, and even a covered open-air water playground with inflatable slides and buckets of water that fill, then douse the kids. Ocean Park still runs Summer Splash every year; in 2016, it teamed up with Nickelodeon for two months to run the city's first SpongeBob Water Party, which among other things, included space for friends to fling water balloons at each other.

Two years after we introduced Summer Splash, Hong Kong Disneyland rolled out their own version of wet entertainment, a parade called 'Mickey's WaterWorks', which they marketed to the public as a way to stay cool. During the parade, the Green Army Men from Toy Story and other characters turned hoses and water guns on the spectators. Disney ran the water parade for six out of seven years between 2007 and 2013. Ocean Park's summer numbers were beating Disney, so I guess it's not surprising they looked to us, then tried to put their own spin on it.

There is another classic tale of imitation, having to do with birthday celebrations. I don't want to give everything away in these opening pages, so suffice it to say, we've learned over time that if Disney — the world entertainment giant — copies you, you must be doing something right!

❖

Not only has Ocean Park proven its early critics wrong, it has grown to become one of the most popular — and respected — theme parks, not just in Hong Kong or Asia, but worldwide. In 2012, the company's industry peers presented it with the prestigious 'Applause Award' — the highest accolade in the attractions business — for "setting a great example for the whole industry" and operating "with a strong vision, a high sense of quality and a dedicated leadership". In 2015, despite a 5% drop in attendance from a year earlier[13], Ocean Park was the 15th most popular attraction in the world, four notches ahead of Hong Kong Disneyland.

Ironically, we realise that Ocean Park's success would not have happened, if it wasn't for Disney.

In 2004, three million people visited a Hong Kong themed attraction. Ten years later, attendance at Hong Kong parks was more than fifteen million. Disney's arrival in Hong Kong expanded the market, and in the process, forced Ocean Park to compete for attention. After years of being the only offering in town, like many monopolies, Ocean Park had become complacent. The threat of competition, especially from a megabrand like Disney, obliged Ocean Park and its stakeholders to contemplate a thorough renewal. Innovation became obligatory. Today, the two parks complement each other and enhance Hong Kong's status as a tourist destination.

An Unexpected Career

When I was 17, I applied for a summer job at Disneyland in California. Disney rejected me because I was under-18. As a parting shot, though, the screener told me I wouldn't have gotten the job anyway, because my

---

13 Attendance figures dropped in 2015 due to a decline in Hong Kong tourism, that was in turn linked to political and currency issues. I discuss this more in Chapter 7 (Control) and in the Epilogue.

hair was too long; it touched my collar, a violation of Disney's 1970's-era grooming policy.

Since I needed a job, I went down the road to Knott's Berry Farm, where I was promptly hired to sweep the streets of the family-owned theme park. I discovered from that experience that I wanted to work where I was wanted and where I could make a contribution. Over time, I also learned that being in the shadow of a giant like Disney can have its benefits. I was forced to be fleet of foot and to act on opportunities immediately. While there was magic in the Magic Kingdom, it quickly became apparent that there was magic to be harnessed outside of it as well. I have since spent a career finding ways to achieve success — with smaller budgets, less resources, and fewer opportunities — in the shadow of the castle.

When I entered the theme park industry in 1977, I did not aspire to make it a career. Like many others I've met in this industry, I thought I would finish university, then get a 'real job'. But what began as seasonal employment to pay for school books, tuition and gas, turned into a fruitful, enjoyable career transforming attractions, often in the face of overwhelming competition. I started aspiring to each new opportunity, taking risks and consistently expressing interest in doing new things that would allow me to grow and make an impact.

The Ten Principles

Over the course of this career — which now spans five decades, starting as a teenage cleaner and rising through the ranks — I have identified Ten Principles to manage and transform a business:

1. Understand
2. Value
3. Measure
4. Plan

5. Be Relevant
6. Control
7. Lead
8. Disrupt
9. Be Genuine
10. Aspire, Then Expect

Over the course of the next ten chapters, I will introduce each of these ideas and show how they helped a relatively small local company stand up and beat an international giant. Regardless of the industry in which you work, applying these leadership principles will help you and your company succeed.

Before we dive into the Ten Principles, let me begin with a salient lesson about the importance of words.

Hope is Not a Management Concept

You may recall that during my interview, I recommended Ocean Park terminate its contract with an outside food vendor and bring F & B operations in-house instead. In 2005, we did just that. We implemented this decision a couple years earlier than expected, which as you might imagine created its own set of opportunities. (While some people might prefer the word 'challenges' in that last sentence, I am not among them.)

Things were moving fast — with Hong Kong Disneyland's opening just months away, much of the team was occupied with aspects of the soon-to-be-adopted Master Redevelopment Plan, without much time left to outfit the kitchens, prepare the staff and take care of other details. I instituted 5-minute standing meetings to receive updates on where we were in the transition. Sit-down meetings have a place, but they add at least half an hour, and we didn't have time to waste.

Kenneth Lau, a jack-of-all-trades whom I could always count on, was leading this project. I set three main goals for his team: (1) we should obtain the highest possible certifications for food hygiene and safety, (2) the food should be delicious and moderately priced and (3) Ocean Park should be able to prepare and serve everything from hot dogs to caviar.

Kenneth was doing a fantastic job, but he had a habit of always saying "we hope" during his presentations. "We hope to open the canteen by next month," or "We hope this new recipe will be popular".

During one of these meetings, Kenneth was reporting on the progress of the new kitchen. "The stoves should be delivered on Tuesday. We hope to have them installed and the staff trained to use them by Friday."

"Kenneth," I said, "do you hope or do you expect that the kitchen and staff will be ready by Friday?"

He looked back at me.

"I need to know that you believe in this," I continued. "If we only hope for something, it's not going to happen. We have to expect it. So are you hoping or can we expect that the kitchen will be ready on time?"

Turning to the rest of my team, I added, "We're embarking on something that we are absolutely committed to and that we therefore expect to realise. Let's remove 'hope' from our vocabulary."

And so we did. Nobody heard the word 'hope' in relation to project management again.

At this point in Ocean Park's journey, we were still an aspirational organization. We set targets like attracting five million visitors a year (up from just three million) and becoming a top-class marine attraction, recognised by international peers. These were stretch goals — achievable, but beyond anything the company had accomplished before. I needed to make sure that the team took the goals seriously and did not think they were flexible or that it would be acceptable if we fell short. Similarly, I needed everyone to realise that this was not a one-person job — I could not transform the park on my own — we all needed to be committed to delivering the ultimate vision.

Over time, Ocean Park's nature changed. The team became accustomed to achieving company targets. Rather than aspiring, they now *expected* success.

This shift from aspirations to expectations affected the way in which we ran the company, from the language used in our vision statement to how we set employee KPIs (Key Performance Indicators). It helped us push the envelope, to set more aggressive goals, to drive the sales team to new markets, to provide better service, and offer an exemplary guest experience. The pivot from aspirations to expectations begins when you realise that Hope is Not a Management Concept.

❖

A word about myself. I am a voracious reader and learner. I observe and listen. I also love what I do. Some of the ideas presented in this book are 'Mehrmannisms', but I cannot claim to have invented all ten principles. There are too many great leaders and thinkers who have come before me. I've been fortunate to learn from the likes of Stephen Covey (author of *The 7 Habits of Highly Effective People)*, Warren Bennis (a leadership scholar and adviser to four US Presidents), and former UCLA basketball coach John Wooden. I've worked with accomplished managers, as well as some who provided examples of what not to do. I've also been influenced by academic research and corporate studies — work done by IBM, INSEAD, and McKinsey & Co. come to mind. In some instances, what I've read confirmed an idea I already had; in others, reading provided a completely new perspective. Regardless, I put my imprint on these ideas, making them my own — something I trust you will do as you adopt these principles to transform your businesses and move from Aspirations to Expectations.

PRINCIPLE 1

Understand

Seek First to Understand,
Then to Be Understood

In 1989, I was a young manager at Knott's Berry Farm in charge of ride operations, when a businessman and educator named Stephen Covey published a book that would inspire millions of readers. *The 7 Habits of Highly Effective People* would go on to sell 25 million copies in 40 languages, leading *Time* magazine to name him one of America's most influential Americans. At the time that Covey visited Knott's Berry Farm, though, soon after his book's publication, he was still relatively unknown.

My CEO, Terry van Gorder, had read *The 7 Habits* and was so impressed, he invited Covey to speak to the park's staff. More than a hundred of us gathered in Independence Hall, a brick-by-brick replica of the famous Philadelphia building where the United States' founders signed the Declaration of Independence and U.S. Constitution. The building was a project of passion for Knott's founder Walter Knott, who wanted to bring the earliest days of U.S. history closer to people on the West Coast, a continent away from the country's first capital.

While I never really knew Walter Knott — he retired from park management after his wife died in 1974 — he was an inspiration. Then California governor Ronald Reagan noted that while Knott had successfully climbed to the top of the ladder of success, he had "always been careful to see that he left each rung of that ladder in good repair, so those who followed after would have less trouble in climbing life's ladder than he had"[14], an example of being genuine, not just generous.

Walter christened Independence Hall in 1966 and, to this day, admission is free. The attention to detail is astounding — from fingerprints in the handmade bricks to the original colour of the paint and placement of the crack in the replica Liberty Bell. Some 100,000 school children pass through the doors here every year to study history, nature and science in a Knott's Berry Farm educational programme.

On this day in 1989, though, the lessons were of a different sort. Stephen Covey spoke passionately in the second-floor theatre about being proactive, beginning 'with the end in mind' and putting 'first things first'. He also challenged us to listen with empathy, to truly listen to someone — from their frame of reference — with the 'intent to understand'[15]. This was the basis of one of the Covey's 7 Habits that resonated most strongly with me: Seek First to Understand, Then to be Understood.[16]

Long before I read Covey's book or heard him speak, I made a point of seeking to understand other people's points of view, so that they would feel heard and their views could inform my own. Hearing Covey articulate this practice on stage, though, was an Aha! moment for me. I realised, *'Yes, I do this . . . but maybe not all the time'*. I wanted to remind myself to think about listening, about understanding and to make these habits intrinsic to who I was. It was an important turning point for me in my career and personal development.

The thing about Covey's ideas is that they're common sense. At the core, he reminds us how people want to be treated, as he presents his thoughts in ways that are clear, concise and easy to remember.

---

14 "Ronald Reagan and Knott's", Knotts in Print, knottsinprint.blogspot.sg/2011/01/ronald-reagan-and-knotts.html

15 Using Emphatic Listening to Collaborate", Fast Company, 26 December 2011, www.fastcompany.com/1727872/using-empathic-listening-collaborate

16 Stephen R. Covey, "The 7 Habits of Highly Effective People", 1989.

Knott's Berry Farm bought copies of *The 7 Habits of Highly Effective People* for its staff. My management peers then formed a book club: we met once a week over lunch to discuss Covey's principles and how we could apply them in our daily work. Nearly twenty years later, I gave the book to my executive directors at Ocean Park and asked our Learning and Development Department to integrate its principles into the company's leadership development programmes. Internalising Covey's concepts has made us all better leaders.

So what does it mean to Seek First to Understand, Then to be Understood?

Covey writes that most people skip the first step. They seek to get their own point across, to be understood, rather than to understand. They listen with the intent of replying, thinking about what they will say next, rather than truly hearing the person speaking.

For me, 'seeking first to understand' starts with taking the time to learn about a situation, the people and processes. How did we get to where we are today and what's needed to correct a problem, if corrections are required? Don't come in with guns blazing, telling people what to do. Instead, have an open mind and open ears. Listen, ask questions, process the information.

I see it as a 3-step process:

First, listen, truly listen.

Second, reflect back what you've heard and verify if you understand correctly.

Third — and only after completing the first two steps — share your own thoughts about an issue's resolution. It's at this point that leaders should seek to be understood — to propose an action plan that either continues in the same direction or along a new path.

I've been practising this principle for years, but Covey made it convenient for me to reference.

Understanding Ocean Park

When I arrived at Ocean Park in 2004, the company had already embarked on a master planning effort to redevelop the park. It was a little haphazard, though, and lacked focus. There was no real direction — plenty of ideas, but none had really stuck.

This was an opportunity to apply the principle of understanding.

I asked my chairman, Allan Zeman, to give me 100 days to assess Ocean Park's status, what we need to do, where we should be going, and to evaluate the team.

Even before my contract was finalised, I began by holding one-on-one meetings with key members of Ocean Park's team. These conversations provided us the opportunity to get to know a little bit about each other. I also needed to understand what they saw as the park's opportunities and weaknesses, where they thought we should be focusing, what they felt worked well in the company and what did not, as well as their thoughts and expectations of a new leader.

I quickly discovered there were some anxieties about the impending change.

My first meeting was with my predecessor's assistant, Wendy Ngan, and her first question to me was, "Are you going to fire me?"

"No. Why would I do that?"

"Every new boss wants to bring in their own people."

"I have no intention of doing that," I assured her. "I don't even have anybody to bring in."

Wendy became a trusted colleague, helping me navigate Ocean Park's currents throughout my twelve years at the helm of the company.

After meeting with Wendy, I spoke with my deputy CEO, Matthias Li, and then with each of the department directors. In each discussion, I asked questions, but let my new colleagues do most of the talking. Towards the end of each meeting, I recapped their concerns and interests, recounted my experience in the industry, described where I intended to take Ocean Park, and how I saw them as a valuable component of the journey. Their world was about to change; I wanted them to understand they had no reason to feel insecure.

Their feedback was resoundingly upbeat. I don't think my predecessors had taken the time to understand their individual contributions or how they could work together to be better. A lot of people in the company were expecting me to change the management — to change everything — and were surprised when I held on to every single member of the team. I added a couple of people, but did not eliminate a single position.

Because I entered Ocean Park seeking first to understand, I quickly realised I couldn't find another team like this. They were steeled by their past and had an intimate understanding of the company's successes and failures. They had worked with the park when it was achieving new records and building cash reserves, from the mid-1980s through the Hong Kong handover in 1997. They had also been through an incredible period of lows that included outbreaks of Bird Flu and SARS, as well as the 1998 Asian Financial Crisis, which contributed to a record loss at Ocean Park of HK$85 million (nearly US$11 million). I looked at their leadership qualities and their attitudes, and saw a fantastic group of individuals who simply needed a jolt of confidence and direction.

The initial round of conversations took about a week. After that, I began to share what the Board was expecting of management and embarked on several parallel tracks of exploration to understand different aspects of Ocean Park's business. I continued to discuss career development with my staff. I walked the park with my head of engineering and chatted with his team, while also visiting each shop and area, learning about their challenges and the support they needed. The company's animal husbandry experts spoke to me about issues related to acquisition and the daily care of animals, as well as facility design and procedures for disease prevention.

The longest and most intense conversations were related to the park's redevelopment. The company had already invested time and money in the project; there were many players involved, including consultants and a Redevelopment Committee. I needed to understand what had been done so far, what was good about the current plans, and what needed to change if the park was to not only survive, but thrive, in the face of competition from Disney.

While the process of seeking to understand never ends, this initial phase took about a month. That left me with another 70 days — out of the 100 my chairman had agreed upon — to develop the framework for a new course for Ocean Park's future.

❖

This initial period was not without its missteps.

Before Hong Kong Disneyland opened, I was worried they would poach people from Ocean Park. We were the only place in town where they could find qualified staff with theme park experience. I assumed we were going to lose people if we didn't take action.

So I brought in some experts — consultants from Hewitt (now AON Hewitt), who specialise in human resource issues — and asked them to put together a retention programme that could tie people to the company and prevent attrition. They developed a proposal based on the same philosophy used by firms going through mergers and acquisitions.

The first step was to identify Ocean Park's most poachable employees — we came up with a list of about 200 — then to offer them a bonus if they stayed with the park for at least one year after Disney opened. We developed a really good plan, then presented it, along with the financial impact, to the Board of Directors.

The Board meeting wasn't until the following week, but it didn't take long for my phone to start ringing. The first call was from my chairman, Allan Zeman: "What are you doing? What is this? I don't like it at all!" Before long, the deputy chairman and other board members called to voice their displeasure as well.

I didn't understand the opposition. The retention plan seemed fundamental to me. During the board meeting, the Hewitt consultants joined me and we presented the paper. The Board slammed it!

"How can you isolate 200 people? What about the other 400+ employees?" they asked. "What will you tell them if they find out why they haven't been offered anything? This isn't going to work. It's divisive and could create all sorts of acrimony throughout the company."

I had had blinders on. The Board's critique was absolutely dead on. They agreed that talent retention was an issue, but now challenged me to find another way to address it.

Back at the drawing board, we decided to survey the company's staff to determine what drove their engagement with the park. Were they there only to collect a pay cheque, or was there something more? We polled every employee, posing more than 100 questions focused on three areas: Would they say good things about the park? Would they stay through tough times? Would they strive for success?

The results were incredibly positive. More than 90% had high engagement ratings; nearly two-thirds were completely engaged. We realized we had this incredible group of people who had been through real hardship — multiple years of being down in the business, in the red, cutting costs and yet finding ways to survive. The experience had steeled and bonded them into a relationship with the park and each other that was unbreakable.

As we looked closer at the numbers, we found that pay was a fairly low motivator for working at Ocean Park. It only ranked 9th. More important were intangibles such as job recognition and ability to grow.

Money for some, those we thought were 'poachable', was not the answer; the staff were instead telling us that they wanted to clearly understand the criteria and competencies required for being hired and promoted. This led us to develop competency models, which informed employee KPIs. More about this, though, when we talk about Principle 7, Lead.

As it turns out, Ocean Park did not lose key staff to Disney. All of the park's directors remained. Out of a company with more than six hundred employees, thirteen Ocean Park staff left to take jobs at Hong Kong Disneyland, and of those thirteen, eight returned to Ocean Park within a year.

As a new person coming in, I overlooked one of Ocean Park's key dynamics — the bond and pride employees had in the company. In this case, I had rushed to impose a solution that didn't match the problem at hand. I also failed to lobby the Board; I didn't spend time with the chairman or his deputy to talk about the programme. I just assumed it was the right approach. I had not adequately listened; I had not sought to understand before being understood.

Understanding the Community

In previous examples, I've shared how leaders need to understand the inner workings of their company, and how such understanding can be gained by listening to employees. Understanding is a principle, though, with value beyond internal management. Effective leaders apply it in relations with all of their business' stakeholders, including members of the public.

Let me share a couple of examples from earlier in my career.

In 1991, I moved to Bloomington, Minnesota — about fifteen minutes south of Minneapolis — to help start an attraction inside the soon-to-be completed Mall of America, a shopping complex so large that it could theoretically house seven professional baseball stadiums. Knott's Berry Farm sent me to set up an indoor amusement park called Camp Snoopy, which would be the entertainment anchor of the mall. It was a homecoming of sorts. Snoopy's creator, Charles Schultz, was born in Minneapolis and many of the Peanuts' storylines are based on his childhood growing up in St. Paul.

Today, the Mall of America houses the United States' largest indoor theme park alongside 520 shops, 50 restaurants, an aquarium, and other attractions. It's one of the world's most successful fusions of entertainment and retail, attracting 40 million people and generating US$2 billion in economic activity annually.

But while the Mall of America has become an integral part of Bloomington's economy, it was initially opposed by members of the local community who didn't see the need for a new mall when they already had one. They were concerned about traffic, and upset that the shopping complex was being built where the old Metropolitan Stadium — home to the Minnesota Twins and Minnesota Vikings baseball and football teams — had once stood. There, Harmon Killebrew, an Idaho native who played most of his career with the Twins and was inducted into the National Baseball Hall of Fame in 1984, had once hit a 520-foot (160 m) home run, one of the longest in baseball history.

While my job was to oversee theme park operations, it also fell on me to hold a series of neighbourhood meetings with Bloomington's citizens. I would arrive at someone's home carrying pizza, beer, and a slide projector. After ringing the doorbell, my assistant, who was from Minnesota, would apologise that we hadn't brought a homemade dish for the pot luck. Once inside, we'd hang a white bedsheet in the garage or living room and use that as a screen for our presentation.

Thirty to forty people would turn up, mostly husbands and wives, working class folk with jobs at Cargill, Honeywell, and General Mills;

some in manufacturing, others in insurance or even farming — almost all were opposed to the new mall. Even though we were outnumbered, I never felt nervous or worried.

"How many of you have ever been to Knott's Berry Farm?" I would ask at the beginning of these meetings. A few hands would usually go up. The Knott's family had their roots in the Midwest and Knott's Berry Farm was a popular vacation destination for people from the area.

I'd describe how we were going to blend the lines between inside and out, with live trees and animals, some local, others exotic, like African grey parrots and Southeast Asian cockatoos. I talked about how we're celebrating Charles Shultz and how the attraction would be a great place to take kids in the winter.

Going into these gatherings, we already had an idea from letters we'd received about the issues that would be raised, and we had taken a lot of these ideas on board to help put the heart and soul back into the mall and connect the community to it. So, when faced with questions, I tried to address our neighbours' concerns head-on:

"I understand you're concerned about the traffic," I'd say. "Well, we've built ramps that bypass your neighbourhood and connect directly to high-speed parking structures."

"You're worried about the impact on Southdale Mall. We're not going to put it out of business. There's enough room here for more than one mall." (Southdale — which, by the way, was the world's first fully enclosed shopping centre — is still flourishing today.)

"For decades, Metropolitan Stadium was part of your community. I understand. You want to commemorate that, and so do we. Camp Snoopy is actually big enough to house the old stadium. We've put a home plate where it used to be and seats up on the wall where Killebrew's longest home run would have hit."

The meetings would run a couple hours, until about 9pm, and while I had my stock answers — "the mall is employing 13,000 people", "it will help your tax base" — I was really there to listen and ensure that the community members felt heard. The Mall of America, with Camp Snoopy at its heart, had the endorsement of the local government and was definitely going ahead. But I realised I was the first face these people were seeing connected to a big corporate organization that was going to transform their community. No one else had taken the time to explain what was being built, what it was all about, and to answer their questions.

I was young and probably exuberant about the project. I think my excitement was contagious — or the pizza was really good — because by the end of the night, there was never any animosity, just thank-yous and appreciation.

Several years later, when I arrived in northern California to be the general manager of an attraction, I encountered another situation where listening and understanding were also the keys to being a good neighbour.

❖

Drive half an hour north of San Francisco, assuming no traffic jams on the road, and you'll reach the city of Vallejo. There, you'll find a beautiful area called Lake Chabot for picnics, fishing, hiking and other outdoor activities. There used to be a golf course here, with lovely custom-built retirement homes on a ridge alongside it. Then in the mid-1980s, in an attempt to bolster its economy ahead of the impending closure of a US Navy base, Vallejo invited an attraction called Marine World Africa USA to set up shop in the area.

Marine World Africa USA lasted about a decade, then ran into cash flow issues. Vallejo turned to Premier Parks to take over the attraction, because the city was also saddled with the park's debt. Not long afterwards, Premier Parks purchased Six Flags — a company much larger than itself — and took over the Six Flags name. It also decided to invest US$170 million in the Vallejo facility and rename it Six Flags Marine World.

It was at this point that Premier Parks / Six Flags hired me to oversee the transition and build the business. We added 35 new rides to the Vallejo animal attraction, including an inverted roller coaster called Kong that flips riders head over heels twice in two seconds, after dropping them nearly 110 feet.

Seriously, not for the faint-hearted. The park grew from 1.1 million visitors in 1997 (the year before the acquisition) to more than 2 million in 1999.

When I arrived in Vallejo, there were two parts to the park that Six Flags had agreed to develop and manage — an established area that we would redevelop, and another piece of land that had been part of a golf course, which had closed to make way for Marine World Africa USA. The expansion Six Flags was planning required new infrastructure to accommodate the influx of additional visitors.

"Do you see that green field, just beside the houses?" Six Flags' Chief Operating Officer asked me on my first day in the office. "We're going to put in a parking lot there. The people in the homes, well, they're not thrilled. You need to go out there and talk to them."

So that's what I did. My Construction & Facilities manager and I drove to the other side of the lake, parked the car, and walked door-to-door to meet our neighbours.

"Hi, I'm Tom Mehrmann. I'm the new GM of the park. This is my colleague, Fred Beiner. Can we come in and talk with you for a few minutes?"

Once inside each home, I'd explain that the old park was failing and that if something wasn't done soon, the taxpayers of Vallejo would be on the hook to pay off the debt. I also told them about Six Flags' plans to turn the park around. I knew my hosts weren't happy; they had bought and built homes overlooking a golf course, not a parking lot. I couldn't give them the golf course back — and the parking lot wasn't negotiable either — but I could let them choose the colour of the wall separating the parking lot from their homes. We carried colour samples with us. I admit it's not the same as a scenic view, but it was a start.

As we chatted with the residents, we learned that many were concerned about noise as well, be it from cars or the park itself.

One house was owned by a firefighter and his wife, who worked at City Hall. Some time after our initial meeting, the husband called me to complain that their marital relationship was being affected by noise from the park. He asked me to come to their house, so I went. When I got there, the firefighter escorted me to their bedroom, where the windows were open. He had me sit down on the bed alongside the two of them, then after a moment said, "There! Hear that?!" I didn't hear a thing, but I must admit, I was probably a bit desensitised to theme park sounds. My office at the time sat in the infield of a major roller coaster, which zoomed by my window every thirty seconds.

While the situation felt a bit odd, sitting there with the firefighter and his wife on their bed, I suggested they might consider closing the windows when they were intimate. "We don't like to do that!" The firefighter was indignant.

"I understand the noise from the park bothers you," I replied. "These are our hours of operation." I handed him a card. "Tell us what you hear the most and I'll take a look at it. Maybe we can move a speaker or adjust the bass or change a show time." Six Flags wasn't going to buy their house, but I would see what we could do to reduce some of the noise from the source.

Another gentleman lived with his terminally ill wife, who was bedridden. He probably called me the most. "I can hear the train whistle and my wife is not sleeping well," or "The announcements at the end of the day are too loud," he would tell me. So, we started talking about what we could do. I met him probably once a month. He liked pizza, so I'd bring a pizza over, sit in his living room and chat. Initially, he wanted Six Flags to buy his house or at least new soundproof windows or water fountains to mitigate the noise. "I'm sorry, we can't do that for you," I'd say, "but we will look into what's disturbing your wife". This may have meant greasing the train track to reduce squeaking or making some other adjustment, but mainly he wanted to be heard and to see that we were making an effort.

After I left Six Flags Marine World to take a post in Spain, my replacement called me a few times to gripe about a local resident who complained incessantly. "Yeah, I know him. I used to have pizza with him. If you talk to him regularly, it will be OK. He really just wants someone to listen."

"I don't want to do that! That's not my style!"

Like it or not, sometimes you just need to listen.

Glendale

In 1999, Six Flags purchased part of Warner Brothers' theme park business. I was still running the marine park north of San Francisco, but Six Flags asked if I would also lead the effort to launch a new attraction, to be called Warner Bros. Movie World Madrid, which was still in the planning stages.

The Madrid city government wanted a world-class theme park that would top the attractions in Barcelona, Seville and Valencia. They invited companies with famous intellectual property, like Disney, Paramount and Universal, to bid on the project. Warner Brothers won the tender and planned to open an attraction with rides inspired by DC Comics and Looney Tunes characters, like Batman, Superman, Bugs Bunny and Daffy Duck.

Then Six Flags acquired the project, to the surprise of the client in Madrid.

I would fly to Spain to introduce Six Flags, but first I needed to understand the work that had been done to date. We had an inkling that the project was running over budget and behind schedule — there had been some veiled references — but to find out more, I travelled to southern California to meet the former Warner Brothers team that had won the tender and been working on the concept design.

I knew the meeting would be tense. They had been working on the project for two years and had had no say in the acquisition. They were as skilled as Disney Imagineers and, frankly, they thought Six Flags was second-rate.

When I arrived, everyone was cordial, overly so. It was like walking on egg shells — not a conducive working environment. Yet I needed to understand the extent of the overruns, how we got there and what we could do to fix the problems. I needed the former Warner Brothers crew — who were now part of my Six Flags project development team — to understand that as the new project owner, we took these issues very seriously.

"You obviously have issues with Six Flags buying you," I told them. "Let's talk about it. Let me understand what your concerns are."

We cleared the air, but as we peeled the layers of the onion, it became evident that this project was US$30 million over budget and six months behind schedule. On top of this, the majority shareholders in Spain didn't know about the overruns yet, and I'd have to be the one to tell them! By that point, I wanted to have a plan firmly in hand. I needed to be able to walk into that meeting in Madrid with the costs and schedule under control.

One day, I was talking with the former Warner Brothers team about these issues and how we would communicate them to the client.

"We haven't told them yet and we're not going to — not until the design has reached a stage where they can visualise the potential and will feel compelled to accept it," the leader of the team told me. He was a tremendous designer, who has gone on to work on attractions across the globe, but in this case it was clear his approach was not going to mesh with ours.

"What?!" I replied. "Has this worked for you before?"

"Yes, definitely. It may not be an easy discussion, and you need to have the designs in front of you to defend the additional costs, but it's the best way to ensure you don't compromise the final product."

"That's not going to fly! We're going to be transparent. Six Flags — which is now running the show — has actually invested money in this project. When I go to Spain to meet our partners for the first time, I'm not going to tell them we are over budget. I'm not going to tell them that the park will open late. Just the opposite. We're going to give them a better park than they expected."

"Our job is to get this below budget, introduce more product than initially planned and get it done on time," I added for good measure.

Sometimes, when you seek first to understand, the solutions suggested by those you're listening to are radically different from your own. You might find that the other solutions are better, but that was not the case here.

Over the next half year, I spent three weeks a month in the Glendale office. Each time I arrived from San Francisco, someone from the former Warner Brothers team would pick me up at the Burbank airport. I never knew in advance who it would be, but almost always, they had an agenda — don't cut this cost, don't change that part of the project — and would work to persuade me during the half-hour drive. There was a lot of positioning going on and people who wanted me to know that they were not part of the overall problem. I always listened and just personally worked through each person and each process.

As my oversight of the design and planning progresses, I run through Covey's principles in my head. We were being proactive. We were beginning with the end in mind. And we were going to put first things first. On top of that, I was seeking first to understand, then to be understood.

You might say I entered the Glendale office preaching from the Book of Covey.

That was a mistake.

One morning, as I was going over the project and perhaps quoting a bit too closely from the *7 Habits of Highly Effective People*, there was grumbling.

"Oh great, Covey! We've all been through that," the team leader said, exasperated.

The textbook approach may have motivated and been appreciated by my previous staff, but this group was rejecting it. They were too senior and too experienced. So I backed up, dropped the Covey quotes, and took a more humanistic approach. My goal was the same, though — to understand, then be understood.

"Listen, I'm here to represent the company that bought your company," I told the team. "I want to make the most of this. Help me make the most of this. Whether you agree with Covey or not, let's just take this piece by piece. Tell me where we are, tell me how we got here, and what you believe the solution should be."

Unfortunately, what I heard over time was absolutely out-of-sync with where we had to go. This was a case where separation was the best course. When your passion is so strong and you are as deeply engaged in something as the leader of the Glendale team was, change is the last thing you want. He was used to larger budgets and being given a free hand, without anyone really questioning his approach. When it became apparent that we couldn't achieve our objectives with the full Glendale team in place, I suggested an exit strategy. While I'm sure it was difficult, he understood the rationale and was professional about the process. He went on to set up his own successful company, while Six Flags retained a number of key people to assist with the transition.

In the end, we did get the project back on track. Warner Bros. Movie World Madrid opened on time in April 2002, with more attractions than were in the initial design, and US$13 million under budget.

Dominating Disney: The Role of Understanding

When I arrived at Ocean Park in February 2004, I needed to gain the confidence and buy-in of the directors and staff who knew the company inside-out. Some CEOs in my position would have considered bringing in their own team and starting with a fresh slate. That was certainly a fear held by some at Ocean Park. But I knew the company needed their collective knowledge and wisdom. I would not hesitate to send someone on a separate path if needed — as I had done in Glendale, California — but first I needed to authentically listen to each member of the team. Only then could we accurately assess how the company got to where it was and chart a transformative route for the future.

As we set out to redevelop the park, I needed to understand where our team felt we were positioned, what they believed would be culturally relevant, and how they thought we connected to the community. As we talked, I articulated and reflected back what I believed I was hearing and what I believed would be the right position for the company. These conversations informed the park's redevelopment as well as the design of our marketing strategies.

It was only by continually applying this principle that we were able to develop and implement the plans that led Ocean Park to dominate Disney.

At times, this meant readjusting in mid-course.

Take the case of Ocean Park's Master Redevelopment Plan. Within the first year, we had a good idea of how we wanted to position Ocean Park relative to Disney. With the help of a master storyteller, we developed a short animated video to provide our stakeholders — the government, legislators, financiers — with a look at the Ocean Park of the future.

We planned to implement the new concept in two phases over four years, and hired an accomplished project director to lead the HK$5.5 billion (US$700 million) redevelopment. After he reviewed the blueprints and spreadsheets, however, he led me to understand that we would need to make changes.

When we hired him, Randy Kalish had more than three decades of engineering experience, including fourteen years with Disney. He had actually been one of the project managers working on Hong Kong Disneyland.

"You've obviously wowed people," Randy told me, "but there's a lot of 'eye wash' here."

That expression — referring to some of the plan's more expensive elements — caught my attention.

"I don't see a budget for escalating costs," he continued. "And while there is a contingency budget for unexpected construction expenses, we calculated this differently at Disney. The long and short of it is, what you've set aside — I don't think it's going to be enough . . . How do you intend to cover these shortfalls?"

So much development was going on in Hong Kong at this time that construction costs changed almost daily. Randy was right, but by this point our budget was set and raising additional funds wasn't feasible. We were going to have to take a very hard look at the entire project.

My team and I had been caught up in the 'dream stage' of what Ocean Park could become, but Randy had technical knowledge and was a realist. As he had just joined the company and hadn't played a role drafting the original plans, he was looking at it with fresh eyes.

This was going to be a huge effort. We needed to retrace our steps, redefine the concept and amend the project parameters to ensure that we wouldn't over-promise and under-deliver. The final result had to be equally exciting; the team needed to feel the same passion for it, or we would come up short.

This was definitely not a case where a leader could say, "You've told me the problem, now let me tell you how to fix it." Instead, with Randy's guidance, we collectively sought to rework each step of the Master Redevelopment Plan — the blueprint that would successfully attract more people each year to Ocean Park than Hong Kong Disneyland. We were able to do it. The final product was just going to look a bit different and take a little longer — six years instead of four, eight phases instead of two — to roll out.

❖

Over the years, I have often been asked how I achieve success in 'foreign' markets where I am an outsider. As I discuss in more depth in Chapter 7, I strongly believe a company should be relevant to the community it serves. But as a *guiri* in Spain, a west-coaster in Minnesota, or a *gweilo* in Hong Kong, how do you do that?

Understanding is key, because without it, without genuinely listening, there is no trust, and without mutual trust, you will not receive honest feedback — which in turn is essential for understanding whether a plan or action will resonate with your company's consumers.

Consider the celebration of Halloween in Hong Kong. You might think this is an American holiday, but Ocean Park takes it to another level. We set up eight haunted houses and run thirteen live shows, while 666 monsters roam the park during a six-week period that attracts more visitors than any other Halloween event in the world. About 1.2 million people experience Ocean Park Halloween annually. It takes nearly 1300 people to run the festival. I even get into the act, literally, with layers of makeup transforming me each evening into a ghoul of the underworld.

During my first year at Ocean Park, we were preparing for the fourth Halloween festival. It was a good bit smaller then — three haunted houses instead of eight, and only one live show.

My marketing team approached me at the time with the storyboard of a commercial they wanted to run: A young boy is playing outside his housing estate near a squeaky carousel. He stands there, his foot on top of a soccer ball, gazing into space like something is possessing him. His mother approaches and shakes him. (This is all done in black and white, with eerie lighting.) When his mom finally wakes him from the trance, he says 'Papa!'.

The storyboard says "So scary, he doesn't recognise his own mother."

Although they had translated the story from Cantonese to English, I didn't get it.

"It's a Hong Kong expression," explained Vivian Lee, who was with the marketing department. "When something is so scary, so nerve-wracking, you won't even recognise your mother."

"How would you say it in Cantonese?"

She repeated the line. This time, everyone around who had not yet seen the ad, started laughing. "Oh my God, that's the greatest!" they exclaimed.

The ad was clearly a hit.

"Vivian, this is perfect. You don't need my input," I told her. "This is a great example where I have to trust and defer to you. If it's relevant to the culture we serve, then we should run with it. I'm glad you shared it with me and thank you for helping me to understand, but don't let me influence the ad to be more American. I don't want it to be anything different from what you've presented, because it's perfect."

This 2004 ad campaign helped boost Halloween attendance 10%, as compared with a year earlier, to 310,000 people; much smaller than now, but the highest festival attendance for Ocean Park at that time.

This is a good place to note that Vivian has been a key player in the Ocean Park story. Subsequent to her role as a Marketing Manager, she was promoted to Marketing Director, then in 2014 to Executive Director for Sales & Marketing.

In my first year, we also learned two other key lessons about Halloween, including one from the media.

The entertainment manager who had driven Ocean Park's first three Halloween festivals was one of the few people who left the company to join Disney, so as we planned this year's event, I asked the rest of the marketing and entertainment team for an update about the previous year's festival, and what materials we still had in-house. Then I suggested, "Why don't we do the Mirror Maze house again? We could reuse some of the pop-up and animatronic effects."

Months later, when journalists arrived for the media preview, they remarked, "Hey, that's the same haunted house as last year! Why should we come again? There's no reason. We've already seen it!"

That was an Aha! moment. I had not understood the need for each year's event to be new and fresh. In other markets, repeating a popular attraction would not have been a problem. We did it all the time at Knott's Berry Farm. But the Hong Kong market demanded a different approach.

Fortunately, the journalists' critique did not make it into print. However, from that point onward, we decided never to repeat a haunted house again. We just had to explore how to make it different and exciting each year, and do it economically.

Meanwhile, through surveys and feedback forms, we learned that our guests were generally entertained by Western ghosts and frightened by local ones. We asked the event sponsors about this during a thank-you dinner. One person shared that there was a ghost in his office at the end of the hallway who takes over the photocopy machine every night at 8pm; he made sure to always get out of the building before then. Someone else shared a story about a ghost in their housing estate. It turned out that everyone at the table had a ghost story to tell, be it their own or an urban legend, like the haunting of the former marine police headquarters in Hullett House (which has since been converted into a hotel and shopping complex).

We wanted to produce scary Halloween entertainment at Ocean Park — not just fun photo moments — so we shifted our focus away from Western tales to local ones.

❖

I believe that one of the first steps required by any new leader in an existing business or business unit is to understand the company's human resources. What do the people working with you require to achieve success? Does there need to be a change in corporate culture? Do they need more or less oversight? How about their budget?

The first step of 'seeking to understand' required me to truly listen to my colleagues, people who had been working hard in the company long before I arrived. My new teammates appreciated that I wanted to hear their ideas and did not simply wish to impose my own. The fact that I listen to them — and rearticulate their ideas — in turn makes them more open when it comes time for the second step, when I wish to be understood.

This principle and process plays a key role in managing human resources throughout the year, including when it is time for the annual performance review.

At Ocean Park, ten people reported directly to me. (In January 2005, when I first conducted assessments at Ocean Park, I had eight direct reports. Later, we added two new portfolios: one for In-park Revenue and another for Project Development.)

Prior to my arrival, I don't think my staff had ever experienced a performance review process like the one in which I engaged them. I don't simply prepare a one-pager and conduct a fifteen minute meeting. The process is significantly more comprehensive. The longest review to prepare, and the longest meeting, was with the company's finance director and corporate secretary, Matthias Li, who had been with the park since 1994 and had a broad ambit of responsibility.

"Matthias, how do you feel you did this year?" I began the meeting.

"I don't know. I thought you were going to tell me," he replied dryly.

"No, I'd like to understand first how you feel about your performance. What do you think you did well? Where can you work harder or produce better results?"

Over the course of a two-hour meeting, we covered every aspect of his job, topic by topic, hitting the high points of each area. I listened. I shared my perceptions. I encouraged him in areas where he was doing well and offered suggestions on things that could be done differently. None of this was much of a surprise, though. We'd been chatting about these items in weekly meetings all year.

Later, Matthias could read my evaluation of his work — a lengthy document that took about six to eight hours to prepare. Today, with an automated review system, members of our team see their leader's assessment in advance. They also submit a self-evaluation. A blend of the two papers guides the discussion.

Some team members engage in this process more than others. If someone is particularly quiet during a performance review, I tell them, 'Why don't you take the assessment with you, review it, and let me know later if you have any thoughts on it. We don't have to close the discussion right here." Some people react better when they have more time to reflect.

Some time after that first review with Matthias, I was at a social gathering when his wife, May, leaned over and told me, "Matthias is so happy with his job, so happy. He really appreciates the feedback you gave him. No one has ever taken the time before to do a review like that."

When your colleague's spouse tells you how happy he is at work, you know you're doing something right. That's some of the best feedback you can ever receive. Matthias, meanwhile, has always been one of the company's top performers, which is why he's now succeeded me as Ocean Park's chief executive.

Applying Understanding to Your Business

Whether you are in a start-up, seeking to transform a business or leading a successful enterprise, applying the principle of understanding will help you and your company succeed.

As you practise this habit, it becomes self-reinforcing. I find myself seeking first to understand not only when there is an issue to resolve or decision that must be made, but also when fielding questions from the media or even coaching my staff. I also remind my team to avoid running into a situation, offering answers without stopping for a moment to ask questions and listen carefully to the replies.

What happens if you do not practise the principle of understanding in your business?

You risk animosity among your staff, poor morale and team members who do not 'own' leadership solutions and direction.

You've likely seen situations like this. The boss walks into the room and says 'this is what we're going to do'. The whole team agrees. But in reality, they do not. After the meeting, there's grumbling, griping, and dissension. When these team members convey the instructions to their colleagues, they preface it by saying "the boss says we need to . . . " conveying that they themselves are not on board. The project may or may not fail, but it certainly will not succeed as it should have.

Effective understanding requires that your colleagues are part of the process and do not somehow feel removed from it. From the beginning, there also needs to be mutual trust that all parties to the conversation can speak freely.

Let me share a few words now about how to implement the principle of understanding in your business. Earlier in this chapter, I listed three steps:

1. Listen
2. Reflect & Verify
3. Share

The hardest step is often reflecting and verifying what you're told. As you listen, consider taking notes, then repeat the main points. This may take some time, but it's essential to ensure there are no misunderstandings. Here's one way to verify your understanding — after listening, fill in the blanks in this script:

"This is what I am hearing . . . And this is what I am understanding from what I am hearing . . . Is this correct? Have I captured the essence of your concerns and views?"

If your staff agrees that you understand their views, you can then discuss how to address them.

"Now that you've shared this with me, what would you like to see happen? How would you like to address this? How can we improve the situation or solve the problem? What role would you like me to play? How can I help?"

You may not agree with the solutions being offered, or perhaps you hear a glaring weakness. In these cases, consider the following:

"In my experience, when I come across a situation like this, this approach has proved to be effective. Have you tried this? Do you think this would work here?"

As you talk through the solution, you can model it out on a tablet or white board. If there's still hesitancy, you can finally add, "I have a view that we should take this approach. Do you think you can accommodate it?"

More times than not, this is a very effective way of being understood.

📌 Remember This

1. Seek First to Understand, Then to Be Understood.
2. Listen, ask questions, process the information.
3. Practise reflective listening — reiterate what you *hear* to verify that you understand correctly.
4. The process of seeking to understand never ends.
5. Practise understanding with all stakeholders, both inside and outside the company.
6. Understanding is not the same as Agreeing, but it's best to be on the same page before proceeding together (or parting ways).
7. Effective Understanding requires all team members to be part of the process, and not feel removed from it.
8. Mutual trust is a precursor to understanding. Employees must believe they can speak without fear of reprisal or they will not share freely with their employer.
9. Mutual trust is also a result of understanding. When people feel heard, acknowledged and accepted, trust increases and individuals become more creative and productive.
10. If you seek first to understand, you can learn from anyone.

PRINCIPLE 2

Value

Make the Competition Irrelevant

When I interviewed at Ocean Park, not quite two years before Hong Kong Disneyland's opening, the prevailing mentality among the company's Board and staff was that we needed to compete directly with Disney.

I challenged this assumption.

"You don't want to pick a fight with an 800-pound gorilla," I told the Board. "Disney has incredible intellectual property. They have an astounding ability to execute this intellectual property (I.P.) in just about any format imaginable — films, rides, retail, you name it. They've got more money, more I.P. and a better ability to implement their I.P. than just about anyone else. We should play to our strengths, not theirs.

"We need to complement Disney, not compete with them."

The strategy that I suggested — and one which I believe can provide both a compass and flight plan for any business facing a competitive market — was to focus on Values, specifically on two types of values: Core Values and Differential Values.

Core Values — together with a company's vision and mission — provide direction and a common rallying point. This is your compass. Core principles become a part of your company's essence and culture. They guide its development and become a defining framework, a reminder of why you're doing what you do. Successful companies stay true to their core values, no matter what happens with the business.

Differential Values, on the other hand, allow you to distinguish your company from the competition. What makes your product or service unique? And what is the consumer's point of reference — what do they compare you to?[17] The answers to these questions become your flight plan. For Ocean Park, articulating our differential values meant staking out positions that clearly showed how a day at Ocean Park was different (and better) than visiting Disney.

Through the first 25+ years of its history, Ocean Park had never fully defined these key guiding principles. The impending arrival of a new competitor, along with the start of my tenure as CEO, provided an opportunity for Ocean Park's directors and staff to reflect, discuss, and articulate these values in writing.

We began with the Vision Statement. Take a moment to close your eyes and imagine you're ten years in the future. What does your business look like? What does it do? Where do you excel? What does your company represent to the members of your community?

As we conducted this exercise, my team initially identified four key values: Fun, Safety, Service, and Conservation/Education. Over the years, we continued to take stock of the corporate vision, mission, and values during our annual off-site strategic planning sessions, to make sure that they remain relevant to our business as it grows and evolves. Only once in twelve years, though, did we update the values, and this was only recently as the park is growing into a resort. We affirmed the existing values, and added two more: 'Show Value' and 'Respect for People, Community and Animals'.

Back in 2004, we collectively determined that these core values define Ocean Park. This then led us down the path to discuss values

17 The EMM Group suggests that three components be 'brought together' to determine a product's differential value: a consumer's frame of reference, your product's unique offering and the price tag. See www.emmgroup.net/insights/delivering-value-vs.-delivering-differential-value

that would differentiate Ocean Park from our main competitor. This was an interesting exercise, because while Ocean Park and Disney are in the same attractions space — and while both parks provide wholesome entertainment for families (a shared value) — the contrast between our two attractions and our two companies is quite stark.

Disney is about fantasy — about Mickey and Minnie Mouse, Pluto and Donald Duck, about animation and action figures — while Ocean Park is about reality and nature, sharks and dolphins, giant pandas and (later) penguins.

Disneyland's famous icon is the fairytale castle. In Hong Kong and California, it's the 'Sleeping Beauty Castle'. Inspired by the homes of European nobility — like the 19th century Neuschwanstein Castle in Germany — you'll find a version of this fairytale castle in every Disney park.

Ocean Park's most famous icon, on the other hand, is the cable car. The rounded six-seater glass and steel cable cars offer stunning views of Hong Kong Island's mountainous terrain and the South China Sea some 670 feet below. Up until 2009, the 8-minute ride was also the only way to travel between the park's two major areas, the Waterfront and the Summit (previously known as the Lowland and Headland, respectively). Until the Ocean Express funicular system opened that year, it's safe to say that every Ocean Park visitor rode the cable car — and it was often the first thing they did after entering the park.

Another important difference between Disney and Ocean Park is cultural: Disneyland is America, while Ocean Park is Hong Kong. Disney was bringing a particular type of American entertainment to Hong Kong. While they publicly tried to appear somewhat Chinese, everything from the cartoon characters to the food to the design of the park is distinctly American, beginning with Main Street U.S.A., the themed area situated just past the entry turnstiles. Modelled after Walt Disney's turn-of-the-century, early 1900's hometown in Missouri, the look of Hong Kong Disneyland's Main Street U.S.A. is nearly identical to that of Disney's first park in Anaheim, California.

In contrast, Ocean Park is 'distinctly Hong Kong'. The park also has a generational connection with parents who visited Ocean Park as children and now bring their own families to visit. These parents want their kids to experience what they themselves did as children. We remind Hong Kongers that we have grown up together and Ocean Park is 'Hong Kong's People's Park'. This generational value, a key distinction between the two parks, taps into a collective memory and emotional point that will take Disney decades to cultivate.

From a corporate perspective as well, Ocean Park and Disney couldn't be more different. Disney is Goliath, a slow-moving, global behemoth. The tiniest decision can require approval from their headquarters in Burbank. Ocean Park is David, a small, local, not-for-profit company that can be fleet of foot. If I want our mascot, Whiskers, to wave with his left hand instead of his right, we can make that change and implement it right away, but if the team at Hong Kong Disneyland believes Mickey's shoes should be red, not yellow, because red is a lucky colour here, they can expect a multi-year, multi-dimensional analysis testing every conceivable impact on Mickey's character and the Disney brand. Before you know it, the opportunity to change is lost.

We didn't need to copy Disney — and we certainly couldn't compete with them dollar for dollar — but recognising these differential values enabled Ocean Park to grow by focusing on its strengths and being true to itself, rather than trying to be something it wasn't.

Differential Values	
Ocean Park	**Hong Kong Disneyland**
Animals	Cartoons
Nature	Movies
Cable Car	Castle
Family	Family
Hong Kong	America

A first-look at Ocean Park's differential values, as discussed in 2004

❖

'Save the best and improve the rest!' This became a guiding principle as we developed a new master plan to modernise and transform Ocean Park. We began to identify all the things we needed to change in order to bring the park into the 21st century, without losing the essence of what made it unique. This really came back to our founding principles — conservation, education and entertainment — keeping in mind that the animals were the core of the park and a key differentiator between us and Disney.

Despite striving to always keep our differential values in view, it didn't take long before we ran headlong into a conflict.

Ocean Park, at the time, had a number of popular attractions — the cable car, aquarium, giant pandas, and a few rides — but no thread connecting them together.

In 2004, we hired a renowned storyteller, Adam Bezark, to develop these links. Over the years, Adam has collaborated with a Who's Who of Hollywood and theme park brands, including Steven Spielberg, Tom Hanks, Cirque de Soleil, Disney, Universal, Paramount and LEGOLAND, to name a few.

Adam proposed that Ocean Park build a state-of-the-art simulator — like a 4D or 5D movie. Perhaps you've enjoyed one of these experiences in a theme park, or even in a shopping centre. You put on glasses to watch a 3D movie, but in addition to that, the seats move at key points during the film, while special effects inside the theatre mimic wind, rain, and other sensory experiences, perhaps even someone blowing on your cheek. The content of these films varies. Some attractions license films from distributors, as Ocean Park did in its early days. The animated content that Adam proposed, though, would be unique to Ocean Park and take viewers on a simulated marine world journey.

Simulators were actually not a new idea for Ocean Park. The park installed its first high-tech theatre, called Film Fantasia, in the 1980s. The cinema had 100 hydraulic seats that could tilt in four directions: forward, back, left and right. (Later cinemas would add 'up and down' to the high-tech seats.) The early content consisted of imported films.

Then in 2002, two years before my arrival, Ocean Park commissioned a US$9 million upgrade called Whiskers' Wild Ride, which was the first locally-made animated production of its kind in Hong Kong. The nearly five-minute film featured Ocean Park's mascot, the sea lion Whiskers, who took guests on a fly-through of the park by day and night. The film was projected onto a 49-foot high screen — smaller than an IMAX, but bigger than many cinemas — and when Whiskers and his pals plunged under water, viewers were spritzed with water; when they flew to the top of the observation tower, you felt the cool breeze in your face.

Now, Adam was proposing to update the media and give it a marine theme.

It was then that I realized, 'Why are we doing this?'. Why are we spending time and money on a simulation? Our media wasn't that great. Without anything else like it in the market, it was okay, but once Disney opened, there was no way it would stand up to scrutiny. No one does simulators and animated films better than Disney, and the last thing we needed was for future visitors to draw unfavourable comparisons.

"Adam, we can't do this," I said, after he presented the storyboard. "Our goal is to stand apart from Disney. This isn't differential; it's playing to their strength. Let Disney own that space. We need to get out of the simulator business."

Borrowing a phrase from my days at Knott's Berry Farm, I added, "The difference is real." Knott's Berry Farm, which is located about seven miles from Anaheim, California, had successfully co-existed with Disneyland for decades by leaving the fantasy space to Mickey and staking a claim to entertainment based on the California Gold Rush and American history.

"If you want the fake mouse, go to Disney," I told Adam. "If you want the real one, come to Ocean Park. We are not a fantasy. We are about real life and connecting people with nature. We need to keep our goals — conservation, education, entertainment — in focus. Disney isn't going to have live animals. That's where we can have an advantage

"Disney has the animated mouse, we have the real one," I repeated.

We pulled the simulator theatre and re-focused our planning on attractions that were in line with Ocean Park's differential values.

❖

Sometimes it takes an outsider to notice what's obvious.

Ocean Park has always been Hong Kong's 'People's Park'. Opened in 1977, initially as a subsidiary of the Hong Kong Jockey Club, Ocean Park today is a place where parents can relive their childhood memories and share the experience with their own children. This generational connection was so intrinsic to the park that my directors didn't notice until a newcomer arrived to point it out.

Understanding that we were "Distinctively Hong Kong" yet "Uniquely Ocean Park" shaped our redevelopment, our programming, and the company's communications and marketing campaigns. To this day, Ocean Park stays true to its Hong Kong roots, while also taking steps to make sure visitors from the mainland and elsewhere feel at home.

My Hong Kong team initially didn't see Ocean Park's 'Hong Kong-ness' as a strength. They were trying their hardest to come up with ways to compete with Disney, rather than complementing it.

"Let our differences be our strength," I told them.

"We don't need to work on immersive experiences like simulators or 'dark rides'," I continued, using an industry term for indoor theme park rides that use some sort of coaster or train, like Disney's 'It's a Small World' and 'Pirates of the Caribbean'.

"Our attractions should be about celebrating nature and the environment."

Ocean Park's core values grounded us, while we focused on the differential values that would set the attraction apart from Disney. The largest piece of the new US$700 million Master Redevelopment Plan would be Aqua City and the construction of one of the best aquariums in the world, home to some 5000 fish, providing visitors with the chance to watch and learn about over 400 species including hammerhead sharks, manta rays, and the hermaphroditic Napoleon Humphead Wrasse (who begin life as females). When Ocean Park's Grand Aquarium opened in 2011, it set a record for the largest underwater aquarium viewing dome, a source of pride not just for its size, but for the great views that it provided.

Aqua City would take half a dozen years to realise. In the interim, we launched other new animal initiatives to generate buzz and stand out from Disney. At first, we created new educational programmes and closeup encounters with animals, featuring Ocean Park's existing resources. The Honorary Giant Panda Keeper programme, for example, began in 2004 and remains extremely popular with parents and children, who learn how to prepare meals and make toys for the pandas, all while learning more about the threats to pandas in the wild. They can enter the panda enclosures (when the pandas are safely back-of-house) and get closer to Ocean Park's panda residents — An An, Jia Jia, Ying Ying and Le Le — than other park-goers, though they are always separated by a translucent safety barrier.

Jia Jia, by the way, was the oldest panda living under human care until she died in October 2016 at the age of 38. In human years, she was a centenarian — 114 years old. While her vision was affected by cataracts and she took medicine for hypertension, she was otherwise healthy until the end, enjoying a daily diet of fresh bamboo shoots and fruit. She was with Ocean Park for eighteen years and we miss her dearly. Jia Jia and An An were given to Hong Kong by Beijing in 1999 to mark the second anniversary of Hong Kong's return to China after more than 150 years of British colonial rule. Ocean Park's youngest pandas — Ying Ying and Le Le — came to Hong Kong in 2007, to celebrate the 10th anniversary of the handover. All four giant pandas are from Sichuan, China. We've encouraged Ying Ying and Le Le to mate. They've shown some interest, but so far, no cubs.

If you're wondering what sort of toys giant pandas enjoy, these are usually puzzles with treats in the middle or items suspended from a tree that require the panda to climb and discover. Our Honorary Giant Panda

Keepers make toys out of rope, cloth, PVC or even pumpkins; inside, they place bamboo hearts, biscuits, or fruit to attract and maintain the pandas' interest. The puzzles challenge the pandas' dexterity and ability to think and manipulate items.

In addition to this giant panda programme, we also created Breakfast with Pandas, a Dolphin Encounter, summer school programmes, and the Ocean Park Academy for students, teachers, and learners as young as three years old.

The first brand-new animal attraction launched by my team was Sea Jelly Spectacular, in April 2006. We converted a small, unused space — about 5,000 square feet — into a themed attraction to showcase the jelly fish. Ocean Park funded the US$1 million project with cash reserves in order to offer a new differential product and stay in the news at a time when we were preparing to tear up parts of the park for redevelopment.

Since jelly fish are not sensitive to light or sound, we used music, lighting and special effects to create a theatrical experience. It's really something to watch the sea jellies, with their umbrella-shaped 'heads' and long tentacles trailing behind, swimming through the vividly-lit tanks of Ocean Park's 'underwater garden' in sync with choral music. These creatures, who are 95–98% water, have "drifted along on ocean currents for millions of years, even before dinosaurs lived on the Earth"[18]. At Ocean Park, there are more than 1000 sea jellies of all shapes, colours, and sizes from across the globe.

For the launch, Ocean Park's chairman Allan Zeman wore a giant pastel-coloured sea jelly costume. All you could see of him, underneath the huge bonnet and bright flowery pinks and turquoise of the outfit, was Allan's face and wide smile. He looked ridiculous, but Allan was always a good sport when it came to promoting the park. The media loved the outfit and it helped to generate a lot of coverage, much more than Disney was receiving at the time.

The public response was spectacular. In the first three weeks of operation, we saw a 350,000 incremental jump in attendance, as compared

---

18 National Geographic Kids: http://kids.nationalgeographic.com/animals/jellyfish

with the same period a year earlier. Families were coming to the park specifically to see the jelly fish and were willing to queue up for more than an hour to get in. The attraction paid for itself within three weeks of operation, which is unheard of in the theme park industry.

❖

While we welcomed new animals to the park and offered innovative ways to interact with them, we weren't about to forsake the entertainment side of Ocean Park's mission, as it had always been part of the company's DNA. Our rides were all open-air, providing guests with the chance to enjoy great views and a wonderful time outside. In December 2011, we would add a new carnival-themed area called Thrill Mountain, with games of skill and Hong Kong's first floorless rollercoaster, which offers breathtaking vistas in addition to hurling guests through multiple inversions. Even our oldest roller coaster, the Mine Train, was special, not because of its speed, but because of its unique location — perched on a 280-foot cliff overlooking Aberdeen Harbour!

Disney simply can't offer this type of experience; they don't have the topography. Hong Kong Disneyland is built on reclaimed land — and it's flat.

As Disney's grand opening in September 2005 approached and we looked for other ways to stand out, my team and I decided it was time to supersize an Ocean Park tradition: Halloween! As I mentioned in the last chapter, Halloween is one of the most exciting times of the year at Ocean Park. It's an iconic festival that entertains and scares hundreds of thousands of park-goers every year.

In this case, we knew Disney would not do anything special for Halloween — the holiday would fall just a few weeks after their debut. After launching in September, there was no way in the world they would come back in October and change their product to put an event in place. Not only would it be too much work, they also had to allow time for the market to get to know them and experience their core offering.

Ocean Park, on the other hand, could ramp up its Halloween celebration. For the first time, we offered a single Halloween admissions ticket, instead of charging for entry to each haunted house. We added a charity preview, a Halloween Fun Run and a grand-scale daytime finale with 50 ghoulish characters, in addition to creating five new haunted zones. Ocean Park's Halloween ghouls and monsters also surprised Hong Kongers in the city when they roamed the streets of Mongkok and Causeway Bay to promote the festival.

As Ocean Park's Halloween Bash was timely and completely different from Hong Kong Disneyland's offerings, we were able to make noise in the market just one month after Disney's opening and actually take market share away from them. The publicity also reminded the public that Ocean Park was home-grown and 'at it again', creating something new and different. While the festival is a fun, escape-oriented event — which on the surface has nothing to do with conservation or education — one dollar of every paid admission still went to conservation research. More about this when we discuss Principle 9!

Dominating Disney: Core and Differential Values

Focusing on Ocean Park's Differential Values while staying true to our Core Values, guided the park's transformation and without question enabled the company to not only respond to the arrival of a major competitor, but to dominate it in the process.

Identifying and focusing on Ocean Park's unique strengths mandated a change of course from the one that my predecessors and Board of Directors had previously set. We would no longer try to out-Disney Disney. They might be a competitor for discretionary time and money (just like movie cinemas or a trip to visit the Big Buddha on Hong Kong's Lantau Island), but they would not be a competitor for product.

As my former boss at Knotts Berry Farm, Terry van Gorder, used to say, and as I repeated to my team at Ocean Park, "The difference is real." Disney has the animated mouse; we have the real one.

When Ocean Park was the only themed attraction in Hong Kong, it could build a simulator and attract visitors. Once it faced competition, the simulator was no longer unique and would in fact be second-rate. It was time to shut it down.

Allowing Core Values to be our compass and Differential Values our flight plan led Ocean Park to renew its commitment to animals, nature, and Hong Kong. These focal points drove the design and selection of new attractions, as well as the company's marketing plans and public communication.

Disney's arrival pushed us to transform Ocean Park into a world-class destination, while always offering value for money. We benefited by the influx of tourists Disney attracted to Hong Kong, yet stayed several steps ahead — in visitor numbers, profitability, publicity and community engagement. Focusing on our differences became our strength.

I'm proud of the fact that through the entire redevelopment, we never lost sight of the founding values of the park: conservation, education and entertainment.

The marketplace has changed since 2004. Hong Kong Disneyland is no longer Ocean Park's sole 'competitor'. In 2014, a Chinese company called Chimelong opened a marine resort near Zhuhai, across from Macau, just a 70-minute ferry ride from Hong Kong.

Unlike Disney, Chimelong's Ocean Kingdom is in the same space as Ocean Park. They have a large aquarium, animals and entertainment. But they don't stress education and conservation like Ocean Park does. They are not an internationally accredited animal facility. They lack Ocean Park's breathtaking topography and generational connection with people in their target markets.

Once again, we needed to assess Ocean Park's Differential Values, but this time, with an eye on both Disney and Chimelong.

Applying Values to Your Business

In 2005, two INSEAD business professors, W. Chan Kim and Renée Mauborgne, published a book about creating uncontested market share and making the competition irrelevant. They called it "Blue Ocean Strategy". The idea is that if you're competing with other companies in the same water — offering the same product and services — the water will become bloody. But if your company can differentiate itself, it can find a 'blue ocean', a space all to itself.

From my experience, the first step to create a Blue Ocean where your company can thrive is to revisit your Corporate Vision and Mission statements. Are these well-articulated and up-to-date? Do the statements convey and adequately express the essence of your business and its DNA? These statements should influence the development of your business' Core Values. Do these values then resonate with your employees, partners, and clients? Does the public associate these values with your brand?

If your company is a monopoly or already working in a niche, you may not feel pushed to go farther. That was the case with Ocean Park initially, until the Hong Kong government reached a deal to bring Disney into the territory.

The moment a competitor enters your market — or better yet, the moment you realise a competitor will enter the market — it is time to take stock of the Differential Values that make your company stand apart. If you don't want to compete solely on price, ask your team the following questions:

- How do we differ from our competitors?
- How do we provide greater value to our consumers than our competitors?
- What makes our company unique?
- Can these differences be our strengths?
- If so, how can we leverage these differences to have a competitive advantage?

The answers to these questions shape the Differential Values that will enable your company to stand out and take market share. For your company values to have impact, they must be much more than words on a web page. They need to be genuine; they need to withstand scrutiny and the test of time. Too many companies simply tick the boxes or frame a document on the wall listing values like honesty, integrity and respect. These are all good values, but they don't mean anything if they are not acted upon and reinforced. You and your company need to be sincere. There needs to be passion. You need to believe and live the values, then they can be reflected in your strategic planning and daily business. Your company's Core Values become a compass, and the Differential Values a flight plan for planning and decision-making.

At Ocean Park, we regularly reinforced and restated our values across the company in a variety of ways, including: discussions and management meetings, employee newsletters, employee orientation programmes, and training programmes for tour guides and corporate trainers. You'll know you're successful when team members honestly believe the values and implement them in their own work.

There will be times when sticking to the company values may force a difficult decision — such as dropping a product offering or abandoning an area of development in which you've already invested — but it will be the right decision to make and, in my view, one which will be in the best long-term interest of the business.

Review the company values at least once a year. The market changes and so does your business. New competitors can enter your ocean; if they do, how do you ensure that you continue to occupy a unique space?

Be careful — if your company does not adhere to its Core Values, your employees and the public will know. And if it fails to adopt or implement Differential Values, newcomers to the market are likely to surpass you and leave your company behind.

🖈 Remember This

1. Core Values are your compass.
2. Differential Values are your flight plan.
3. Core Values should reflect your corporate DNA and provide a daily reminder of why your company is in business.
4. Differential Values clearly show how your company is different (and better) than its competitors and enable you to play to your strengths, not theirs.
5. Differential Values create a 'blue ocean' where your competitors are irrelevant.[19]
6. Let your differences be your strengths.
7. Complement, don't compete.
8. To have impact, values must be more than words on a page; they need to be reflected in your strategic planning, your daily business and embodied by your staff.
9. Use all forms of internal communications to reinforce and restate corporate values.
10. Review your Core and Differential Values at least once a year to ensure they remain relevant in the face of changing market conditions, new competitors and your company's evolution.

---

19 As mentioned earlier in this chapter, the phrase 'Blue Ocean' was coined by W. Chan Kim and Renee Mauborgne in the book "Blue Ocean Strategy" published in 2005 by Harvard Business Review Press.

Measure

If You Can Measure It, You Can Manage It

About eight years into my career, I was transferred from the admissions' department at Knott's Berry Farm and promoted to be manager of Ride Operations.

As a kid I had enjoyed going to Knotts Berry Farm — which is located in Orange County, California, not far from where I grew up — to ride one of the first log flumes in America, marvel at the Wild West shows and be captivated by headline entertainers in the John Wayne Theatre. Park lore has it that Knott's Berry Farm got its start as a place to visit in 1934, near the height of the Great Depression, when Walter and Cornelia Knott, struggling to make ends meet, served eight homemade fried chicken dinners followed by Boysenberry Pie on their wedding china to motorists driving by on State Route 39. Before long, travellers were lining up for more.

Six years later, the Knotts added their first attraction: a cyclorama depicting a panoramic view of the family's journey West. "The Covered Wagon Show" was set in the lobby of an old mining hotel that Walter Knott relocated from Prescott, Arizona. The hotel and show were the start of Knott's Berry Farm's first themed area, Ghost Town, which would later include storefronts with peek-in windows, a post office, saloon, livery stable, Borax mule train, jail, print shop, blacksmith, corn mill, waterwheels, gun and knife stores — all purchased in abandoned towns, then rebuilt on his property. Today, the park is one of the most visited in North America. The Chicken Dinner Restaurant is still a big draw, too, serving 1.5 million people a year.

After my first job as a teenage sweeper cleaning the park grounds, I eventually worked my way up to become Vice President of Park Operations and Entertainment at Knotts Berry Farm. Back in 1984, when I was an operations newbie, my boss Joe Meck pulled me aside to talk about efficiency. Joe's vision had been shaped by his early years in the business, at an attraction located about seven miles down the road: Disneyland. Joe taught me the three P's: "Guests should never have to wait to pay, pee or park," he said. Sound advice.

No matter where they are in the park, long lines can be a headache for visitors. As I embarked in my new role, Knott's Berry Farm CEO, Terry Van Gorder, asked me to consider how we could improve the guest experience. He passed me an old study done for another theme park by the consulting firm McKinsey & Co. It looked at how many rides should be offered per guest per hour during peak times. The rule of thumb was a minimum of two rides per guest per hour. Anything less could lead to grumbling.

This was an Aha! moment for me. I realised there's science behind the business, math propelling the fun. Because if you can measure it, then you can manage it.

At Ocean Park, we continually measured everything, from the time that visitors spend in the park to which rides are most popular at a given moment, to the number of taxis that drop off and pick up guests.

I can't stress enough the importance of metrics. I wasn't a math major and have never been a statistician or analyst, but I've always found that if I can break something into its core elements, then I can understand and quantify it in terms that make sense for our business strategy. The right metrics enable you to set targets and key performance indicators. Measuring enables you to hold yourself and others accountable.

What happens if you don't measure?

Management becomes driven primarily by gut feelings and a 'seat of the pants' mentality. You leave yourself exposed to random things, and when there are problems, it's a lot harder to identify root causes, much less set targets for improvement. Feedback to your team and employees throughout the company ends up being driven by personal observation, which makes it harder to gain buy-in when changes are needed.

Back at Knott's Berry Farm, after reading the McKinsey report, I realised we couldn't just look at the number of rides per hour. Yes, our guests enjoyed riding The Corkscrew and spending time with the Peanuts gang in Camp Snoopy, but they also came for the chicken dinners and hard-to-find replicas of historical firearms in the Overland Gun Shop. I couldn't focus on rides alone, because Knott's Berry Farm is one of the very few parks where people say they're actually coming for the food!

I needed to think bigger. If I was going to come up with an accurate measure of the park's offerings, I needed to take into account all the attractions — the rides, the shows, the saloon, and the dining. So I came up with a new metric which has served me well throughout my career: 'Entertainment Units'.

Once we had a core metric, how would we use it to ensure that, mathematically at least, guests wouldn't have to wait longer than half an hour for an attraction during peak hours? There had to be enough entertainment offerings.

Every park — indeed every attraction, be it a shopping centre, movie theatre or theme park — has a maximum capacity. At Knott's Berry Farm, the magic number was 30,000. So we had to have at least 60,000 entertainment units in order to assure 2 attractions per guest per hour.

To give you an idea of how we reach 60,000, you need to count how many people can ride each roller coaster in one hour, how many seats there are in each live show, the hourly capacity of key non-ride non-show attractions, how many people can eat in the restaurants each hour, etc., and then add them all up.

It's important though not to count something which is not actually entertainment from your guests' perspective — more about how this can trip you up in a moment.

When I arrived at Ocean Park in 2004, we calculated that there were 35,000 Entertainment Units. But the park's instantaneous capacity — as set by Hong Kong law — was 36,300 people. This meant that during peak hours, we couldn't even offer one attraction per guest on an hourly basis. This was dreadful! Nowhere close to the best practice of at least two attractions per hour. No wonder a lot of visitors were less than happy.

Whatever our redevelopment was going to be, it was abundantly clear that we needed to focus on adding entertainment units to the park. We needed to double the current offerings, and then some.

I began to introduce the concept of Entertainment Units to the team and to our designers and developers. I needed to make sure that this thrust would drive the park's new strategy. By the time Ocean Park's Master Redevelopment Plan was complete, the park offered 85,000 Entertainment Units — and more than that during months when we were running a special event like Halloween.

To this day, Entertainment Units feature in Ocean Park's Daily Operation Update. The number varies depending on the frequency of live shows, whether an attraction is closed for maintenance or bad weather, and the number of guests who visit the park that day.

❖

Identifying a core metric is important, but it's only the first step. Here are two important corollaries:

1. Stay True to your Essence

Imagine if at Ocean Park we had just blindly built more rides. On paper, it might have looked good. Our core metric, Entertainment Units, would have improved. But this alone would not have ensured the park's success. We also needed to stay true to who we were, to the business' values and mission.

At its heart, Ocean Park is an animal-based park. About two-thirds of the Master Redevelopment Plan budget financed conservation and education-based attractions, including new animal exhibits. The remaining third was spent on creating entertainment and themed areas, like the Polar Adventure facade that resembles icebergs.

2. Some Units are More Equal than Others

Two of the most popular attractions at Ocean Park are the Grand Aquarium and Polar Adventure, where there are hundreds of penguins, sea lions, snowy owls, and arctic foxes.

Imagine if you set aside a day of your weekend or holiday to visit Ocean Park with your family. Your kids are excited to watch the penguins play, while you and your spouse like to marvel at the manta rays as they glide through the aquarium.

But when you arrive at the park, you find out that both of these exhibits are closed for the day. Plenty of other attractions are still open, but the ones you were most looking forward to are not. How would you feel?

Some attractions are more equal than others.

At Knott's Berry Farm, we realised that having two or more iconic attractions offline at the same time was a cause for concern, even if the total number of entertainment units still passed the key threshold.

We also decided that if the park's entertainment capacity ever dropped below 85% — again, regardless of the overall number of entertainment units — we would need to consider adding additional capacity, such as another live show. Otherwise, visitors might feel cheated.

❖

From my earliest days in park operations, I thought of assigning different values to attractions based on their appeal to the public.

"I think we could spread out the downtime and maintenance schedules of rides and attractions throughout the year," I told my boss at Knott's Berry Farm, "so that we never have too many closed at once. That way, we'd ensure that we're always providing sufficient entertainment value to our guests."

"What do you mean by value?" he asked.

"Well, if every attraction is assigned a value from 1 to 5, we can easily calculate the total entertainment value of the park if everything is open," I explained. "Then imagine we start closing different attractions. How does this diminish the value to guests?

"We could also look at combinations of attractions — water rides vs. roller coasters, thrill rides vs. kids' rides — and assign numbers to them to ensure that there's always sufficient entertainment for every group."

I may as well have been speaking a foreign language. My boss looked at me like I was nuts.

"What are you talking about?" he replied. "That's not the way this business works!"

Well, I wasn't ready to give up quite yet, even though I felt like a lone voice in the woods. I approached Tom Cluff, a creative guy who worked in the entertainment division. Tom and I used to produce the largest Halloween attraction in California, Halloween Haunt, together. He also reported to the same boss. In the mid 1980s, spreadsheets were not that common yet, but Tom was quite good with computers. When I shared my idea with him, he said, "Of course you can do it. Look at this!"

Tom quickly put together a spreadsheet. We went through the entire park and assigned a value to everything. We came up with scenarios to manage maintenance, while paying attention to the guest experience. We set targets and quantified something that many of our peers thought wasn't possible. We never actually got the head of our department to buy into this method, but I applied it everywhere I went after that.

Disney Lost the Plot

Now, I'm not the only one to apply this sort of methodology.

The Walt Disney Company has long employed industrial engineers to optimise processes and reduce waste in its theme parks and resorts. They help establish operating hours, set sales goals, and build simulation models. "Our goal is to constantly improve the guest experience using solid analytical techniques," Walt Disney Parks and Resorts' director of industrial engineering Kathy Kortte Kilmer told a publication at her alma mater, Purdue University. "(Industrial engineers') span of support across all units makes us uniquely qualified to solve even the most complex challenges.[20]"

---

20 "Putting IE skills to work for Disney," Eric Nelson, Purdue Engineering Impact Magazine, Fall 2009

But when Hong Kong Disneyland opened in 2005, the lines were so long that the park faced a barrage of public criticism. It was classic Economics 101: they did not have enough capacity to meet demand. There weren't enough rides and attractions. They didn't have enough seating. The experience was horrible. Government officials even suggested that Disney let fewer people in through the gates.

"A charity day on Sunday that was supposed to test the park's ability to run at near its capacity of 30,000 people turned into a fiasco of hour-long lines for rides, food shortages, inadequate parking and even the partial closing of a large area of the park because of overcrowding[21]," Keith Bradsher wrote in The New York Times.

From Day 1, Disney was on its heels, trying to increase capacity, fight negative perceptions, and somehow be more culturally relevant to the market, despite the fact that some of their best industrial engineers had worked tirelessly on the project for years.

What happened?

Disney simply didn't offer enough entertainment. If you look at Hong Kong Disneyland's first year map, they only had about 13 rides, shows, and attractions. I calculated that they had about 20,000 Entertainment Units, not counting the nightly fireworks, which meant that at peak times during the day they could only offer visitors 1 attraction every 90 minutes.

If you looked at their internal models, though, you certainly would have seen a different picture. Disney wouldn't have allowed the park to open the way it did, if the models had accurately portrayed its lack of capacity.

What likely happened is that Disney's budget started running thin. The project team had to conserve money and started working the numbers. They broke a cardinal rule: Disney tried to value everything in the park as a top attraction, even if it wasn't.

---

21 "It's a small park: Hong Kong Disneyland faces overcrowding," Keith Bradsher, The New York Times, 8 September 2005

Take the Fantasy Gardens, a pretty area with flowers and gazebos that is used as a backdrop for photos with Disney characters. Disney's industrial engineers would have measured the size of the garden, calculated how many people it can hold and then applied this capacity to their models. A similar approach would have been taken with the park's retail stores and restaurants. While this type of accounting helped the modellers meet capacity targets on paper, they forgot what's really important: guests were buying tickets to enjoy the *real* attractions — the rides and shows.

Disney forgot about the guest perspective and counted the wrong things.

Cedar Fair's Focus

In 1997, Cedar Fair purchased Knott's Berry Farm. By this time, we had implemented quite a few metrics across the entire park that helped us determine how, when and where to deploy our staff.

Cedar Fair, which had started in Ohio and was really just starting to expand, had a different approach. The new General Manager instructed me to stop measuring ticketing wait time and staffing. "We don't do that at Cedar Fair," I was told.

Our new owner had their own set of reports that we were required to complete, but these were focused on procurement and costs. They wanted to know, for example, how many toilet paper rolls and paper towels were in every restroom in the park as well as how many we went through in the course of a year. Perhaps this made more sense at Cedar Fair's other properties. They were seasonal attractions and the company didn't want to have a big surplus on hand at the end of the summer. Knott's Berry Farm was their first year-round theme park operation.

Calculating toilet paper consumption by toilet isn't going to help measure or manage the guest experience at all. Of course, you never want to run out of toilet paper. That would violate the 3 P's rule ("Never make a guest wait to park, pay or pee!"). But it's simpler to just make sure there are always spare rolls in the cabinets, and to procure at an overall level for the park that meets historic guest demand and projected needs.

Cedar Fair, on the other hand, wanted to measure paper product consumption so that it could consolidate its purchases. They would issue a single tender for paper products in all nine of their properties. They knew the volume requirements and could get a better price by buying in bulk. Cedar Fair was so driven by the bottom line, though, that they lost focus on the guest experience. They were measuring the wrong things.

As the sociologist, William Bruce Cameron, wrote in 1957, "Not everything that can be counted counts.[22]"

Lunchtime at Movie World Madrid

Sometimes the problem is not knowing what to count, but how to count it.

In 1999, when I moved to Spain to start up Warner Bros. Movie World Madrid, it was a brand new project that would take three years to bring to market. We opened with rides inspired by DC superheroes like Batman and Superman in 2002, as well as cartoon characters like Bugs Bunny and Daffy Duck. It's now one of the top parks in Europe and consistently wins safety awards. But one area we did not get right at first was food.

When designing a theme park, you need to know how long visitors will spend eating lunch or dinner, so you can calculate the number of restaurants needed, the number of seats, and how many servers and cooks to have on duty to ensure that the waiting time is not long.

We knew that eating patterns would be different in a Spanish theme park, but didn't grasp how different they are from the United States.

In the US, people generally spend 15 minutes in a fast food restaurant, half an hour in a cafeteria buffet and 45 minutes to an hour for a sit-down meal. We started with these metrics, and then visited Spanish restaurants to

---

22 See Quote Investigator: quoteinvestigator.com/2010/05/26/everything-counts-einstein/

study table turnover patterns. There weren't any comparable theme parks in Madrid at the time, so we observed people eating in shopping malls and other venues. We went to McDonald's, Burger King, KFC, neighbourhood restaurants, shopping mall eateries and sit-down restaurants. We also visited Port Aventura in Barcelona and Isla Magica in Seville, to get a sense of Spaniards' eating habits in other theme parks.

We thought we nailed it. We planned for 20 minutes for fast food, 45 minutes for buffeterias, and 90 minutes for sit-down dining.

But from the day Movie World Madrid opened, it was clear we didn't have enough capacity. Visitors were spending significantly longer in every type of restaurant in the park. We needed more seats.

What went wrong?

First, just about everyone in Spain eats lunch at the same time. Come 2:30 p.m., they stop what they're doing and go to eat. We didn't expect this habit to carry through to the theme park, but it did. No matter what special shows or events we programmed at this hour — anything to divert the crowds — it didn't matter. The cultural pull was too strong. Very few parks can handle 70–80% of their guests eating at the same time, but we had to adapt.

Second, more people wanted a sit-down meal and fewer opted for fast food than we expected.

Third, we conducted our research at the wrong times. We went to Barcelona and Seville to visit competitive attractions on weekdays. While we knew this wasn't a peak time, we thought we could extrapolate the behaviours we witnessed. As we walked around Port Aventura, we saw empty and closed restaurants. We thought they had over-provisioned and were sitting on dormant facilities. But, in fact, we didn't observe the true dining patterns.

In Spain, it's really feast or famine when it comes to entertainment (excuse the pun). On weekends and holidays, attractions are packed. On weekdays, it's another story. We didn't understand that at the time.

We should have visited Port Aventura and Isla Magica during their busiest times, to see how they managed the crowds. Instead, we chose times that were more convenient to our workday.

We knew what to count — how long people spent eating. In Spain, though, we just didn't know how to count it.

Transforming Qualifiable into Quantifiable

When you look at your own business, you may be thinking there are important aspects that can't be measured. After all, perceptions are subjective and not everything can be quantified, right?

Can you quantify what you stand for?

Yes, you can. But it may take some work and creative thinking.

Take, for example, Ocean Park's mission. A key part of what Ocean Park stands for is Education. Our mission states that the park should provide all our guests with "memorable experiences that are educational" and that we should "promote life-long learning".

But how could we measure if Ocean Park's guests were actually learning?

Well, one way would have been to test them as they left the park, but that's not very practical. We wouldn't be able to gauge if visitors retained what they learned a week or a year later. Plus, to really understand if the guests learned, we'd have to know what they had already known before visiting the park.

I shared this dilemma with Ocean Park's Education team.

Isabel Li, a bright Education Manager who joined the park in 1999 as an educator, spoke up.[23] She's passionate about influencing Hong Kongers' habits, to encourage sustainable living. She's been a driving force behind many of Ocean Park's campaigns to stop people from eating shark's fin soup and, like many of our educators, she wanted to know that her work was making a difference.

Isabel proposed creating a new metric called Education Units, along the same lines as the park's Entertainment Units. We could use these to

---

23 Isabel Li has since been promoted to Education Director.

quantify the amount of education available per guest per hour in exhibits and attractions with educational messaging.

"We could measure both passive and active learning," Isabel explained. "Passive learning occurs when a guest walks by an educational panel and reads it. Active learning requires interaction."

The team took Isabel's idea and ran with it. We created Passive Education Units based on the number of guests exposed to information panels in the aquarium and other animal attractions, and Active Education Units that measure the potential for guests to interact with Ocean Park educators or interactive, interpretive models (like the 'Shark X-ray', a translucent screen that visitors swipe to generate images of a shark's digestive, reproductive, and sensory systems).

If we weren't focused on measuring, we could have just put signs up and figured that some people would read them and some wouldn't, and that would have been the end of the story. Creating these two new metrics, however, allowed us to define quantifiable targets for our education staff. While we couldn't measure education directly, we measured the exposure points and optimised those experiences. Setting targets then helped determine how to staff the attractions, as well as the goals and KPIs set each year for the Education team.

There are plenty of examples of things that appear too subjective to measure, but if you think about it carefully, you'll find ways to quantify it or at least proxies that help you do so.

How, for example, can we judge whether the park is clean? Subjectively, this is visual. Do I see dirt or trash on the ground? Objectively, we can gauge visitor feedback. Are there any complaints? What do visitors say when surveyed? We can also track how frequently the cleaners make their rounds. Do they pass through heavily trafficked parts of the park often enough to ensure that it's clean? The frequency of their work is quantifiable and can be adjusted if needed.

Meanwhile, like most marine parks and theme parks, Ocean Park produces several shows every day. Visitors can watch birds of prey up close, travel along with a brave adventurer in 'Ocean Wonders' to learn about marine life and reducing marine debris, interact with sea lions, or sing and dance with Ocean Park's iconic mascots in Whiskers Theatre.

How can we tell, though, whether the shows are any good? How do we measure their quality? I might think a show is well-written, well-produced, and a great addition to our lineup, but that's subjective.

What we can do is measure a show's popularity. Is the house full? Are there any walkouts during the show? What about guest feedback? I can deduce an objective position — whether the show is good or bad — based on certain quantifiable metrics: attendance, walkouts and comments.

It is still important to be careful not to make a wrong deduction. There are other factors that can affect attendance, such as showtimes. Perhaps guests aren't in that part of the park at that time of day, in which case we would reschedule the production.

At the end of the day, if a key aspect of your business seems difficult to measure, you need to ask, (a) can it be broken down into measurable parts, and (b) are there easy-to-measure proxies that will answer the bigger questions.

Dominating Disney: The Role of Metrics

When Hong Kong Disneyland opened in September 2005, it was the attractive, highly-publicised, much-anticipated new kid in town. But once people entered the gates, they realised the product didn't match the hype.

At the time, Ocean Park had 35 rides, shows and attractions. If you compared the two parks — as local newspapers like Apple Daily did frequently — Ocean Park basically had triple the attractions at half the price. Even today, while Hong Kong Disneyland claims to have 100 shows and attractions, if you actually count them, it's more like 27 to 30, about one-third of Ocean Park's offerings.

Three weeks after Disney's opening, it was time for Ocean Park's month-long Halloween celebration. We added an additional twenty specialty attractions and a separate evening admission ticket. While Disney was criticised for not being ready and offering a sub-par experience, we offered a hugely popular, world-class Halloween celebration that stood in sharp contrast to Disney's failure. We were more than capable of meeting demand and providing a fantastic day or night out. Halloween reminded the public that Ocean Park was truly Hong Kong's 'People's Park'.

During the first year, Ocean Park and Hong Kong Disneyland's attendance numbers were more or less dead even. In year two, we eclipsed them by more than 1.2 million people.

The metrics drove Ocean Park's success. When we identified our core metric, we put in place a fundamental principle that hadn't existed before, and from then on it drove everything we did. It shaped our Master Redevelopment Plan (MRP) and informed plans to add new attractions and additional capacity every year for six years running.

With each new ride, with each new animal exhibit, with each seasonal festival, we were in the news, reminding Hong Kongers that they had a new reason to come back and visit the park. We were continually in a 'must see' position, relative to Disney, all because we had focused on being relevant to the market we serve and committed to increasing the entertainment offerings.[24]

By the time the MRP was complete in 2012, we had 85 rides, shows, and attractions, and 85,000 Entertainment Units. Without adding additional shows, Ocean Park could offer 2.3 EUs per guest per hour when the park was filled to capacity.

Once the metric was in place, we didn't have to change the measurement model again. We just needed to keep our eye on the ball and make sure we hit the targets. Recently-added wifi and automated counting processes provide real-time information about the utilisation of facilities, and enable the park to share information and direct visitors to areas with shorter waiting times. Daily reports show how many attractions we are offering per guest per hour during peak times. If we miss the mark, we can determine where we're missing it and what we need to change to achieve it.

By applying this same philosophy to all aspects of our business — not just the bottom line — we were able to transform Ocean Park into a world-class destination that consistently tops its better known competitor.

Applying Metrics to Your Business

Start by asking a few fundamental questions:

- How do you define and measure success in your business?
- How do you measure whether you are accomplishing an objective?
- Are there areas in which you are failing to meet your personal objectives?
- Are you getting too many guest complaints? Why are you getting them?
- Is your business performing at optimum levels?

---

24 For more about relevance, see Chapter 6.

It may be easiest to focus on the bottom line, but your business' optimum level can also be measured in repeat purchases, client feedback, public perception, safety records, etc.

As you begin to look at how you are performing against these indicators, can you break them down further to identify elements that will help you execute better?

Identifying the right metrics and continually taking stock of relevant measurements will shape your business strategy. You can then set overall targets for the business (and design a strategy to achieve them) as well as Key Performance Indicators for yourself, each department, and individual members of the team.

Once the metrics are in place, it becomes a matter of staying true to them.

But never become so focused on the numbers that you lose your sense of judgment. More about this in the next story.

A Difficult Decision: Metrics vs. Judgment

Jagged fingers of rose jasper and grey basalt rise from the beach of the Shantar Islands in the Okhostk Sea. Nine-foot high Kamchatka brown bears climb the cliffs and fish for salmon in the streams. With the exception of a few lonely souls at the weather station and the passing crew from commercial fishing vessels docked in its waters, these isles are uninhabited.

In the mid-1800s, at a time when the US was fighting and recovering from a bloody civil war, American ships hunted bowhead whales here. At least three whaleships crashed on the islands, not surprising given the tumultuous weather, unpredictable fog and ice floes that often encircle the terrain.

The sub-arctic waters are home to colonies of seals, sea lions, and one of the world's most charismatic animals, the white beluga whale, a beautiful creature with a toothy smile, round, protruding forehead and an amazingly flexible neck. The beluga are social animals. National Geographic calls them "vocal communicators (who) use a diversified language of clicks, whistles and clangs."

I've never actually travelled to the Okhostk Sea, but in 2006, Ocean Park commissioned conservation research there, to ascertain the state of the beluga population and potential impact of bringing several of the wondrous creatures to Ocean Park.

At the time, beluga whales were listed as a 'vulnerable' species by the International Union for Conservation of Nature (IUCN). We thought they would be an incredible ambassador for conservation.

"It is through the depth of our affections," writes the environmental advocate, David Orr, that people "set boundaries to what we do and direct our intelligence to better or worse possibilities." If you see a beluga up close, you'll understand.

Visitors form an emotional connection with Ocean Park wildlife. They're more likely to recall conservation messages and more open to considering the impact of their actions, according to Ocean Park consumer surveys and scientific research by groups like America's National Research Council and the U.S. Commission on Ocean Policy.

Our Master Redevelopment Plan called for the acquisition of up to eight animals — a mix of males, females, young and old — so that we could start a breeding programme and educate the public about the challenges faced by polar animals as climate change is melting the ice caps. We expected the beluga would be a tremendously popular feature of Ocean Park's new Polar Adventure, which was set to open in 2012, the grand finale of the Master Redevelopment Plan that had been adopted half a dozen years earlier.

I should note here that not everyone agrees with this assessment. As early as 2005 when the plans were announced, animal rights activists voiced their opposition to Ocean Park's plans.

When it comes to acquiring animals, especially endangered species, Ocean Park's policy is to exhaust all other opportunities before going to the wild. Our first choice is to adopt animals from other zoological facilities, through breeding loans, animal exchanges, purchases, or rescue programmes. Preferably, these are also animals that are not suitable for release, such as those born under human care.

At the time that we were undertaking this project, there were less than 150 belugas under human care worldwide, and no facilities with surplus stock. Acquiring the animals from a zoo or aquarium was not an option.

We could have simply bought beluga on the open market, as some attractions were doing. The Russian government provided whale quotas to fishing companies, who would have been more than happy to sell to us immediately. But we actually wanted conservation to justify the population size and confirm that a sustainable take was viable.

If it's not possible to obtain animals from another facility, Ocean Park will only acquire animals from the wild if research clearly shows that this will not affect the sustainability of the animal population.

Unfortunately, no such research existed in Russia. So I flew to Moscow, along with the head of our zoological and education unit, to meet a professor who was well-known for studying polar animals in his facilities, as well as researchers who could do a population assessment.

Together with the Georgia Aquarium and several other marine attractions, we engaged a respected, well-known, local academic to study the issue. Dr. Olga Shpak was a research associate with the Institute of Ecology and Evolution at Russian Academy of Sciences. The China Daily wrote that "few people in the world know and love beluga whales as well as Olga Shpak."

We asked Dr. Shpak to answer the question, "How many beluga whales, if any, can you legitimately take from a population without impacting their ability to thrive and continue growing?"

Since Ocean Park was paying for the research, we were conscious that it might be viewed as biased, so we insisted that the work be scientifically peer-reviewed and made a four-year advance commitment to fund the population assessments. A Canadian institute, the Group for Research and Education on Marine Mammals (GREMM), monitored the work.

Dr. Shpak and her team conducted cross-sectional flyovers of the Okhotsk Sea, to count belugas. They tagged the whales, tracked their movements by satellite to monitor migration patterns, and took genetic samples.

After four years compiling a tremendous amount of data, Dr. Shpak concluded that the number of beluga in the western Okhostk Sea more than surpassed what was necessary for us to arrange a sustainable take. Her report estimated that 145 belugas could be removed from that area over a five-year period without adversely affecting the population. We needed 8.

Animal activists from groups like the Whale and Dolphin Conservation Society, the Hong Kong Dolphin Conservation Society and Green Sense were still opposed to Ocean Park's plans, so we decided to take the research a step further. We asked the International Union for Conservation of Nature (IUCN) to review the numbers, as well as Dr. Shpak's methodology. No one had ever done this before. No marine attraction had ever sought IUCN's support, because the organization is typically opposed to animals under human care. We approached them knowing full-well that they might reject the report and our beluga plans would be scuttled.

Two of the world's foremost cetacean experts, Bob Brownell and Randy Reeves, reviewed the study. (Cetaceans are an animal group that includes whales, porpoises, and dolphins.) Not only did they give the research a passing grade, but Brownell held the report up to me and said, "This is the kind of research every government should be doing before they give their quotas to fishermen. I want to use this, if you don't mind. I'm going to take this back to the governments so that when IUCN is advising them on quota-setting, I can show them how a real population sustainability assessment should be done."

Brownell backed up what he said in his report's conclusion. Here's an excerpt:

"Effectiveness of international conservation agreements depends on credible population and removal data and on accurate reporting of trade in wildlife and wildlife products. It is rare that the beneficiaries of such trade are seen to invest in the research and monitoring needed to ensure long-term sustainability. In the case of Sakhalin-Amur beluga live-captures, it is important to acknowledge the institutions that supported the work under review, and also to commend them for making the methods and results available for critical, independent scientific evaluation."

IUCN commended Dr. Olga Shpak's "dedication to conservation of Okhotsk Sea belugas through the pursuit of good data and appropriate analyses" and thanked Ocean Park's head of zoology, Suzanne Gendron, for "her personal commitment to this process."

Obviously, we thought this was fantastic. But before bringing in the beluga, we thought we should survey public sentiment on the issue. The first results that came in were markedly in favour of our plans. We noticed there might be some bias in the questions, though. So we asked a well-known research group to rework the survey and do it again. Again, the public appeared to solidly favour Ocean Park.

Activists continued to make noise. They were small in numbers, but increasingly attracting media coverage. The Hong Kong government, specifically the Tourism Commission, was getting a little nervous. No matter what the numbers showed — no matter how sustainable the wildlife catch, no matter how popular the belugas might be with the public — we had to anticipate the possibility that the beluga attraction might hurt the goodwill that Ocean Park had built up with the Hong Kong public.

Ocean Park had spent US$700,000 funding the population assessments[25] and untold hours planning and preparing the ground for the North Pole Encounter. We first shared the artist renderings and concept with the public in 2005. Six years later, the data said 'yes', but our judgment said 'no'. I made the final call. On 29 August 2011, Ocean Park announced that it would not acquire belugas from the wild.[26]

---

25 Ocean Park Hong Kong spent US$700,000 from 2006–2012. The expenditure for 2011 and 2012 had already been pledged when Ocean Park decided not to acquire beluga whales.

26 Ocean Park had an 'option' to acquire beluga from Russian collectors. These beluga had already been captured in the Okhostk Sea, but not specifically for Ocean Park. From the start, we explained Ocean Park's process and the need for sustainability research, before a purchase could occur.

We could have justified it, but it wasn't worth the headache and potential risk. We wanted to keep focus on the park, not on a specific species. The overall goal is to connect people with nature, and we felt we could keep doing that even without belugas in the mix. Ocean Park continued to support beluga research in the Okhostk Sea, and by 2016 had spent nearly US$900,000.

Ocean Park's zoological team was deeply disappointed and still is to this day, but it was the right decision. Just take a look at what happened at the Georgia Aquarium in Atlanta, which proceeded with plans to expand its existing pod of beluga whales, with the hope of creating a self-sustaining population. The Georgia Aquarium spent US$6.5 million to care for 18 belugas housed in Russian sea pens, while trying to import the animals in the face of public opposition. After taking a beating in the press, the aquarium announced in June 2016, nearly five years after Ocean Park's decision, that it was dropping the project.

📌 Remember This

1. If you can measure it, you can manage it.
2. Identify your business' core metrics.
3. Don't get so caught up in targets that you forget what makes your business unique.
4. Use graduated scales because not all units are created equal.
5. Never make people wait to pay, pee or park.
6. Count from your consumer's perspective.
7. Not everything that can be counted counts.
8. Ask yourself, "Am I counting this the right way?"
9. Subjectivity can be quantified.
10. Good judgment is more important than numbers.

Plan

ACE Your Planning:
Anticipate | Communicate | Execute

N obody plans to fail, but many people fail to plan.[27]

When I arrived at Ocean Park in 2004, I discovered a planning process that had been languishing for months. There was a consensus that Ocean Park needed a significant overhaul, but discussions about the new design were not advancing. There were no decisions, no coherent storyline, and nothing that seemed to resonate or excite the team. Nor had a proper business case assessment been done to test the ideas that were in play to see if they were feasible.

I started work on February 1st. By early summer we had agreement on a rough outline for a US$700 million Master Redevelopment Plan (MRP) that would firmly establish Ocean Park as a world-class premier tourist destination. We would increase the number of offerings in the park by more than 225% and add five themed areas plus a funicular express that could transport 10,000 people per hour. We refined the plan in the ensuing months and in November, filmed an 11-minute promotional video

---

27 This is an old saying; it's unclear who said it first.

highlighting Ocean Park's generational connection to the community and our plans to 'save the best and improve the rest!'.

The MRP itself was 1000 pages, consisting of eight books and weighing about 25 pounds. At 120 slides, the keynote presentation was hardly short either. Our board approved the plans in December, and just one year into my term as CEO we were making presentations to the Hong Kong government and financing partners for their approval.

Projects of this scope can often take years to develop and longer to obtain the necessary authorisations. The speed at which we developed the Master Redevelopment Plan was extraordinary. So how did we reach agreement, draft a detailed plan, and obtain multiple levels of approval so quickly?

We applied a management philosophy that I call ACE: Anticipate — Communicate — Execute. At the risk of sounding corny, let me tell you how we aced our planning — and how you can too.

Anticipate

The key question for Ocean Park in 2004 was When Disney comes to town, what is this going to mean for us?'

We needed to anticipate the implications of Disney's entry into the market. Would Ocean Park's attendance go up or down?

To answer that question, we took a step back and asked, "What will be Disney's impact on tourist arrivals to Hong Kong?" The government expected that Hong Kong Disneyland would attract millions of new visitors, particularly from the mainland, every year. How many of those tourists would visit Ocean Park, particularly once new attractions were launched?

At the time, our annual attendance was 3 million people. We anticipated that it could rise to 5 million.[28] Was this realistic? And if so,

---

28 Annual attendance in 2012, the year the Master Redevelopment Plan was completed, was 7.4 million, well above our initial target. We actually topped 5 million visitors in 2006.

what would our guests expect? With Disney next door, comparisons were inevitable and visitor expectations of Ocean Park would undoubtedly rise. We recognised that our guests were often waiting more than an hour to enjoy attractions. They were also spending just two and a half hours, on average, in the park, which in turn was depressing per capita spending. This was unacceptable. We needed to give visitors a reason to stay longer. We needed to increase the park's ride and attraction capacity, particularly if we anticipated higher attendance. As a result, the MRP focused first and foremost on creating enough Entertainment Units[29] within the park to meet what we believed would be the future demand.

Anticipating what sort of new rides and animal attractions would attract visitors was only part of the equation. We also needed to test the business case for planned additions. Could we afford them? Would the park generate enough revenue to merit the investment? What about the timing — would we be able to pay back the loans on schedule?

You can get a sense of how Anticipation helped shape our plans. These same sort of questions were applied to every aspect of the MRP. We also needed to anticipate the potential risks of new products, the permitting and approval requirements of various agencies, the interest of banks to finance the project, and how the market would react to it.

Like all successful projects, big or small, Ocean Park's redevelopment began with a vision. In our case, the vision was to create a world-class marine attraction that would complement Disney and attract 5 million guests a year, while connecting them to nature. This vision was linked to an opportunity (what some people characterized as a challenge). We first anticipated all sorts of wonderful possibilities to realise the vision — a Blue Sky approach that is unconstrained by practicalities. We then anticipated these practicalities and examined how to bridge the gap. In the end, you want to ensure that the project is aligned with both vision and resources. To do this, anticipation is linked closely to preparation (this is why the MRP was 1000 pages!).

---

29 See chapter 4 for a discussion of Entertainment Units (EUs).

Communicate

Once a goal is set, you have to share it — indeed, you need to 'sell' it — to all relevant stakeholders, which in the case of Ocean Park included employees, the Board of Directors, the Hong Kong government, banks and the public.

Before we even reached that stage, I faced a communications challenge while drafting the master plan. Prior to my arrival, Ocean Park had engaged a design firm — let's call them "Design Attractions" — to be the lead consultants for the project. The Design Attractions team had some good ideas, but there wasn't enough communication between them and Ocean Park. Part of the blame for this fell squarely on our side. There seemed to be an over-reliance at Ocean Park on external consultants, a mindset that we could simply hand them a problem and they would revert with the solution, end-of-story, no need for further discussion.

But planning requires constant dialogue. I wanted my team to understand that project design is an iterative process. Information, suggestions, and feedback are needed from every department — and at Ocean Park, that meant Finance, Design & Planning, Engineering, Human Resources, Operations, Project Development, Sales & Marketing and Zoological & Education. However, as I brought the entire team into the flow and discussion, I realised that our vendor had a more formulaic approach. They weren't actually looking for operator input to inform the creative process, nor was Ocean Park actively providing it.

While Design Attractions' approach had served their past clients well, I strongly believed that the Ocean Park team needed to 'own' the plan and believe in it, in order for it to succeed. For that to happen, we needed to be active participants.

At the same time, Design Attractions' proposal wasn't resonating within the context of Ocean Park or reflecting our differential values. They were cutting and pasting from other work they had done, without creating a story that would set us apart from Disney. This was actually a long-standing problem for Ocean Park, which had popular attractions — an iconic cable car ride, the aquarium, giant pandas, a roller coaster and log flume — but no thread connecting them together.

We needed to write that story and to do that, the process for producing the master plan had to change.

❖

"Allan, hi, it's Tom. I'd like to talk with you about the redevelopment plans." Two weeks into the job, I was calling my boss to communicate the need for a major change.

"We need to switch gears," I said. "There's no continuity to our planning. It's a mixed bag of 'let's do this and let's do that'. We're not getting the creativity we need. I'd like to suggest that we get a storyteller, someone who can help us frame a basic tour for our guests. An imaginary family comes in and we want to guide them through the park.

"We're a real animal attraction, but we can still tell stories. We can educate, entertain and promote conservation in a way that is responsible and gives back to the community, while doing all the things we're chartered to do as a company.

"I realise we've gone a far way down the road with Design Attractions, and they're trying hard, but I think we need a different approach. We need to create a continuity that's lacking in the proposals we're receiving. Design Attractions is geared heavy as well. They have a big team that needs to be fed; they're generating work and billing to keep things moving.

"Let's bring in a storyteller. And let's work with a smaller design team, one that will incorporate our input better."

Allan was very receptive. "You know what? You're right. The designs we're seeing aren't creating the right energy. We need to rethink this. Ocean Park has the potential to be so much better. The park needs to be 'shit hot'. We have to focus on the things that make us strong and different, and build on those."

Together, Allan and I placed the call to Design Attractions to tell them we wouldn't be using them anymore.[30] We then hired the renowned storyteller, Adam Bezark, and a 15-year old boutique design company, Vertex Productions.

Of course that last paragraph simplifies the story. After talking with Allan, I needed to communicate the change in direction to my management team to ensure their support. We then had to develop a paper to present to the Redevelopment Committee, the Board of Directors and the Hong Kong government, to explain the need for this change, seek their approval to end one contract and enter another, and change the scope of work and put in place a more accelerated timeline.

While no objections were raised, my communication skills were being put to work from the outset.

❖

Communicating the change in vendors provided a foretaste of what would be required once the draft MRP was ready for approval. From a technical standpoint, there would be blueprints, computer-aided designs, multimedia presentations and slides to prepare.

Internally, we needed to debunk fears that people were going to lose their jobs. While I had convinced the board not to shut the park down entirely during the redevelopment, inevitably some areas would be closed for extended periods of time. Members of the staff thought that if their area was shut down, they would be out of a job. I was committed though to not retrench anyone, and I'm happy to say that no one lost their job due to the redevelopment.

We set up a room with a model of the completed park, to sell the MRP to legislators, government officials and the media. I ended up using that room to speak with every employee in the company and walk them through the details of the redevelopment.

---

30 While the 'Design Attractions' team didn't like our decision, they were professional. I respect their work; it just wasn't what we needed at the time. ('Design Attractions' is a fictionalised name.)

"We'll find a way to absorb you somewhere else in the company, if your attraction closes," I told the team in a series of meetings. "Once it's rebuilt, we'll return you to that area or teach you new skill sets so you can work elsewhere."

We recognised that if employees didn't buy into the plan, it didn't matter how I sold it to the outside world. I needed them to be as passionate about the redevelopment as I was.

Externally, we needed to obtain the buy-in of key leaders in the legislature and government. This didn't simply mean selling them on our vision. We needed to listen and understand their comments and concerns, then reflect them in subsequent revisions of the plan.

Finally, once we successfully navigated the channels of government to obtain their approval and persuaded a consortium of banks that Ocean Park's renovation was a good investment, another key communication task remained: conveying the vision and technical requirements in a series of tender documents to choose our vendors. And this brings me to the third part of the planning trinity: Execution.

Execute

After numerous rounds of the anticipate — communicate feedback loop, it was time to take the master plan and develop a detailed, executable programme that would allow us to achieve the MRP on time, on budget and at a quality level that would meet or exceed expectations.

How do you do this?

The first step is to ensure that everyone who's involved with the project is working toward the same desired outcomes. In my experience, the key is to establish a clear set of objectives from the very beginning of the execution phase so that both employees and vendors understand what's needed to realise the plan. The next steps include:

• Awarding contracts
• Managing vendor performance to achieve desired objectives

- Managing budgets, schedules and the quality of deliverables
- Coordinating the appropriate permits
- Developing a marketing communications strategy to ensure the market knows what you're doing
- Having a detailed handover programme from vendors to our operations team, and
- Promptly following up on any issues that may arise once the project is up and running.

The second step is to apply Anticipation and Communication to the individual elements of the plan.

As we turned concept into practical application, we needed to make adjustments. This can happen in any project, particularly one that unfolds over multiple years, but it was perhaps more of an issue for us, due to the speed at which we were moving.

Fortunately, we had built a degree of flexibility into our plan. We also had a chairman who staunchly believed that we must adjust to market conditions, and that the imperative was to deliver the essence of the project, not the exact details. The essence for us could be summarised in three words, all of which were identified during the Anticipate phase: Capacity, Cost, and Quality.

To achieve those last two criteria — to ensure a quality outcome and keep the project on budget — Ocean Park uses a double envelope tender system to select vendors. It narrows down the bidders based on technical qualifications, and only then looks at their price. While this takes time, it's the fairest and best way to choose vendors. If we are tendering for something straight forward, like an auditor, we may place a greater weight on price, but for contractors — where there is a wide variety in experience and competencies — we emphasize technical ability.

As we executed the MRP, the biggest change we had to make was related to the project's timeline. We initially expected the redevelopment could be implemented in two phases over four years. However as we examined this approach, we realised it wasn't practical. It would take too much of the park out of circulation. So we decided instead to divide the plan into smaller bites and spread it out over a longer period. In the end, we rolled out the MRP in eight phases over six years. This longer time frame proved to be beneficial. It gave us more marketing hooks, more ways to keep Ocean Park in the news, top-of-mind, and relevant as a tourist destination.

Table 3: Applying ACE to the Master Redevelopment Plan

Anticipate

The following provides an overview of the types of anticipation, communication, and execution required to develop and implement Ocean Park's redevelopment:

a. Anticipate Disney's offering.
b. Define a differential position. (Propose an idea or vision, as well as attractions that will complement and be different from Disney's anticipated offering.)
c. Define the master planning parameters, including the guiding principles for the project and the metrics to be achieved.
d. Anticipate associated risks & develop a risk assessment, particularly for untried products. (In a marine attraction like Ocean Park, this is particularly important for new animal acquisitions.)
e. Assess the business case, including costs and available budget, market demand, financial impact and viability of the proposal.
f. Anticipate and determine financing requirements and assess the interest/appetite of financiers.
g. Anticipate permitting and approval requirements as well as the relevant agencies that will need to be engaged.
h. Anticipate market reaction and plan accordingly, being sure to achieve metrics for safety, service, and show quality.

Communicate

a. Communicate guiding principles, objectives and vision with everyone working on the redevelopment, including master planners, the feasibility study team, quantity surveyors, and service providers.
b. Ensure that all parties are aligned on the vision and objectives by communicating with the management team, project team, affected parties, staff, and related support teams.
c. Communicate with Board Sub-Committees, Board of Directors, Executive branch of government, Legislative Council, financing institution and others to gain approvals, secure support, and assure success.
d. Communicate with prospective vendors to obtain the best possible bids, in terms of both quality and price, and ensure a fair tender assessment process. Continue to communicate with award winners throughout the duration of the project.
e. Communicate with media and all stakeholders throughout the project to ensure accurate and timely dissemination of information.

Execute

Establish a set of objectives linked to desired outcome(s) to ensure successful delivery of the project, then, with an eye on achieving those objectives and the final outcome:

a. Direct tendering processes, award contracts, and manage performance.
b. Manage budget, schedule and quality.
c. Coordinate permitting.
d. Plan marketing communications strategy and engage media to generate awareness, then develop Call to Action messaging to drive attendance after openings.
e. Develop protocol for handover from vendors to the company.
f. Follow-up as needed on defects and liabilities.

Applying ACE: The Case of the Killer Whales

You don't need to be in the midst of transforming your business to apply the ACE methodology. I regularly use it to plan other projects as well. Consider for example the creation of a new animal exhibit at Ocean Park.

As I mentioned above, each project begins with a vision, this time a suggestion from my chairman.

"Let's get the biggest, most impressive sea animal we can. It's got to be first-class," Allan said to me one day. "Crowds will be lining up to see it."

One of the world's biggest marine mammals and strongest predators is the orca, commonly known as a 'killer whale', even though it's actually a dolphin. Black and white orcas can weigh up to six tonnes. They have distinctive white patches above their eyes, large dorsal fins, and are known to hunt in pods, similar to a wolf pack.

If we were to bring orcas to Ocean Park, we needed to anticipate the implications.

First, we needed to consider the logistics and facilities required to care for the sea giants. How big a pool, for example, would be required? There are zoological standards to help answer this question. The depth of the pool needs to be at least one and a half times the animal's length, while the length should be three times the animal's length multiplied by the number of animals. Since male orcas can grow to be more than thirty feet long, we would need a pool at least 45–50 feet deep. The plan called for a pod of four orcas, which meant the pool would have to be nearly 400 feet long, at a minimum.

Ocean Park did not aspire to minimum standards, though; we aspired for excellence. We would need to exceed those standards, and likely double them. After doing the calculations, we determined that the orca pool would need to hold 14 million litres of water, nearly three times the size of our Grand Aquarium.

We also had to consider where to place a pool of this size, as well as the cost, since Ocean Park does not have a lot of free space. In addition, how many staff would be required to care for the animals and what sort of specialised skills would they need to have? Would this addition prove popular with the public, and was it financially viable?

Next, we had to anticipate how we would acquire the animals. As previously mentioned, Ocean Park's policy is to exhaust all other avenues before going to the wild. Only if breeding, rescue and loan programmes are not available will Ocean Park go to the seas, and then, only if peer-reviewed scientific research shows that the animal population can sustain a take.

If we did acquire the orcas, would we be able to present them in a way that was in line with the company's education and conservation values? Some marine attractions cross the line into pure entertainment. That's not Ocean Park's way. While we want visitors to feel an emotional bond with the animals, they should also leave knowing more than when they arrived, all while ensuring the animals' excellent health, safety and welfare.

Finally, we needed to anticipate the risks and opportunities of bringing in orcas, including public reaction. To do this, we prepared a Risk Assessment Register, which is essentially an extensive spreadsheet that lists all the conceivable risks associated with a project, their causes, likelihood, and potential impacts as well as how they could (or could not) be mitigated. We had to ensure that the potential risks did not overwhelm the upside returns of the proposal.

As we anticipated the benefits and risks of acquiring killer whales, we also considered how we would communicate the programme to the public. We had to consider the potential impact of animal rights activists who were increasingly vocal in their opposition to Orlando's SeaWorld and other marine attractions with orcas in their care.

If we did proceed, we needed to prepare several layers of communication, including but not limited to:

• The management team, project team, and related support teams, to ensure that everyone was aligned with the vision and objectives of the acquisition

- The Board of Directors (and relevant sub-committees), the legislative and executive branches of government, and financial institutions to obtain approvals and support
- Prospective tenderers to share the technical requirements and identify the most suitable partners
- Quantity surveyors, feasibility teams and other vendors
- The media, to keep them accurately informed on a timely basis leading up to completion and launch of the new attraction.

As we applied the ACE framework to the orca acquisition, we realised that we could execute the project, albeit with several 'buts': the pool size would exceed the budget allowance, so there would be a financial issue; there were no available orcas in captivity, so we would need to go to the wild and it was not clear that a sustainable take was feasible; and on the communications side, we came back with nothing but negatives.

In the end, not unlike the beluga story, we determined that it would be better to focus our efforts elsewhere.

Unexpected Feedback

As you ACE your planning, you may find you need to return to the drawing board partway through the process. This happened to me as Knott's Berry Farm was developing a new payment system for Camp Snoopy in Minnesota.

Because Camp Snoopy is located inside the Mall of America, visitors can walk through the park without having to pay for admission. The individual rides and attractions are gated, but the park is not. We anticipated that ticketing needed to be quick and easy, as visitors were essentially 'paying' each time they rode a new ride. If it took too long to sell or accept the tickets, visitors would be turned off and go somewhere else in the mall.

We decided to adopt a state-of-the-art payment system — like a subway card — that would be scanned each time they entered a ride or show. Points would be deducted when they went through the turnstile. Visitors could purchase the cards — and add value to them — at automated ticket machines, which accepted both cash and credit cards.

This may not seem all that progressive — not at a time when cities like Hong Kong and Singapore have subway cards that can also be used to make 'flash' purchases in 7-11s and other convenience stores — but in 1991, this payment scheme was extremely innovative, especially for pay-as-you-go attraction management.

After anticipating a need and developing a proposal, I requested detailed feedback from the Finance, Operations, and Marketing teams to ensure that the system would be developed in a way that met each department's needs. We expected Finance would have specific requirements about tracking sales and accounting for receipts, while Operations would want to ensure the smooth flow of people through the park. Marketing would surely need a system that could implement promotions and discounts.

In response to my request for input, the Operations department provided a 40-page detailed list of specifications about how the ticketing system should work. Finance's reply was even longer. Marketing, interestingly enough, submitted the most succinct reply I have ever seen, a 1-sentence specification: "The system should not impede the creativity of marketing."

We went back to marketing several times during the process, but they stuck to their guns. While their reply was not what we were originally looking for, they were not wrong. They were saying, 'Don't give us protocols or bureaucracy. We need the freedom to be creative to be able to sell tickets.' They were challenging the project team to make sure we didn't box ourselves into a procedural corner.

We were forced to accept their feedback and restart the ACE loop, this time approaching the project parameters with a more open mind and in a different way. The Operations and Finance teams rewrote their specifications to accommodate the marketing brief.

To this day, I view that 1-sentence reply as the most brilliant specification.

Bridging Silos

Planning — whether it's for a major overhaul or something much smaller — invariably requires cross-departmental cooperation. Marketing, Finance, and Operations will all have input and a role to play if a project is to be a success. Too often, these teams work in silos, or worse, are at odds with each other.

When I first joined the Admissions department at Knott's Berry Farm in 1984, I found a system where these three teams were responsible for promotions that drive attendance, but there was no process in place to properly manage communication between them. It led to delays, and sometimes disarray, at the ticket counter, which was my area of responsibility.

Imagine approaching the counter and asking the ticket-seller, "Do you have any promotions going on? What's the best deal I can get on tickets today?" The ticket-seller looks down at a clipboard and replies, "Well, we have a 20% discount for Bank of America cardholders. Do you have a Bank of America card? No? How about a California driver's license? Are you a university student? Library card holder? Yes? OK, you have two of those, let's see which one gives you the bigger discount." And the list would go on. All the while, the line behind the customer at the counter was growing longer.

The park was offering too many promotions, some of which were in conflict with each other, while accounting processes were unclear because there weren't any checks and balances in place in the early stage of setting up the promotion.

At the time, if marketing had an idea, they would simply say 'let's do this'. Finance would process marketing's request, and Operations (the ticket-sellers) would have to implement it. No one checked though how many other promotions were already in place or calculated which were most effective. Operations bore the brunt of the confusion and as the promotion sheet grew longer, it became harder to service the guests.

The first thing we did was to whittle down the number of promotions, by applying an 80:20 rule. What were the top tier promos, in terms of consumer redemption? Let's focus on those. The other 80% are just noise.

Then we put in place the ACE system (though I didn't call it that yet[31]) for future promotions. Here's how it worked:

Anticipate: Marketing would anticipate an opportunity to drive attendance to the park. They would communicate their proposal to Finance, which would evaluate whether the promotion was consistent with the financial modeling of the company and likely to achieve its goals. Operations would also have an opportunity to flag issues that could arise during implementation of the project.

If Finance had concerns with the promotion — say, it didn't see a business case for it — it would return the proposal to Marketing, which could either recraft or shelve it.

Communicate: If Finance approved the proposal and Operations had no objections (or their concerns were addressed), Marketing would begin to communicate the promotion throughout the company and to the public.

Execute: As it was already engaged in a discussion about the project, Operations was prepared to execute it.

Everyone one had a role. You couldn't sell a ticket out of admissions unless Finance had approved the promotion number. Finance wouldn't approve a proposal before checking that it didn't conflict with existing programmes. The promotion wouldn't take place without the creativity of Marketing, which had to anticipate a need and communicate it to the market.

---

31 At first, I called this planning model, PACE: Propose–Approve–Communicate–Execute. Marketing proposes, Finance approves, Marketing communicates and Operations executes. PACE helped clearly delineate each department's responsibilities. As we thought about this further, though, we realised that 'proposing' is really part of the anticipation process. ACE is not only faster than PACE (in linguistic terms), it's also provides a broader framework for project management.

Whether your business is manufacturing or services, this same model can be applied to provide focus, create efficiencies, and ultimately get things to your intended market faster. By clearly delineating the roles of each department and providing a framework for them to communicate, we streamlined the process and got all teams working on a common goal, not just their departmental ones.

Dominating Disney: The Role of Planning

Disney Imagineers — a group whose skill sets are cross-departmental — begin new projects with a Blue Sky Approach, before introducing a series of constraints. They review cost, time and scope — three variables taught by business school professors — as well as aesthetics, quality and safety, factors of key importance in the attractions industry.[32]

---

32 There are numerous case studies and articles about Disney's approach to project management. See for example, "How to Create Magic–Project Management Lessons from Walt Disney Imagineering," by Linh Tranh, 24 July 2015, published on InLoox.com.

Yet while Disney has its own project management philosophy, it suffers, in my view, from a grave pitfall: Paralysis by Analysis.[33] The company has grown so large that it over-analyzes and over-studies opportunities, rendering it slow to market.

There's no question that the impending arrival of Hong Kong Disneyland forced Ocean Park to reassess every aspect of its business. Yet without a clear planning philosophy, the company would not have been able to adapt.

By viewing Disney's arrival as an opportunity — one that would increase the overall size of the market by attracting more tourists to the city — we anticipated ways to better attract, please and retain consumers. This viewpoint was critical to development of the new master plan. The ACE feedback loop encouraged timely interaction between project stakeholders, which in turn enabled us to quickly develop and gain approval of a proposal that was imaginative, detailed, and well thought-through, then effectively execute it.

Applying ACE to Your Business

Whether the project is big or small, here are some steps to guide your planning:

1. Start with a Vision.
2. Anticipate what's possible.
3. Explore the opportunity to see if it is as big as you imagine.
4. Evaluate the options, taking into account the costs plus current and future market conditions. If the market opportunity is real, align your Blue Sky anticipations with what you can actually afford.
5. Communicate the proposal internally and with relevant stakeholders.

---

33 The phrase, 'Paralysis by Analysis', was coined by H. Igor Ansoff in 1965 in the book "Corporate Strategy: An Analytic Approach to Policy for Growth and Expansion". Source: Wikipedia.

6. Welcome feedback and revise the proposal as needed.
7. Communicate the proposal again, to ensure support from everyone involved.
8. Establish a clear set of objectives linked to the desired outcome, to ensure successful delivery.
9. Execute the project, keeping a close eye on budgets, schedules, and quality.
10. Build flexibility into the plan, particularly for larger projects.

Two words of caution:

One, I've already highlighted the danger of 'paralysis by analysis'. Some analysis based on information available is essential, but at some point, you need to lead and make decisions.

Two, beware of complacency, particularly when it comes to executing a project. It's too easy to think, "we've done this many times before" and then ignore protocols or best practices. Ocean Park looks at everything — be it an animal vaccination, construction of a new facility, or conceptualisation of a new programme — as if it's the first time it's being done. If you're going to be excellent every single time, you need to make sure you've got the basics right every time.

📌 Remember This

1. Nobody plans to fail, but many fail to plan.
2. ACE your planning: Anticipate, Communicate, Execute.
3. Anticipation — and successful projects — begin with a vision.
4. Anticipation is closely linked to preparation.
5. Effective planning requires constant dialogue.
6. Be prepared for unexpected feedback.
7. Establish a clear set of objectives so all participants understand what's needed to realise the plan.
8. Lead. Make decisions. Avoid 'paralysis by analysis'.
9. Build flexibility into your plan.
10. Complacency has no place in business. To be excellent every single time, make sure you always get the basics right.

Be Relevant

You Can Always Customise
the Software

A theme park must be culturally relevant to the markets it serves," my former boss, Terry Van Gorder, the chief executive of Knott's Berry Farm, used to always say.

For many years, as a young manager in the southern California park, I didn't have a clue what he was talking about. Didn't everyone love roller coasters? Weren't Snoopy and Charlie Brown universal icons? What did cultural relevance have to do with our business?

But in 1994, I got it.

Knott's Berry Farm was struggling. We were attracting about 3.5 million visitors a year, down from a peak of 4 million. I had just returned to Orange County to become the park's vice president of operations and entertainment, following several years in Minneapolis setting up Camp Snoopy in the new Mall of America. I recognised that Knott's Berry Farm needed to improve its local market penetration if we were to attract more visitors.

Southern California is a dynamic, ever-changing region. When Knott's Berry Farm was established, California was predominantly white, but by 1990, the state had become an 'ethnic kaleidoscope'.[34] In our neighbourhood alone, there were amazing pockets of ethnicity. Just down the street, there was a huge Vietnamese population. Koreans lived to the north. Japanese, Chinese, Filipino and Mexican communities were all within easy driving distance.

Knott's Berry Farm wasn't doing anything special to attract these communities. Its marketing wasn't targeted. Campaigns were generic, revolving around a common theme about being 'your park' and 'a part of California's history'. Once faced with a downturn, our marketing department proposed something different, something unique — a Filipino fiesta to coincide with The Philippines' independence day. We would bring in Filipino musicians, offer Filipino food, and market the event directly to the local Filipino community.

We expected 35,000 visitors to attend the weekend festival, but we got that on Saturday alone. More than 60,000 Filipinos poured through the gates over two days, paying an additional US$7 to enter the fiesta areas, on top of the park's normal US$19 entry fee. We had to open an hour early to accommodate the crowd. Fiesta Filipiniana was a rousing success.

"Mabuhay!" I greeted celebrants on Sunday during the opening ceremony. "With this event, we acknowledge the great people of The Philippines. We had our #5 best day in history yesterday for attendance, which tells you how powerful this event has been for the Filipino community."

It was the first time The Philippines' '4th of July' was celebrated on such a large scale in southern California. Hands on their hearts, Filipinos — many wearing the traditional white *barong* shirt that's reserved for formal occasions — sang their national anthem, *Lupang Hinirang* ("Land of the Morning"). They enjoyed Tagalog love songs and home-cooked dishes like *bibingka, puto, pancit malabon, chicharon bulaklak* (rice cakes, noodles and fried pig intestines). In the evening, women in gorgeous

---

34 The academic James N. Gregory uses this term in "The Shaping of California History", published in the "Encyclopedia of American Social History" in 1993.

traditional gowns and their escorts paraded through the Air Field, Ghost Town, and Roaring 20's zone of Knott's Berry Farm for the *Santacruzan*, a Catholic procession commemorating the search for the holy cross by Constantine the Great and his mother, *Reyna Elena*.

"It's like coming home," Joel Dauz told the L.A. Times. "Everywhere you look, you see a Filipino."

Knott's Berry Farm partnered with the Philippines' Department of Tourism and the Southern California Filipino American community, both of which provided sponsorship, as well as a local promoter to identify Filipino performers. While we scheduled the festival on a Filipino holiday, it also coincided with a traditionally slow period in the park. The following year, we expanded Fiesta Filipiniana to two weeks, drawing in the bulk of the local Filipino population.

We didn't have to change the rides or the story of the park, but we could change the software and immediately be culturally relevant.

Subsequently, we organised Korean, Vietnamese and Mexican-American festivals, all of which attracted a huge number of first-time visitors. In addition to revelling in the fiestas, these new park-goers rode the roller coasters, visited Camp Snoopy and enjoyed other Knott's Berry Farm attractions. Once we connected with people in these markets, Knott's Berry Farm was in their hearts. Families who first joined us for special events, revisited over and over again.

By being relevant, respectful and celebrating our communities' cultures, Knott's Berry Farm garnered huge market share, grew its customer base and eclipsed Disney's attempts to connect with California's multi-ethnic population.

This was a lesson that I would carry with me throughout my career.

❖

When I arrived at Ocean Park in 2004, our two biggest markets consisted of local Hong Kongers and visitors from the mainland. As the pie grew, the percentages changed, but the two basic groups remained the same:

40–50% from mainland China, 35–45% from Hong Kong, and the rest from other parts of Asia.

With so many visitors coming from across the border, it has always been essential to ensure that Ocean Park is welcoming, friendly, easy and comfortable to navigate for Chinese guests.

At the same time, we strongly believe that people visit Hong Kong, well, to appreciate Hong Kong. This might seem obvious, but it's also a key differentiating factor from Disney which offers a slice of America. Ocean Park never loses sight of the fact that we are a Hong Kong park: "Distinctively Hong Kong and Uniquely Ocean Park"

So how did we ensure that Ocean Park is relevant to both local and mainland audiences, as well as guests from other parts of Asia?

We started with language. In Hong Kong, the primary languages are Cantonese and English. In the People's Republic of China, the national tongue is Mandarin. Hong Kong uses traditional Chinese characters; mainland Chinese read simplified characters. So from the moment you approach the front gate, the announcements and the signage are all trilingual. As visitors walk through the aquarium and other animal exhibits, the information and displays are also in three languages. Ocean Park does this throughout the park, from the ticket windows to the live shows and restaurant menus.

Speaking of menus, Ocean Park offers a range of dishes to showcase Hong Kong's rich culinary heritage, including Cantonese dim sum, tea-leaf eggs, Hainan curry and hand-made dragon beard candies — a type of spun sugar that is hard to find in the city these days. Other restaurants cater to mainland and western tastes, with roasted pork ribs, gourmet pizza, sustainable seafood, organic dishes and fast food.

To cater to the growing number of guests coming from India, Ocean Park hired several Indian chefs to prepare curries and *paratha*. They cook southeast Asian favourites like *laksa* and satay, while offering halal food to serve the needs of Muslim guests.

When it comes to food, relevance goes beyond region and ethnicity. New menus are prepared to coincide with holidays and special events. One of the more fun dishes is the iconic "coffin dog", an 8-inch hot dog served every Halloween in a coffin-shaped bun. We did have some concerns initially, that the coffin dog would not go down well with superstitious Chinese visitors, but it's turned out to be a big hit.

While Hong Kong's reunification with China occurred in 1997, the currency is still different. There was a time when the Hong Kong dollar was stronger than the Chinese renminbi (the opposite is true today), but we offered a 1:1 exchange rate at the park to mainlanders nonetheless.

Being relevant to our customers goes beyond the 'software', it extends to the very design of the park itself . . . though I can't say this was entirely intentional. Ocean Park's initial growth, from its founding in 1977 through the early 2000s, was organic. Like the city, there was no master plan; one area simply adjoins another. There's no central hub, no main street, the walkways are neither flat nor straight. The topography underneath the development is also just like Hong Kong: rugged, mountainous, beautiful, and a stone's throw from the South China Sea.

After I arrived and we began work on the redevelopment plan, we wanted to maintain the park's intrinsic charm, this Hong Kong mix of East meets West, a blending of old and new, chaos amidst order. The new walkways, for example, were designed to be a bit tighter than in other parks — no wide open boulevards — to provide a greater sense of intimacy and the feeling of the rush of the crowd (while of course ensuring that visitors could get from one place to another quickly and safely).

Later, in 2010, we decided to develop an area between the old walkway and the cable car. When considering what to place there, my team and I returned once again to what makes Ocean Park special, that we are Hong Kong's People's Park. We wanted to celebrate Hong Kong's heritage and decided to build a street that recaptured the vibe of the post-war era.

"Old Hong Kong" opened in March 2012. There's a replica of the Star Ferry Pier clock tower, a retro-fitted tram car, facades of old tenement buildings and 1950's shop fronts. More than seventy local dishes and drinks are on offer. Listen closely and you'll hear the legendary TVB actor, Cheng

Gwan-min, sing "no money to buy bread . . . hungry belly, just like a hungry cat," recalling the difficulties of many families in the 1960s. Or perhaps you'll reminisce about your first love, when you hear the songs of 1970s-era Cantopop stars like Poon Sow Keng and Sandra Lang. Whether it's slurping piping hot fish ball noodles or taking photos on a rickshaw, Old Hong Kong has been a hit, particularly with the city's elders, who are eager to give their grandchildren a glimpse and a taste of the Hong Kong of their own youth. Following the launch of this area, the number of local senior citizen visitors to Ocean Park doubled to about 3500 a week. It's been great fun to watch.

I must admit that when we decided on the Old Hong Kong concept, we also knew it would stand in sharp contrast to 'Main Street USA', the large boulevard that greets visitors at Hong Kong Disneyland.

So, how relevant is Disneyland to Hong Kong? And what about Disney's new park in Shanghai, the first international theme park to be built in China? How relevant is it to the Chinese market?

❖

Disney basically delivered a 1955 Disneyland to Hong Kong. The scale was slightly different, but they started with that framework and essentially never made an effort to be anything more or less than Disneyland.

Which is not to say that they didn't also study the local market. They did — as well as the preferences of consumers in southern China — and subsequently made a few small accommodations.

As Disney started doing more market research, they realised that mainland Chinese really enjoy taking photographs of themselves, their families and experiences, more so than in other markets. So Disney added 'Fantasy Gardens' — where Disney characters could be positioned for photo opportunities — to the original plan. Fantasy Gardens was unique to Hong Kong, until Disney decided to replicate it in Shanghai, where they've built even more gardens and meandering paths for character placements and photos.

(As I discuss more in the next chapter, the construction of Fantasy Gardens in Hong Kong may have lulled Disney designers into believing that Hong Kong Disneyland offered enough attractions to entertain large crowds, something that was evidently not the case when the park opened and was barraged with complaints about excessively long lines.)

Disney also had Mickey and Minnie Mouse wear traditional Chinese *cheongsams* — a fairly simple thing to do — and they tried customising a few dishes, as opposed to offering straight American or Hong Kong fare. One dish — introduced with fanfare — was the '*char siu* burger'. These burgers, which were on the opening menu of Disney's Starliner Diner, combined *char siu* barbequed pork with water chestnuts and burger meat; they used Chinese *mantou* buns for the bread. A Disney chef said they spent months getting the taste right. They should have listened to their focus groups, instead.

"We asked two focus groups in Hong Kong and Guangzhou what kind of food they want," Disneyland executive chef Rudolph Muller told the media during the pre-launch marketing blitz. "Both said they wanted American food." But Muller and his team didn't believe the data. Their fusion attempt didn't go well and it wasn't long before the *char siu* burger and other 'Asian' dishes were quietly dropped from Disney's menu.

One of Disney's biggest mistakes at the time, though, was assuming that everybody in China knew Disney. They didn't.

Disney should have launched a campaign introducing their project to the market, followed by a call-to-action, something straight-forward like 'Visit the new Hong Kong Disneyland!'. Instead, Disney produced a branding ad that was typical of other markets.

Hong Kong Disneyland's very first commercial featured a young girl walking in the park with her dad, holding a red balloon with Mickey Mouse ears. Jump ahead a couple scenes — past the one of her sitting on her dad's lap in a train and another shot waving to the camera, always smiling with the balloon — and she's now inside the eye of a huge sculpture of an old man. While she looks on in disbelief, her father loses the balloon, which

119

floats upward and travels around the park. Finally, Dumbo the Flying Elephant catches the Mickey balloon and returns it to the happy girl.

Viewers didn't know what to make of Disney. The ad confused them and they wondered, "Is this what the Disney park is like? You lose your balloon and a flying blue elephant gives you a new one?".

The problem with this type of campaign, which tries to tug at people's heartstrings, is that it only works when consumers have a basic understanding of your product; they need to already feel an emotional connection in order for the ad to resonate.

It didn't take long for Disney to realise their misstep. Not only did they produce new ads, they also started offering an introductory course, just inside the park, to mainland tour groups to introduce Mickey Mouse, Donald Duck and other Disney characters.

❖

On 16 June 2016, nearly eleven years after the launch of Hong Kong Disneyland, Disney opened its first theme park in mainland China. While the groundbreaking ceremony at Shanghai Disneyland took place in 2011, the park was really decades in the making, part of a long-term plan by Disney to reach China's rapidly expanding middle class.

Stung by criticism that tainted the opening of its parks in Hong Kong and Paris, this time, the Walt Disney Corporation made a tremendous effort to be more locally relevant than ever before.

Disney chairman and CEO, Bob Iger, describes Shanghai Disneyland as being "Authentically Disney and Distinctly Chinese". (Sound familiar?) Going into Shanghai, Iger realised Disney had to take a different tack than it had in Paris and Hong Kong, where it had missed the cultural connections. "We didn't build Disneyland in China, we built China's Disneyland," he told the media.

For the first time in a Disney park, there's no Main Street USA, nor the traditional hub at the end of the street, which has been a signature element of Disney's design and master planning, to distribute visitors to the park's various themed lands.

Instead, visitors enter along Mickey Avenue which leads to a large lake and the Gardens of Imagination. Here, Disney and Pixar characters are presented through the lens of the Chinese zodiac to help provide an introduction to Chinese guests that did not grow up with them. On the other side of the lake is a castle, the largest Disney has ever built. Shanghai's 'Enchanted Storybook Castle' — as opposed to the Cinderella and Sleeping Beauty Castles in other Disney resorts — is said to be inspired by Renaissance architecture, with a few Chinese elements added to 'appeal to the Chinese audience'.[35]

There's no doubt that the US$4.4 billion Shanghai park is a spectacular attraction. But how relevant is it to China?

One area that Disney has been touting for local relevance is the resort's cuisine. Disney says the food on offer is 70% Chinese, 20% Asian and 10% Western. Take a walk in the park, though, and you'll see that this is a huge stretch. In fact, the Chinese and Western numbers are probably flipped. Yes, there is a Chinese teahouse and Mickey Mouse-shaped Peking Duck pizzas, but there is also a giant Starbucks, a Cheesecake Factory and Wolfgang Pucks. Just about every food outlet I visited at the resort was dominated by Western food — and these items appeared to be the most popular.

Disney is clearly selling a story that they have been more sensitive to Chinese culture, but the fact that the park's design differs from that of it other parks does not make it distinctly Chinese — or culturally relevant. Whether Disney's competitors in China — either the new Wanda theme parks, Universal Studios Beijing or Happy Valley Shanghai, which predates Disney's arrival there — will be able to seize on this as an advantage, remains to be seen.

---

35 The Disney Wiki: http://disney.wikia.com/wiki/Enchanted_Storybook_Castle

Dominating Disney: Being Relevant

The Walt Disney Company, with its iconic characters and decades of experience producing quality family entertainment, puts on a great show. There's no doubt about it. But its theme parks are inherently American. It will take more than simply placing a Chinese dress on Minnie Mouse to demonstrate local relevance.

Hong Kong Disneyland — much like Euro Disney before it and Shanghai Disneyland now — overstated the importance of local ingredients in its mix. Visitors to the park — who were initially attracted by Disney's core strength — didn't buy it. When Disney entered the Hong Kong market in 2005, it expected the Disney brand to carry the day. But that mis-step, the failure to truly connect with Hong Kongers and Chinese visitors from Day One, cost Disney. While a lot of people rushed to see the park, they did not hurry back for a second visit.

Disney was offering a slice of America with a bit of Hong Kong. Ocean Park, on the other hand, was already Hong Kong, with added relevance to our Chinese market. As a company, we needed to make sure not to lose sight of the fact that tourists who come to the city expecting a taste of Hong Kong are better served visiting Ocean Park than Disneyland.

We leveraged our positioning to help people understand that the difference is real. Ocean Park continually renews itself to maintain this relevance. Hong Kong youth flock to the park every year for the ever-changing, month-long Halloween Fest. Seniors and their grandchildren visit for the experience of Old Hong Kong. And the park's consistent commitment to education and conservation ensures its relevance to local schools.

The lesson Terry van Gorder taught me at Knott's Berry Farm over twenty years ago has never rung more true than it does today: a theme park must be culturally relevant to the markets it serves.

Applying Relevance to Your Business

Relevance is not only a concept of importance to the entertainment industry. Every business operating in a competitive environment, no matter what sector, needs to constantly and consistently ensure that its products and services are relevant to the markets it serves. If not, it risks becoming irrelevant and eventually going out of business.

As Andrea Coville, CEO of the communications agency Brodeur Partners, writes: "People are awash in choices about where to spend their money and place their loyalty. If you aren't relevant, they will go somewhere else.[36]"

So, how can you tell if your business is relevant?

It starts with asking a fundamental question: "Are you missing market share opportunities?" If so, what can you do to address the gaps?

---

36 "3 Ways to Make Your Company Relevant," Andrea Coville, fastcompany.com, 3 April 2014.

First, take a look at your intended market. This might consist of existing consumers or people who are not currently using your product. As in the case at Knott's Berry Farm, this could mean identifying 'missing' markets of consumers who you think would benefit from your product or service, but currently are not. Your market segment might consist of an ethnic community or it could be defined by other factors, such as age, geography or people with a particular passion.

Second, determine whether your product or service resonates with the intended market segment.

There are a number of tools available to help you determine whether your company or product resonates with your target audience, including customer feedback, surveys, focus groups, market studies and even social media.

With statistical tools that gauge consumer preferences and demographics, marketing today is far more sophisticated than it was twenty years ago, when intuition and personal observations played a greater guiding role. Yet ensuring your business' relevance still begins with the same simple question: do people like what you have to offer? This is a good time to ensure that your offering is consistent with your target audience's values and interests.

Third, consider how you can tailor or customise your positioning and offering to resonate with the desired market.

At its core, your business may have a universal degree of attraction. Take Starbucks, for example. There are over 23,000 Starbucks across the world. Each one sells coffee and snacks. But Starbucks layers elements on top of this basic offering to ensure its relevance with local communities. As I write this, Starbucks Singapore is promoting 'Blossoming Hibiscus Fizzios', Starbucks Philippines is touting Double Chocolate Green Tea Frappuccinos, while their counterparts in the US market a range of 'craft' cold coffees.

When Knott's Berry Farm wanted to increase its market penetration among the area's youth, it created a dance club called Studio K, which attracted teenagers by the thousands. Even a celebration like Halloween needs to be culturally relevant. In California, that meant creating linkages with horror films and popular cult figures like Elvira and Wolfman Jack. In Hong Kong, it means a focus on local spirits, not Western characters like Dracula and Frankenstein.

Finally, stay in touch with the communities you (want to) serve. Ask what's important to them. Listen to their feedback. Pay attention to trends.

Sometimes it also pays to simply keep your eyes open. One day about five years ago, I was walking the park with my Executive Director for Revenue, Joseph Leung. "Take a look at those ladies' legs," Joseph told me. "Huh?! That's not appropriate," I replied, turning to look at him instead. I was baffled; it certainly wasn't like Joseph to suggest something unprofessional. "They're wearing heels," he continued, then after pausing for a moment, added "and carrying so many bags." Still unsure what he was driving at, I asked him to tell me straight-out.

"They're wearing heels and carrying so many bags," he repeated. "Their feet and arms must be very tired. I think our retail stores should start selling flat shoes and rolling luggage." I had never heard of a theme park selling luggage and shoes before, but Joseph had a good point, so we gave it a try. Both items are now hits with Ocean Park's female consumers.

📌 Remember This

1. Your business must be relevant to the markets it serves.
2. If it's not relevant, consumers will go elsewhere.
3. Even if you can't change the hardware, you can still customise the software.
4. Language, food, music and brand positioning can all be tailored to resonate with your company's consumers — and those who are not your customers yet.
5. Ensure that your offering is consistent with the target audience's interests and values, as well as those of your company. Don't just create a marketing campaign.
6. Relevance extends beyond culture and demographics.
7. Don't claim to be culturally relevant, if you're really not.
8. Integrate relevance into your corporate strategy and new offerings.
9. Even if you're a big brand — *particularly* if you're a big brand — don't assume that people in a new market know and understand you.
10. Stay in touch with the communities you serve.

Control

Control the Controllable

On a Sunday night, in late September 2014, tens of thousands of Hong Kongers took to the streets, to demand universal suffrage and protest a Beijing plan for more limited elections. Frustrated with the implementation of the 'One Country, Two Systems' plan — that provided the framework for Hong Kong's reintegration into China in 1997, after 150-plus years of British colonial rule — and moved by a belief that China was reneging on its promises, protesters blockaded major roads around government buildings and key commercial areas.

For 79 days, students and other protesters faced down official calls to disband, hoisting umbrellas instead to deflect police tear gas and pepper spray. At its peak, more than 100,000 people joined the 'Umbrella Revolution'. A number of areas were paralysed by protest, including Admirality, which happens to be the site of a key bus interchange — and the only place for most Hong Kongers to board public transportation to Ocean Park.

While bus services were soon diverted to Tin Hau down the road, the street demonstrations marked the beginning of a sustained decline in Chinese tourism to Hong Kong, driven in part by anti-mainlander sentiment.

Tensions between Hong Kongers and mainlanders had been growing for a long time. They appeared to hit an ugly peak in October 2015 when a tourist from northeast China was killed outside a jewellery store. His Hong Kong tour guide was convicted of assault eight months later.

While none of this was good for tourism, two other factors were also drawing Chinese travellers to choose new destinations for their holidays.

First, currency shifts were making Hong Kong a more expensive place to visit relative to other destinations. The Hong Kong dollar is pegged to the US dollar, so as the US dollar began to appreciate in late 2014, so too did Hong Kong's currency. Yet during this same period, while Hong Kong was becoming pricier for Chinese tourists, the renminbi was gaining strength against the euro, yen and other Asian currencies, making those places more attractive destinations for Chinese tourists.

Second, around the same time, Europe relaxed its visa restrictions for China, leading an increasing number of Chinese tourists to make long-haul trips to the continent.

There were 1.4 million fewer Chinese visitors to Hong Kong in 2015 than in 2014. And during the critical 'Golden Week' Chinese New Year period, visitor arrivals were off 26% in 2016 as compared with a year earlier.

All this was bad news for the attractions business.

At Ocean Park, mainlanders had accounted for half of ticket sales. It would have been easy to fret about the impact of all these developments on Ocean Park's business. In fact, it would have been all too human. We could have spent endless meetings worrying about the fact that fewer Chinese were coming to Hong Kong. But what good would it have done?

There's no point focusing on things that are out of your hands.

Instead, leaders need to **Control the Controllable**.

In the course of business — and the course of life — you will always be confronted with situations that are driven by external events, but if you remain focused on your objectives, you can still achieve them. The key is to identify areas *within your control* that you can change.

Rather than getting bogged down and discouraged by a problem, spend your energy and time on solutions. Maintain perspective.

Very few things are out of your control, if you break them down into basics.

Political demonstrations and currency fluctuations might be bad for business, but they're not the real issue. The real 'challenges' are how to maintain and increase (a) the number of people visiting the park, and (b) visitor spending, in the face of declining tourism from China.

I can't control the exchange rate, but I can control where we advertise to attract visitors.

In this case, we identified three courses of action for Ocean Park:

First, we could control which markets we focus on in China. The nation is not monolithic. Some areas are less affected by market sentiment than others. We returned to our analytics — as discussed in Principle 3, if you measure it, you can manage it — to see which markets produce the most visitations. We then evaluated whether it would be productive to invest more money and effort in these markets. We made a clear decision not to turn our backs on China, but to select and hone which regions to go after.

Second, while we recognised that China will always be an important market for Hong Kong, we could supplement it with additional local market penetration. Annual passes are a popular item with locals. But not only do we want to sell annual passes, we also want to encourage higher visitation rates. So we examined ways to create more value for money and value-added opportunities for frequent visitors, as well as promotions to attract Hong Kongers who had never visited Ocean Park or had not been there in a long time.

For example, we declared the month of May to be "Lovely Panda Month" and offered discounts up to 25% on tickets to Hong Kong residents whose Chinese or English names contained a P, A, N or D or a character related to pandas. Then in August, we extended a popular birthday promotion — that normally invites Hong Kongers to visit Ocean Park for free on their birthday — to enable anyone born during the entire month to enter the park for free.

These promotions may sound gimmicky, but they drive incremental business. For every ticket given away, we find there are several people who join the fun, accompanying their friend or family member, and purchasing tickets at the regular admission price. Promotions like these have proven to be very popular, not only leading to better attendance numbers, but higher in-park spending as well.

Third, we increased advertising in third tier markets, like India, The Philippines, and Korea, which are Ocean Park's top three markets outside of Hong Kong and China. We also produced new marketing campaigns in Taiwan, Japan, Singapore, Malaysia, and Indonesia.

For this last item, we recognised from the start that we could not do it alone. After all, we were not simply marketing Ocean Park to the outside world, but Hong Kong itself. So we approached the Hong Kong Tourism Board and successfully lobbied it to create a matching fund promotion, which enabled Ocean Park and other attractions to double their overseas marketing reach.

Those are three ways — four if you count our outreach to the tourism board — that we were able to control the controllable by focusing on how to make Ocean Park and Hong Kong as attractive as possible. We kept the issues in perspective, worked to create deals that couldn't be passed up, and put our energy into areas we could control.

The Aha! Moment

The idea to 'Control the Controllable' first resonated with me when I started working in the Admissions Department at Knott's Berry Farm in 1984 and quickly realised that visitor complaints increased dramatically whenever it rained.

Bad weather days were the most hectic for my team at the gate. Once thunderstorms started, the lines at the counters grew, with each person asking — ok, sometimes, demanding — a refund or complimentary tickets, or some other form of compensation because their time in the park was cut short by bad weather and they couldn't enjoy their favourite coasters.

As you might imagine, the admissions team did not like rainy days. We dealt with a lot of grumpy people, which is not what you want to see in the entertainment business. As a supervisor, I thought, 'there's got to be a better way to provide guests with a positive experience, even though we know that bad weather is going to affect what they get'.

It was abundantly clear that we can't control the weather. But I realised we could control the guest experience on bad weather days.

After all, we knew what a wet day in the park is like. Internally, there were protocols that specified which rides needed to shut down in the event of rain or heavy wind. But we failed to do two things: proactively communicate with park-goers and offer alternative forms of entertainment.

We needed a rain plan that we could activate quickly, instead of scrambling at the last minute. For example, Knott's Berry Farm offers lots of live entertainment. While some of these shows were outdoors and would be cancelled in the rain, we could still move the Gun Slingers, Saloon Girls, dancers and other performers to sheltered areas to pose for photos and interact with visitors. While park-goers wouldn't see the whole show, we could still entertain them. We'd just give them a different experience on a rainy day. We could also add extra shows on bad weather days. For example, in 1987, we opened a 3D underwater adventure film called Sea Dream. It normally ran five times a day, but on wet weather days, we could double this without needing additional personnel.

The other half of the equation was communication. When I arrived in the Admissions Department, I realised we didn't share enough information with guests. Park-goers had no idea which rides would be shut down during inclement weather. Even our staff on the switchboard weren't prepped on how to reply to questions like these.

In these pre-mobile, pre-internet, pre-online booking days, I thought it would be a good idea to prepare a 'Rain Card' with this sort of information on it. We could hand them out to guests before they bought their tickets, managing their expectations in the process.

I shared my idea with Jack Schrecengost, Knott's Berry Farm's operations manager and the last line of defense when it came to disgruntled visitors. Jack was a tough, grandfatherly figure. Orphaned at a young age, he had migrated west as soon as he could. A former boxer with a broken nose that had never been properly reset, Jack had spent time in the military and had a gruff demeanor that disarmed guests, but he was as soft as could be once you got to know him.

Jack had been working in the attractions industry for at least twenty-five years; first at Disneyland, then Knott's Berry Farm. When I showed him the Rain Day Card, he was unimpressed.

"You don't need that!" he told me gruffly, pointing to the card. "Watch this, goddammit!" He strode up to the gate, looked across at the crowd of people lining up to buy tickets, raised his hand to his mouth and shouted, "Now listen up everybody! I am Jack Schrecengost. I'm the Operations Manager today. If you have a problem, you come see me. I just want you to know right now, though, that if it rains, you are not going to get anything. If anything goes wrong today, you will not get anything. So if you want anything, just come see me at the end of the day."

Jack walked away from the gate, turned to me and said, "That's how you manage expectations."

I had to laugh (though I held my smile until later). We still handed out Rain Cards that day. I can't tell you if it was the cards or Jack's speech that did the job, but guest complaints went way down after that.

Taking Control, When A Business Partner Says 'No'

In the world of business, it's not just the weather and big political and economic trends that can be outside your control. At times, the thing you can't control is how someone else is going to react.

Take, for example, a meeting I had with a catering partner soon after joining Ocean Park in 2004.

Michael Wu Wei-kuo was a sharp, young, Brown-educated businessman who had taken over the helm of his family business — a popular catering and restaurant chain called Maxim's, known for its bakeries and dim sum outlets — from his grandfather a few years earlier. Michael was responsible for bringing Starbucks to Hong Kong and southern China, acquiring the largest sushi chain in the city, Genki Sushi, and expanding the company. Under his leadership, Maxim's was flourishing.

At the time, Maxim's also provided all of the food in Ocean Park. But while their fast food division made dishes to order, Maxim's catering division pre-produced food in bulk. Unfortunately, Ocean Park was serviced by their catering division. I wasn't happy with the quality of the food we were receiving and neither were our guests. So when Maxim's contract came due, I wanted to make a change. I was about to learn, though, that Michael had other ideas in mind.

Along with my deputy, Matthias Li, we met in the boardroom at Ocean Park, where I shared our complete outlook for the park's development. I walked him through the master plan and explained all the things we were going to do to respond to Disney's impending arrival — how we would match and balance our offering against theirs so that we would be a formidable competitor. Then we asked for a better deal on the food contract.

Michael listened respectfully, then responded.

"You know, I hear what you're saying. I can see what you're doing and your plan sounds great. But I'm going to put my money on Disney."

Maxim's, we learned, had already sealed a deal with Hong Kong Disneyland to run their bakery, a Chinese restaurant in the park, and their employee canteen. So instead of offering Ocean Park better terms, Michael presented a less-than-ideal counter-proposal.

I was flabbergasted. We had put our heart and soul into the new Ocean Park strategy. While the new plan was still unproven, we believed in it wholeheartedly and knew we had the ability to connect emotionally with our consumers. But here was the head of a distinguished local company who thought Disney was going to kill Ocean Park. He was placing his faith and trust in an import over us.

Going into that meeting, we thought we only had one choice: to work with the Maxim's Group. But Michael's counter-offer would not improve the quality of the food. When customers complained, we couldn't tell them, 'it's their food, not ours'. As far as guests were concerned, the food was in our park, so it was our food. And they were right. It was our issue to fix, not theirs.

We couldn't control Michael's response. We couldn't control the terms offered by the Maxim's Group. But we could take control of the food chain.

Instead of accepting a sub-optimal deal that would generate both internal and external griping — or starting the process over again with another third party vendor — we decided to bring the food in-house.

I had actually always wanted to do this — and had shared the idea with Ocean Park's Board when they interviewed me a year earlier — but going into those negotiations with Maxim's, we didn't think we were ready for such a big step, particularly as our focus was on first redeveloping the park. Michael's response forced our hand.

We hired executive chefs, sous-chefs, we took over the warehouse, the central kitchen, the employee canteen, and we began to create menus and define the experience so that it would be fun and consistent with Ocean Park's theming and values. We strove for excellence at every step along the way, from ordering and receiving to preparing and distributing meals. We obtained the highest possible certification, ISO 22000, for hygiene and food safety.

From that day forward, we took our food to a new level. I set a goal that we should be able to prepare and serve everything from hot dogs to caviar. Our F & B offerings are now among the best of any theme park in the world and rival top-tier hotels. We can also react more quickly to changes in the market, like offering European-inspired pastries and healthy organic foods. (Seriously, who would have ever expected park-goers — who famously enjoyed anything sweet or deep-fried — to request quinoa on their salads?)

Providing great food has a knock-on effect: it encourages guests to stay in the park longer, instead of leaving at lunch time. This increases per capita spending and is good for the bottom line.

Two years later, The Hong Kong Institute of Directors recognised my contribution to Ocean Park and Hong Kong during their annual Directors of the Year Awards. At that point, more than 5 million people were visiting us annually, while Hong Kong Disneyland's attendance had dropped to 4 million. After the ceremony, amidst the interviews, Michael Wu walked up to me.

"Congratulations!" he said, as he shook my hand. My greatest mistake was not listening to you guys. I should have found a way to make that deal work."

I'm glad we didn't. We took control of the park's destiny, no longer allowing a third party to determine how the public perceived us.

Dominating Disney: The Role of Control

While you could bill it as a David vs. Goliath story, in 2005, the Walt Disney Company seemed even bigger in the public eye than the biblical Philistine. Ocean Park would need more than a slingshot to stay alive.

Disney has one of the world's best brands, fantastic intellectual property, and a lot more money than competitors like Ocean Park.

Mickey and Minnie Mouse are iconic. Children across the globe love Cinderella, Snow White, Alice in Wonderland, Beauty and the Beast, Frozen, Moana, Tarzan, Tinker Belle, The Lion King . . . the list of classics goes on, and then there are the more recent Disney acquisitions like Chewbacca, R2-D2 and Iron Man. I love Ocean Park's Whiskers, but our beloved sea lion mascot is not quite so famous.

Disney's deep pockets are legendary as well. In 2005, the year that Hong Kong Disneyland opened its gates, there were only 53 companies in the US with more revenue. The Fortune 500 placed The Walt Disney Corporation at #54, with annual turnover of US$30.7 billion and profits of US$2.3 billion. At that time, Ocean Park had a yearly turnover of less than US$8 million and profits of about US$1.5 million. Just to be clear, we're comparing **billions** with *millions*.

Not only did Disney have significant resources of its own, it also persuaded the Hong Kong government to invest US$3 billion in Disneyland's initial construction and related infrastructure as part of the deal for opening up in Hong Kong.[37] Later, in 2015, it successfully lobbied the government to invest another US$220 million in a new hotel, Disney's Explorers Lodge. In 2016, Hong Kong Disneyland announced a US$1.4 billion expansion; Hong Kong will pay US$750 million of this.

We could control neither Disney's allure, nor its budgeting.

But we could control the experience that visitors receive when they visit Ocean Park.

We knew we couldn't spend at the same rate as Disney, but rather than fretting about this, we stayed within our zones of strength. We focused on Ocean Park's differential values (as highlighted in Principle 2) by remaining culturally relevant to the markets we serve.

We kept our focus, controlled the experience, and ultimately, the results.

No sense worrying about what you can't change. Control the Controllable.

---

37 The New York Times provides a good explanation of costs, the government's rationale and criticisms raised. See "Mickey and Minnie Go to Hong Kong; A Proposed Disney Park Raises Queries on Tourism and Cost" by Mark Landler, New York Times, 3 November 1999.

Applying Control to Your Business

Whether you're in the boardroom or part of a departmental work group, it's easy to be distracted by events or factors that are outside your control. Work groups, in particular, are susceptible to spending time in the wrong places. As leaders, we need to keep perspective and encourage our teammates to do the same.

Applying Control to your business does not mean ignoring outside forces. Rather, it's a question of focusing on objectives and finding ways that *you* can adapt to achieve the goals.

Let me return to the example of Hong Kong's Umbrella Revolution. On a macro level, we needed to assess how the protests would affect park attendance and then take actions to mitigate a potential drop.

On a micro level, we needed to review the impact and implications for every aspect of our operations. Was there enough food on hand for the animals? Would street blockades prevent new deliveries from reaching the park? Two Australian Kookaburras (a type of Kingfisher bird) were due to be delivered on the 29th and several koalas a few days later. Did we need to find alternative routes to ensure their safe arrival?

Ocean Park's annual Halloween festival — which employs about 2000 performers, backstage crew members, and logistical staff on top of our regular staff — is one of the most popular local draws of the year, and was already underway. Would employees skip work to join the protests? Did we need to arrange for new forms of transport to help them get to work? What would be the impact on group and individual tours? Did we need to condense our offering, to close some rides and attractions? And if we were offering fewer attractions due to staffing shortages, would we need to reduce the ticket cost?

I convened a meeting of Ocean Park's Emergency Response Team. Fourteen department leaders joined me in the boardroom as we drew a grid to assess the situation, determine steps that had to be taken, and make contingency plans. We ranked the likelihood of potential risks, assigned responsibility to members of the team, and focused on ensuring the smooth running of the park. The meeting took one hour. We convened again for 30 minutes in the late afternoon and continued to meet periodically over the next ten days, each morning before opening and again in the afternoon, to assess the impact and implications of that day's protest.

By focusing on the details and breaking the impact of the demonstrations into manageable pieces, we were able to concentrate on areas within our control. We anticipated consequences and likelihoods, then addressed the immediate and potential impacts of the demonstrations. While we needed to initially defrost some food and order additional bamboo for the animals, there was no noticeable impact on our business.

Communication throughout the organization — from part-timers to the Chairman of the Board, as well as with our vendors — was also key to managing the situation. (See how to 'ACE Your Planning' in Principle 4.)

While you cannot anticipate every contingency, it helps to plan in advance. I always tell my team, "If you prepare for the worst, you'll never be disappointed". Develop a profile of inherent risks (such as inflation, political uncertainty, changes in consumer sentiment or the weather), then determine how to mitigate them. After doing this, what are the residual risks?

In some cases, no matter what actions you take, you may find that there is no longer a business case for your project. If after taking every possible precaution, every reasonable mitigation, you find that an initiative is still headed south, take a step back and ask 'what are the odds that this scenario will occur?'. If the likelihood is high, even with every mitigation in place, then you probably shouldn't be pursuing the project at all.

📌 Remember This

1. Control the Controllable.
2. Maintain perspective.
3. You can't control the weather.
4. There's no point focusing on things that are out of your hands.
5. Identify areas within your control that you can change.
6. Stay focused on objectives and figure out how you can adapt to achieve your goals.
7. Very few things are actually out of your control, if you break them down into basics.
8. Applying Control to your business does not mean ignoring outside forces.
9. Your time and energy are best spent on solutions, rather than getting bogged down in the problem.
10. Prepare for the worst and you'll never be disappointed.

Lead

Be a Present Leader
Begin with the End in Mind
Catch People Doing Things Right

Soon after I started work at Ocean Park, I turned to my assistant and asked, "Where do the staff eat?"

During peak season, Ocean Park has about 5500 employees — from the ticket sellers at the front gate to the accountants in the back office. While the theme park is not far from residential and industrial areas, I knew the staff needed to eat somewhere on the grounds — it would take too long and be too troublesome to leave the park every day for lunch.

"They eat in the staff canteen," Wendy told me.

"Where's that?"

"Near the central kitchen area by Wong Chuk Hang Road," she replied. "Why?"

"It's lunchtime. I'm thinking of going there."

Wendy audibly gasped. "Chief executives don't eat in the staff canteen. No CEO here has done that before."

"Now I have to go!"

As I approached the canteen, I could see through the windows that the room was full. It was noisy too, filled with laughter and friendly conversation. No one took much notice of me. I think the diners thought I was going to walk by, but when I opened the door and stepped in, the whole room fell silent. 'Awkward' would be an understatement. "This is a moment of truth," I thought to myself. "I can either turn around or continue inside." I took a breath and did the latter.

When I approached the counter, I saw that the menu on the wall was only in Chinese. I was still new in Hong Kong, so I ordered the only dish I knew how to say: Char Siu Fan, barbequed pork rice. The young gal behind the counter smiled and chuckled. My pronunciation was probably all wrong, but she understood me.

Then the next moment of truth arrived. I could either eat in the canteen or order takeaway and walk back out. I made a decision to stay. When I got my food, I took the tray, turned around, walked to one of the tables, and sat down with a group of employees. They were stunned. I asked someone, 'how are you?', but he was shy and didn't know what to do. Plus there was the language barrier. Eventually, a manager who spoke a little better English, walked over and joined me.

Before lunch was over, I took a good look around the room. I noted that it was filled with second-hand stuff from across the park. The TVs weren't working. The chairs and tables didn't match. There were all sorts of styles and sizes. Apparently, if something broke or was replaced, it got sent to the canteen.

After lunch, I called my human resources and operations managers. "This is a travesty," I said. "We expect Ocean Park employees to deliver world-class service, but we treat them like this. It would seem to me that we can spend a little bit of money to make sure that they have a comfortable dining environment. Let's give the canteen a fresh coat of paint, put some photos up that are representative of the park, change out every table and chair and make sure the TVs work."

The makeover was done within a week.

I then made a point of taking every one of my company directors to lunch in the canteen. Not only did I feel it was important to encourage interaction, I also wanted the staff to know that what they eat at work is as important to me as it is to them. I felt a responsibility to provide the team with as good a product as possible, and I knew that my continued presence in the canteen would help drive the quality.

Throughout my tenure at Ocean Park, I rotated between the park's different restaurants, but continued to regularly frequent the staff canteen. To this day, my successor, Matthias Li, has the same habit.

Being Present

Imagine, for a moment, having two bosses. One is always accessible, no matter how busy she is. The other is nearly impossible to reach. The first boss makes it a habit to visit branch offices and walk the floor of the company when she's there. Not only does she get a first-hand perspective, she also chats with employees and is open to their ideas. The second boss rarely visits. But when he does, everything stops and focuses on him.

Which boss would you rather have?

In the course of my career, I've worked for both types of people, but I made a commitment early on to be like the first boss, an accessible and Present Leader.

Being present, in the management context, has two connotations. The first is similar to the Buddhist concept of 'mindfulness': do one thing at a time, truly listen when someone is speaking. (Remember Principle 1: Seek First to Understand.) To quote Deepak Chopra and one of his spiritual advisers, the Thai monk, Arjarn Ekachai, "Keep your attention on what is here and now.[38] The most important way to create the future is to be present now[39]."

The second connotation of being present in the management context has to do with accessibility. A good leader cannot solely manage from behind a desk. You can't just wait for people to come to you. Whether your business is in a factory or a service line, it's important to get out in the field and visit with your staff in their place of work. When I have

---

38 Deepak Chopra, "Ten Keys to Happiness," www.deepakchopra.com/blog/article/4930

39 The Venerable Arjarn Ekachai, as quoted at meditationbenefits.co

a meeting, I often schedule it to take place in my colleague's office or I suggest that we have a discussion while walking the park together. I encourage my team leaders to do the same with their direct reports.

Being comfortable in the field means that I get to know the staff and they get to know me. Even if language is an issue, we wave and smile. Not only do I eat in the canteen, I also visit the staff break areas, locker rooms and workshops. I don't do it to catch anyone doing something wrong. On the contrary, I prefer to acknowledge good work while keeping my ear to the ground and being accessible to my staff.

You don't always have to be on the shop floor to be present. My chairman, Allan Zeman, is a great example. I knew that I could call him at any time and he would be present and available to assist. And he knew that I would only call if it was important.

Regardless of your business, people are at the core. A good leader takes note of what's happening on the horizon and can shift directions or apply more resources if needed, while simultaneously providing guidance and support to the team. Being a Present Leader is a start.

Lead by Example: Do the Right Thing

Whenever I walk through Ocean Park, if I see a piece of litter on the ground, I bend down, pick it up and throw it away in the nearest trash bin. Ensuring a clean park is a part of our company's ethos. And while we have sweepers and cleaners, they can't always be the first to see a discarded cup. It's the responsibility of every staff member, including me, to pitch in.

As a leader, you are constantly being watched by everyone in your company. Any executive who says otherwise isn't paying attention. Let's say I'm entertaining a visiting dignitary — an ambassador from India or even Hong Kong's Chief Executive — and I'm giving them a tour of the park. I spot a tissue on the path. I could ignore it and continue my conversation, perhaps even lead my visitors in a different direction, or I can pause for a moment. Either way, someone in the park will see me and note my choice.

Employees constantly observe leader decisions and how they make them, whether it's choosing a new product line or something as simple as pausing to pick up litter. Effective leaders lead by example. Their actions reverberate throughout the company. Managers do things right; leaders do the right thing.[40]

Consider another example. I'm in a meeting with my leadership team. The discussion is tense. The issue has to do with money. A decision is reached. I ask the people in the room, "How are you going to deliver this message to your working groups?"

One person replies, "I'll tell them, 'Listen up. There's going to be a change. The boss says we need to. . .' "

I stop him right there.

"If you go back and tell your staff that I told you to do this, you are disowning the decision and it won't survive. You're basically saying you don't believe it's going to work and your staff will be the first to pick up on that. You need to lead by example. If you can't deliver the message as your own, you don't own it."

It's OK to have disagreements during a discussion; these need to be aired upfront. But once a decision is reached, insist on collective ownership. If not, expect trouble.

During the course of meetings, I often pose another question, "If you owned the business, what would you do? What would your view be? Would you act differently if you were the owner?".

A good decision should survive not only the chain of command, but a change of leadership as well. I reiterate the message to my staff by telling them not to do something because I've told them to, but because it is the right thing to do.

---

40 This saying has been attributed to several management experts, including Peter Drucker and Warren Bennis.

Catch People Doing Things Right

For too many bosses, criticism is easy while praise is scant. I actively take a different approach.

At Ocean Park, we created a system for staff to recognise the positive contributions of their colleagues. As it was initially conceived, supervisors and other managers gave Ocean Praise cards to line level staff who were doing a good job — for example, to a ride operator who helped locate a lost child, or a cable car engineer who was meticulous with maintenance. In addition to receiving a written commendation, recipients could also drop their card in a raffle box to win prizes like movie tickets or even a trip overseas.

After some time, as we assessed the programme, front line staff asked if they could give out the Ocean Praise cards to their colleagues as well. My Learning & Development and Human Resources teams were against the idea.

"You can't let hourly staff hand these out. They'll abuse the system. They won't do it right."

I disagreed. "Let's give it a try," I told my team. "Let's give the cards to everyone, so that line level staff can recognise each other or even praise their supervisor if they feel something is done well. If it doesn't work, we can always pull back."

Later, as we assessed the programme again, not only was there no abuse, we found that line level employees were probably more judicious with their praise than the supervisors.

❖

Ocean Park generates a monthly Guest Services Report based on all of the comments received from visitors, including feedback cards submitted in the park as well as emails, website and social media comments.

I make it a point to write a personalised thank you note to every employee who receives a written compliment. I don't want my thank yous to appear like a form letter, so each note is handwritten and specifically acknowledges the positive action taken by the recipient. I usually sign off in a similar manner, "Thank you for your exceptional service. You make us proud!".

I include a signed 'Ocean Parkner' card with each thank you note, so the recipient can enter the monthly Lucky Draw. ('Parkner', a fusion of 'park' and 'partner', is part of Ocean Park's internal vocabulary.) After our first year of doing this, the Learning & Development team came back to me to say there was a problem. There was a poor redemption rate on the Ocean Parkner cards. So they pulled together a focus group of employees to talk about it.

"Employees aren't participating in the Lucky Draw because they want to keep the card with your signature as a souvenir of the recognition they've received!"

This was a pretty good problem to have. We fixed it by creating a two-part card: one half that I sign and another that they can drop in the raffle box.

❖

One afternoon, I was walking into the park from a back-of-house area, up a hill on the way to my office when a young F & B employee started gesturing at me. She was with a group of three colleagues who were going off shift. Waving and smiling, she clearly wanted to speak with me, though we both realised there was a language barrier. As she walked up to me, her girlfriends stayed a few steps back. She reached into her handbag and pulled out one of my letters. Smiling, she showed me that she had laminated the thank you note and always carried it with her.

This has happened a number of times over the years. Most recently, a part-time server named Liu Sik Yu, who is part of our Senior Citizen employment programme, approached me while I was having lunch at Panda Cafe. Sik Yu asked me to wait a moment, ran to the back of the restaurant to her locker, pulled out her thank you note and hurried back. She wanted to take a photo with me and the note!

❖

Around 2012, after several new areas of the park were launched, the number of compliments received from guests increased exponentially. One day, after returning from a week-long business trip, there was a huge stack of thank you notes waiting to be written on my desk.

"Would you like me to prepare these, so you can just sign them?" my assistant, Wendy, asked.

"No, I can't do that," I thought, reflecting back on that first laminated thank you. "It wouldn't have the same meaning. I need to write these myself."

During the course of my tenure at Ocean Park, I wrote nearly 15,000 personalised notes to thank employees for their great service. The number rose steadily from a couple each month the first year I arrived, to 46 a week in 2016.

❖

People are the core of any business and how you treat them speaks volumes about you and your corporate values.

"People do what you inspect, not what you expect," my former executive director for marketing, Paul Pei, was famous for saying.

I agree with Paul, though the key for me is not to inspect for errors, but rather to catch people doing things right.

Empower the Right People

When I was a young manager in the 1980s, I went to a trade industry conference in Orlando and attended an education session about human resources, led by someone from Disney. The gentleman giving the presentation covered all the normal things about Disney's HR programmes, but when it came time for the Q & A, a man in the audience raised his hand and said, "I have a question for you. How do you make your people so darn nice? That's what I want to know."

The speaker from Disney was silent for a moment, allowing the question to hang in the air.

Then he replied, "Well, we don't."

He paused again, then added, "We hire the right people."

"I can't make a grumpy person nice," he explained. "I don't have to say no to him. We can put him in a role where he won't interact with guests. He might have the right skills for the kitchen or warehouse, but we won't place him in a service position. Our goal is to cast people in roles that fit their personalities, skill sets, and desires."

It was a brilliant exchange, a fundamental reminder that a company needs to hire the right people.

Sometimes, you need to take a step back and remind yourself that a certain profile is required for a job. In our industry, you need people who are happy to engage with guests, who don't mind working outside, and won't be bothered by humidity (even at the director level!). Too often, in large organizations, people are hired to fill a spot, rather than being cast for the role where they can blossom and best serve.

Now that you've hired people, the next step is to determine which staff members to empower with more responsibilities and authority.

❖

Soon after I joined Ocean Park, we conducted an Engagement Survey. Every employee in the company participated. While the results were incredibly encouraging — more than 90% had high ratings and some two-thirds were completely engaged — we saw that employees wanted better information about career paths in the park, namely, what it takes to be hired and promoted.

This feedback led us to articulate eight 'core competencies' applicable to everyone in the company and five 'leadership competencies' that must be met by managers, division heads, and above. Typically, frameworks like these are generated by top management or someone in the HR department. I'm quite proud that Ocean Park's Corporate Competency Model was developed directly from employee input. After conducting the Engagement Survey, we held a series of small group meetings with the help of an external facilitator, to share the results, gauge employee reactions and gather further input. During these sessions, a list of common traits and competencies, that the staff felt should be required of our company's leaders, became apparent.

Table 4: Ocean Park's Corporate Competency Model	
Core Competency	**Leadership Competency**
Planning & Organizing	Strategic Perspective
Teamwork & Partnership	Decision-making
Communicating Effectively	Innovation & Improvement Orientation
Change Orientation / Flexibility	Respect for Diversity
Customer Orientation	Building People Capacity
Quality Orientation	
Goals/Performance Driven	
Problem Solving	

We define each competency as well as positive behaviours associated with it. We also detail 'proficiency levels' for each competency, which is a corporate way of saying that what's expected of a division head is more than that of someone on their team. It would be too complicated to dive into each competency and proficiency, but here is an example from Core Competency #7, Problem Solving.

The positive behaviours associated with this competency include:

• Applying common sense to identify problems and taking initiative to generate solutions (a core requirement for every employee)

- Acting quickly and independently in critical situations (a requirement for supervisors)
- Growing the business by identifying and resolving key business problems (a requirement for managers)
- Challenging existing industry concepts and developing new ones to create a competitive advantage for the company (for division heads and above)

There are other criteria at each level, but you can see how the expectations for problem solving rise with authority. These competencies and the behaviours associated with them are shared widely throughout the park. They inform how employees are rated each year during assessments and provide a guide as to what's expected of them in order to advance. Within this framework, leadership traits are encouraged and assessed, like someone's propensity towards innovation, respect for diversity and people-building capabilities.

Being clear with your staff about what's expected of them is important, but not enough. One, it's crucial that your company provide employees with opportunities to demonstrate their capabilities. Two, show that people are promoted from within, that top jobs don't always go to outsiders. And three, develop a good learning and development programme.

At Ocean Park, we established the 'Ocean Parkner' platform (the latter word is a fusion of 'park' and 'partner') to teach professional mindsets and skills. As employees participate in these in-house trainings, they acquire Ocean Parkner stickers, certifications, and management recognition. In addition to grooming leaders, the programme ensures that everyone in the company is on board with the corporate mission and values. Every staff member participates in the first tier — about safety, service, show, and sustainability — and can then decide which courses to take after that. Ocean Park's employees have been quite receptive to the programme and even refer to each other as 'Ocean Parkners'.

❖

Once you hire and promote the right people, it's crucial to empower them. To promote without empowering provides social elevation, but no new authority. The new job title may provide employees with a short-lived boost, but it's unlikely to ensure commitment over the long-term.

To effectively empower someone, you need to delegate authority (though final responsibility always rests at the top). It's a matter of clearly laying out goals and providing the necessary tools and resources to achieve them. Along the way, we review progress and, at times, adjust the targets. In addition, it's extremely useful to apply another principle, which I learned early in my career... and which is the topic of the next section.

Begin with the End in Mind[41]

I've always been a visionary with a small 'v'. I don't claim to predict the future — other people make their living thinking about that — but I do enjoy envisioning what a finished project or venture may look like, what it may achieve, before we've even started work on it.

The writer, Stephen Covey, has a phrase for this, "Begin with the End in Mind". I've always done this, but after I met Covey and read his book, his saying reinforced my practice and subsequently helped me ingrain the concept in the leadership habits of my colleagues.

Beginning with the end in mind has played a key role in the transformation of Ocean Park. About one year into my term as CEO, we announced the US$700 million Master Redevelopment Plan. Over a six year period, we would more than double the number of animal and ride attractions from 35 to over 80, and firmly establish Ocean Park as a world-class, must-see, premier tourist destination.

To achieve the level of detail in a 1000+-page plan, we started with some very general questions: Where do we want to be? What will the

---

41 Stephen R. Covey, "The 7 Habits of Highly Effective People", 1989.

company look like when we're done? We set top-level targets — both for the company and our impact on the Hong Kong economy — and then worked backwards from there. We envisioned:

- Educating and entertaining 5 million visitors every year
- Being able to offer at least 2 'Entertainment Units' (EUs) per guest, per hour during peak times[42]
- Annual revenue of US$175 million
- Per capita spending of at least US$35
- A US$13 million annual surplus[43]
- An Internal Rate of Return (IRR) of 16%
- Complementing Hong Kong Disneyland
- Adding 0.5% annually to Hong Kong's GDP
- Creating 17,700 construction jobs and 37,100 total jobs by 2022
- Economic benefits of over US$18 billion over a 40 year period

Thanks to the work of a financial adviser on Ocean Park's board, we already had a budget in mind. As we conceptualised the MRP, we committed to completing the project within this budget, on time and at top quality.

After setting these targets, we then asked, 'What will it take to realise our goal?'.

How will we increase park attendance from 3 to 5 million? What additions will attract more visitors? How much will they cost? Will there be enough entertainment offerings to meet our EU metric and ensure that lines in the park are not too long? What type of retail and food outlets do we need to increase in-park spending? What are the expected revenue and costs? Will the changes be consistent with our core values and differential values?

---

42 See Chapter 5 for more details.

43 As a non-profit entity, Ocean Park does not report a financial profit, but rather an annual surplus (or loss) instead.

We applied these questions not only at the macro level, but also when considering new rides and animal attractions. As we conducted feasibility studies, we referenced the objectives that had been agreed upon and ensured that they would be supported by the new product mix and our base market.

By beginning with the end in mind, we were able to frame the end result and define the park's redevelopment.

In the end, we surpassed almost all our initial targets. In 2013, the first year after the MRP's completion, Ocean Park welcomed 7.5 million visitors, generated nearly 50% more revenue than expected, and had an annual surplus of US$16 million. We were also recognised by our industry peers as one of the best attractions in the world.

❖

Beginning with the end in mind is also a useful tool for setting deadlines. At Ocean Park, we would regularly hold cross-departmental meetings to plan for the grand opening of a new project. I'd always begin this process with an overview of where we were headed, as in, what the new area would look like and its importance to the company. "This is where we want to be," I'd summarise. "Now let's set a date."

Project managers and creative people are notoriously hesitant to set hard deadlines. After all, a deadline creates a requirement that you finish on time, when there are all sorts of things that could go wrong in the interim.

To overcome this hurdle, we work backwards. If we set the Grand Opening for 15 January, will that provide enough time to complete the construction and safety inspections? How about marketing — does that give sufficient time to create and run promotional campaigns?

After agreeing upon a launch date, we then work backwards to determine a timeline that will enable us to meet our goal.

This is such a useful practice that you would think more business leaders would do it. It's not difficult, but it does take discipline. Oftentimes, people get so caught up in the details — a number on a spreadsheet — that they lose sight of where they want to be at the end of the day. This lack of discipline leads to soft objectives, wandering projects and mission creep.

Communicate Clear Targets

Before I arrived at Ocean Park, the company was on a cost-cutting path to stem its losses, which led the management team to close down parts of the park that they felt were too expensive to operate. In 1999, the company shut down a popular water slide area called Water World. Two years later, it closed the Middle Kingdom, a 10,000 square foot crafts and entertainment village modelled on China's Ching dynasty.

Water World had been situated near Ocean Park's front entrance, the Middle Kingdom by a back entrance. Both were closed without a plan of what would replace them, which meant that guests had to walk by boarded up areas when they entered the park.

This approach had to change. Visitors should feel the magic the moment they enter the park, not several hundred yards later. The company's corporate mentality needed to shift as well.

"We cannot save our way to prosperity," I told the team as we changed tack and began work on the Master Redevelopment Plan. "You have to speculate to accumulate."

To be clear, I do not advocate reckless planning and spending. Leaders need to take calculated risks based on facts and their board or parent company's appetite for risk. As a government-owned, not-for-profit organization, Ocean Park was relatively risk-averse. This did not mean we would not speculate, but rather that our choices had to be grounded in solid market research.

❖

I made it a habit at Ocean Park to hold weekly 'folder' meetings with the director of each department. These one-on-one encounters were an opportunity to discuss operations, programmes, budgets, and anything relevant to that part of the company.

Not long after taking up my new post, I was in one of these meetings with the head of Ocean Park's zoological operations & education, Suzanne Gendron.

"We need to do more to drive revenues," I told her.

Like a number of others who were driven by their love of animals to work at Ocean Park, Suzanne was not yet on the same page.

"Why are we putting such a focus on revenue?" Suzanne challenged me. "Ocean Park is government-owned. It's a not-for-profit organization. I didn't think we needed to make money."

"Not-for-profit is a tax status, not a business plan," I replied.

❖

While I prefer to build a consensus from the ground up, sometimes a leader has to push ideas from the top down. During Ocean Park's 2010 strategic meeting, I announced a new goal: the park would welcome seven million visitors a year.

While I gave my team five years to meet the target, the proclamation was met with groans. The park had just topped five million visitors, a record; how were we going to grow so much further?

"Be hungry for change," I told the team, reiterating a theme that was prevalent throughout the redevelopment period. "We need to set stretch goals. We need to aspire to reach targets that we believe we can achieve. If it were easy, it wouldn't be a goal."

For Ocean Park to achieve this aspirational target, we would need to clearly communicate, promote and reinforce it throughout the company.

"Let's keep this simple," I said. "Let's rally everyone around the number 7."

We started with coffee mugs. We placed a word cloud on it — with terms like honest, transformation, dynamic — and at the centre, in big purple letters, we wrote, "Goal: 7 Million". We applied the same concept to screen savers, mouse pads, the backdrop at the annual staff dinner, and even in back-of-house areas so that every performer saw it before going on stage.

At the same time, we made it very clear that the company would not cut corners. President John F. Kennedy not only said that the United States would place a man on the moon, he promised to bring him home safely. Ocean Park's goal may not have been as dramatic, but in no way could we compromise the company's commitments to safety, service and show in reaching it.

The 7 million campaign was more successful than anyone initially anticipated. We hit the target within one year, not five, and soon had to reprint the coffee mugs, replacing 7 with 8.

Leadership Traits

While I was working at Knott's Berry Farm, soon before being tasked to help lead the development of Camp Snoopy in the Mall of America, I was invited to attend a seminar by Warren Bennis, who had recently founded The Leadership Institute at the University of Southern California.

By the time I met Bennis, his reputation as a scholar and pioneer in the field of leadership studies was well established. He had already advised four US presidents (Kennedy, Johnson, Ford, and Reagan) as well as legions of CEOs, though most of his thirty-plus books had yet to be published. This particular seminar was for family-owned companies, as Bennis was interested in studying the leadership structure of 3rd generation family enterprises. Along with Knott's Berry Farm, there were representatives from Mars, Anheuser-Busch and more than a half dozen other companies.

During the course of the presentation, one participant said, "It seems to me that you can't open a book to learn leadership. In all your years interviewing heads of state, generals, and corporate leaders, haven't you determined any inherent qualities that leaders either have or they don't?"

"If I agreed and told you the answer to that question is 'yes', you wouldn't have any reason to be here," Bennis replied. "You wouldn't have a reason to buy my book or listen to me talk, because it wouldn't make any difference. I may as well fold up my tent and go home."

We all chuckled at Bennis' reply, then he said, "Actually, you're not wrong. I have discovered over the course of time that there are ten innate qualities possessed by successful leaders. I've found them time and time again in presidents, heads of state, and CEOs."

These are the qualities that Bennis shared with us that day:

- Curiosity
- Sense of Responsibility
- Sense of Humor
- Passion
- Courage of Conviction
- Persistence
- Initiative
- Sense of Urgency
- Creativity / Innovative
- Confidence

Bennis believed that everyone possesses these qualities, however they need to put themselves in situations where they are allowed to demonstrate them. Unfortunately, some companies and bosses do not encourage the best in us; they simply want employees to do the tasks assigned to them. A different corporate culture is needed, if you really want people to thrive.

I've incorporated these characteristics into my presentations, because I believe we can all cultivate them within ourselves, and they can be nurtured. I also hire and promote leaders based on whether they demonstrate these ten qualities.

Curiosity

No matter what leaders he interviewed around the world, Bennis said that without fail, they all had a sense of curiosity. They were always looking for something new and different. For me, this is about never being satisfied with the status quo. I'm always seeking opportunities to grow and develop; looking for new ways to drive the business. I enjoy studying trends — what's happening in the realms of education, food, entertainment, technology, and lifestyle — my curiosity is fed by considering which trends have staying power and will help shape the future.

Being curious means asking questions and looking beyond the obvious. Effective leaders' curiosity makes them more aware and better informed. They are willing to challenge routines and don't get stuck in a rut. They ask, "What if we did this? Why don't we try that?"

Without curiosity, mediocrity will set in, but having curious people in your leadership ranks will ensure that you are constantly challenged and your team is always seeking better ways to achieve the company's objectives.

Sense of Responsibility

Leaders have a responsibility to uphold corporate values and ethical standards while striving to serve the company vision and mission. Having a strong sense of responsibility means you never lose sight of your purpose.

At Ocean Park, responsibility for conservation, education and maintaining the company's good reputation can trump the argument for a new project. When I talk about this trait in presentations, the slide always has a photo of an Ocean Park panda . . . because we have a very real responsibility to the individual pandas in our park and to the species as a whole, to prevent it from going extinct.

As a leader, you need to demonstrate your sense of responsibility by showing that you take care of employees as well as the bottom line. Honesty and integrity are an integral part of being responsible. People say that integrity is what you do when no one is looking. I often ask candidates to relate a story about how their integrity has been tested, or a time when they demonstrated a sense of responsibility. This could be as simple as helping return a lost wallet to its owner or being responsible to the staff that report to you.

If you read the news, there are unfortunately too many cases of top executives who have not displayed integrity. And if you don't have integrity at the top, how can you expect it from your team?

Sense of Humor

Did you hear the one about . . . ?

In the context of business leadership, having a sense of humor isn't about telling jokes or making people laugh. A good boss certainly never makes light of a difficult situation. Rather, a leader with a sense of humor is someone who can read the team's mood and say — or do — something to relax people and alleviate pressure. It might be a wry remark or perhaps sharing a box of donuts. The goal is to keep the team focused, without being agitated, tense or distracted by negative news. To this end, I also always remind my team to keep things in perspective and control the controllable.

A willingness to be self-deprecating goes a long way as well, though of course timing is everything. During Ocean Park's 30th anniversary dinner, I dressed up as Elvis and sang 'Love Me Tender' and 'Blue Suede Shoes', even though I had never sung in front of a group before, let alone with a full band and back-up singers. For the park's 35th anniversary, my directors and I dressed up and performed as KISS.

Passion

In his 1989 classic, "On Becoming a Leader", Bennis distinguishes between a boss and a leader. A boss is a manager focused on the bottom line. A leader is a passionate, independent thinker who can steer an organization effectively. Bennis blamed managerial bosses for the private sector's failings, including outrageous compensation packages and an over-emphasis on quarterly results over long-term benefits, both for the company and the community.[44]

---

44 See also the New York Times' obituary, "Warren G. Bennis, Scholar on Leadership, Dies at 89", by Glenn Rifkin, 02 August 2014.

For me, passion feels fundamental. If you are not passionate, it will show in your work. Not only does it affect quality, passion (or a lack thereof) is also evident in someone's attitude, behaviour, commitment and the way someone interacts with their team.

At Ocean Park, there's no way we could have achieved the park's redesign without passion. Each team member understood the importance of the Master Redevelopment Plan for the company's future, its employees, and what it would do for Hong Kong. This generated the passion needed to see the project through. Similarly, if a business and its leaders are going to live up to a company's values, they need to be passionate about them.

Aspiration-based goals are driven by passion; Expectation-based goals are driven by motive.

Passion also fuels our next leadership trait: Courage of Conviction.

Courage of Conviction

Everyone, every business, every leader encounters setbacks and failures. Unless you are surrounded by 'yes-men', you will run into a situation where your ideas or proposals are not supported. What do you do then? If you believe in what you're doing and that it's the right course of action, you should have the courage of conviction to see it through.

My courage of conviction was tested soon after I joined Ocean Park. There were a number of people on the board — bankers more than anyone — who opposed the Master Redevelopment Plan. "You can't spend that kind of money," they said. "How are you going to pay it back?" The naysayers were focused on the financial liability, so we needed to prove that the redevelopment was financially viable. We had to demonstrate, and rightfully so, that a revitalised Ocean Park could generate the attendance and revenue that would be needed to repay the new debt. We also needed to show that if we invested less than our proposal, the results would be insufficient.

Bringing all the necessary stakeholders on board would take time and effort. Fortunately, my chairman was as convinced as I was that the Master

Redevelopment Plan was the right course of action, that the sum of money was the right amount to spend, and that it would return in spades if done right. We shared a courage of conviction that enabled us to overcome resistance and embark on the plan.

Persistence

Coming in to Ocean Park, I didn't realise the full implications of leading a government-owned, not-for-profit entity — that it would require multiple layers of reviews and approvals before we could proceed with new development plans. If I had known how difficult it would be, I occasionally joke, perhaps I would have taken a different job. But we took to heart Bennis' advice that effective leaders have "the strength to persist in the face of setbacks, even failures"[45], and persistence — fueled by passion and a courage of conviction — helped us fight for our belief in Ocean Park's future and navigate challenging conditions.

Similarly, when I led the redevelopment of Marine World in California, I needed to surmount the opposition of animal groups both within and outside the company, who opposed the introduction of rides into the attraction. I argued that without new entertainment, we would be signing the death certificate of both the attraction and many of the animals that lived there. It took time and persistence to build a consensus, but in the end, we were able to successfully redevelop the attraction.

Initiative

Leaders do not wait for something to happen, they make it happen. Before I promote someone, they need to show me that they are willing to make decisions and take action, without waiting to be told to do so.

In some cultures — both corporate and otherwise — there may be a bias against initiative: a boss who slaps people down or a risk-averse civil-servant mentality. In these cases, an effective leader needs to encourage initiative.

---

45 "On Becoming a Leader," Warren Bennis, 1989.

Perhaps it was because the company had been through several down years, but when I first arrived at Ocean Park, nearly every requisition came across my desk, even something as simple as buying brooms. Yet I had well-paid, competent leaders on my team. I made it a personal mission to change the corporate culture, to empower those around me and encourage initiative.

There's an old saying that it takes seven years to change a corporate culture. While there was incremental progress along the way, it was in 2011 — seven years after I joined the company — that I noticed a phenomenal shift. The park was doing well, and the team was seizing opportunities and addressing issues as soon as they arose.

Sense of Urgency

"The trouble is, you think you have time," writes Jack Kornfield, in a quote that is often falsely attributed to the Buddha.[46]

Every year, Ocean Park faces typhoons. Once the red flag is hoisted by Hong Kong Observatory, park staff need to hurry to tie down the rubbish bins, deflate inflatables and move things out of harm's way. If they react too slowly, the park could suffer, and worse, they might not make it home before the storm.

Too many managers believe that time is on their side. That was likely the case at Ocean Park in 1998, when the company found itself upside down from the year before. 1997 was a record time, with a US$11 million surplus. A year later, the company was in the red by the same amount. I often wonder what was going through the minds of the business' leaders at the time, as attendance dropped by a million people.

Whenever you face a change in market conditions — due to new competitors or a shift in the economic winds — you need to act quickly. If you don't, you will find yourself on the bad side of a business result and, possibly like that 1998 CEO, out of a job as well.

---

46 "Buddha's Little Instruction Book," Jack Kornfield, 1994.

If you do not display a sense of urgency in meeting your corporate goals, who will? This sense of urgency goes hand-in-hand with initiative; effective leaders encourage their team to not only realise opportunities, but to seize them.

Creativity and Innovation

Can you take a stalemate and turn it into a victory? Can you overcome barriers by trying a new approach?

In 2005, my marketing team produced an attention-getting, scary commercial to promote Halloween. A schoolgirl on a bus vomits into the handbag of a classmate. The second girl, who is understandably upset, gets another shock when she looks into the bag and a decapitated human head puckers up to give her a kiss.

Unfortunately, Hong Kong's regulatory authority thought the ad was too scary to run in prime time. We didn't want to edit the commercial, so my team said, 'Hey, let's put it on YouTube. Nobody's monitoring the internet!'. This might not sound innovative — and it may seem hard to believe — but YouTube was only founded in 2005 and didn't become really big until Google bought it a year later. This Halloween commercial became Ocean Park's first viral video and set us on the path of doing more digital releases.

If you want creativity and innovation, you need to foster an environment where people feel they are welcome to share their views and input. This will mean leaving your ego at the door.[47] Accessibility helps as well; at Ocean Park, staff feel comfortable approaching me during my daily walks through the park to share their ideas.

"There are two ways of being creative," Bennis says. "One can sing and dance. Or one can create an environment in which singers and dancers flourish. Leaders must encourage their organizations to dance to forms of music yet to be heard.[48]"

---

47 On this point, I'm paraphrasing Warren Bennis, who said this in an interview with Antioch University Los Angeles president Neal King on 27 October 2010. See www.youtube.com/watch?v=ZooDUKGey6o.

48 ibid.

Confidence

Growing up in California, the legendary UCLA basketball coach John Wooden was one of my heroes. I attended his summer basketball camps. I carried around an autographed copy of "They Call Me Coach" until the binding fell apart and I hung a poster of his Pyramid of Success on my bedroom wall.

Wooden always conveyed a quiet confidence that I admired, not to be confused with arrogance or cockiness, which might have been understandable given his unprecedented winning streaks. But Wooden was too classy to be brash or conceited. Coach's Pyramid of Success has 15 blocks and five tiers. Confidence is right near the top of the pyramid, next to Poise; together, they support the apex of success, 'Competitive Greatness'. They are also the product of proper preparation. Confidence, Wooden writes, is "well-founded self-belief. It is earned, not given.[49]"

At Ocean Park, we earned the right to be confident in 2012 — confident in our ability to deliver world-class entertainment and to effectively promote quality conservation and education — when the company earned the Applause Award, the attraction industry's highest accolade. Just as Coach Wooden's teams set goals of excellence and practised hard to achieve them, so did we — and so can you.

---

49 John Wooden, Pyramid of Success, see www.coachwooden.com.

Dominating Disney: Leadership

Disney and Ocean Park have very different leadership styles, and as a result, our organizational structures — the way in which our theme parks are managed — are light years apart.

The Walt Disney Company has an unbelievable golden goose in Mickey Mouse, as well as hugely popular brands like Star Wars in its portfolio, and it takes strong measures to protect this intellectual property. They have a system that works for them, particularly if you factor in movies, television and toys (which are widely believed to be its prime motive for entering China).

For anyone competing against Disney, understanding how they manage their business can enable you to effectively compete, without spending the billions that they do.

Disney brings a legacy history and distant idealism to their theme parks overseas. They have a formula — a cookie-cutter approach — that belies any talk of localisation or cultural relevance. Be it design, administration, or communications, Disney precasts its product and presents it to the local team for implementation. Pride and arrogance get in the way of understanding and being receptive to local market and employee needs.

Disney organises its subsidiaries with a system that business professors refer to as a Matrix Structure. Unlike the movie where Keanu Reeves acts like a free agent, Disney's employees are hamstrung by multiple layers of reporting that ensure that the parent company has the final word. Consider, for example, a director of marketing in Hong Kong. He's going to report to Hong Kong Disneyland's Managing Director, but he'll also take directions from the corporate marketing team in Burbank, California. Not only does this impede his ability to react quickly, but conflicts can easily develop as well.

In contrast, I brought a present, engaged, on-site leadership style to Ocean Park. I took time to understand the local environment and made myself accessible to employees throughout the company. Our organizational structure is simple and flat: straight-line reports between staff and management. Employees are empowered and encouraged to show initiative. I created an environment where staff members think like owners, where integrity is valued and problems are solved starting with the end in mind. Our leaders do not spend time worrying about things they cannot control, and people are celebrated for doing things right, rather than castigated for mistakes. Their passion to consistently deliver on Ocean Park's vision and uphold its values is clear and strong.

As a result, Ocean Park is fleet of foot, quick to market, and more responsive to the needs of consumers, employees, the media and the community.

Applying Leadership Principles to Your Business

Regardless of your business, the first thing that an effective leader needs to do is to understand a company's human resources and what's required of its people to deliver desired results. Leaders must be able to direct and motivate staff by providing advice, guidance, plans and inspiration that are timely and relevant.

Once you recognise that people are the heart of your enterprise, it follows that the working environment should be positive and rewarding. If it isn't already, identify what is wrong and assess how to fix it. If you're new to a company or a location, take time to understand the culture — both within the company (or the local plant) and the community. In this chapter, we've discussed a number of leadership principles that you can apply to create a positive, reinforcing environment where staff are motivated and proud to work together. It takes time, focus, and energy to make things work, but (to quote John Maxwell), 'teamwork makes the dream work'.[50]

As a leader, you will of course face external challenges as well as internal ones. With the entrance of a new competitor — particularly if

---

50 John C. Maxwell, "Teamwork Makes the Dream Work", 2002.

it is a multinational and much bigger company — the first question I would ask is, "what is their organizational structure?". Do they have a matrix structure like Disney, where local directors cannot make a move without home office approval? If so, know that with proper leadership, any action taken by your team can be executed more quickly than that of your competitor. Not every big company organises along these lines, though. Some, like my former employer Six Flags, provide a greater deal of flexibility to their local directors, so they can be more responsive to local market needs. In these cases, your company should still have the advantage of knowing the local market better than the new entrant, even if they are bigger.

✒ Remember This

1. Be a Present Leader.
2. Lead by example.
3. Catch people doing things right, then thank them.
4. Begin with the end in mind.[51]
5. Communicate clear targets.
6. Empower the right people.
7. Provide your management team with the latitude and resources to achieve greatness.
8. Cultivate the Traits of a Leader — both in yourself and others.
9. Encourage employees to think like owners.
10. Confidence is earned, not given.[52]

---

51 Stephen R. Covey, "The 7 Habits of Highly Effective People", 1989.

52 John Wooden, Pyramid of Success, see www.coachwooden.com.

PRINCIPLE 8

Disrupt

Be Disruptive by Nature

In the middle of 2010, construction near the front of Ocean Park was reaching a climax. In six months, we would open Aqua City. At a cost of more than US$140 million, this was the largest single component of the company's Master Redevelopment Plan; it would transform the visitor experience, as well as some operations.

For starters, we consolidated the park's entries and exits into one main gate at the front — closing a secondary access point at the back of the park — to provide all guests with a common themed experience. We added five hundred new parking spaces under the arrival podium and rerouted entry and departure traffic. The new elevated entrance area, accessible by escalator, is punctuated by whimsical sea animal sculptures and topiary shrubs trimmed to look like dolphins, seahorses, dancing pandas, and other animals, all of which are now popular photo points for arriving guests. The government also built a new public train line with a station that opened in December 2016 directly in front of the park.

It's worth noting that when I arrived at Ocean Park in 2004, visitors entering through the front gate had to first walk by large water slides that had not operated since 1999. This seasonal part of the park had been shuttered because it wasn't profitable. You had to walk about 300 yards before reaching an area that was open and functional — not exactly a great welcoming statement. That has all changed now.

Pass through the turnstiles today and there's 15,000 square feet of contiguous themed retail space. Ocean Park never had a proper retail statement before. Now, there are signature shops where you can buy cuddly toy penguins, Ocean Park apparel, Discovery Channel educational products, photos from your day in the park, snacks, souvenirs, and much more. Retail is an important revenue stream in our industry, generally accounting for ten to fifteen percent of an attraction's revenue, and increasing in-park per capita spending was a major goal for us. As Aqua City opened, we set new targets for F & B, merchandise, games and photos, all of which were met and exceeded.

We introduced Ocean Park's first nighttime show, a multimedia spectacular called *Symbio!* where animated images are projected onto a 360-degree water screen (which is just what it sounds like — a screen made solely of water). The tale, which is accentuated by flames, geysers, music, and pyrotechnics, is about two dragons — the fire dragon and water dragon — who symbolise the relationship between humans and the Earth, and the need to live in harmony while conserving precious resources. The storyline is consistent with Ocean Park's values, while the production was cutting-edge when it opened, with the first (and still only) water screen of its kind. More than that, it provides guests with a reason to stay in the park until the end of the day.

Behind Symbio! lies the centrepiece of Aqua City: the Grand Aquarium. Inspired by the architecture of Frank Gehry and designed by a renowned theme park architecture group called PGAV, it offers visitors a look at marine life from the 'sea floor to the sea shore'. From outside, the building is reminiscent of a giant marine creature. Inside, there are 5000 marine animals, including many species that were new to Ocean Park. Our communications department described it this way:

"The new Grand Aquarium brings to Ocean Park and Hong Kong a new iconic landmark that will soon be associated with marine conservation throughout the world. Clad with 244 trapezoid panes

of glass and draped with golden fins across its surface, the egg-shaped Grand Aquarium lights up the Park at night with a cobalt-blue glow, exuding the grace and brilliance befitting the Park's new crown jewel."

The Grand Aquarium is more than twice the size of our previous aquarium — which had been a cornerstone of the park for more than three decades. It can accommodate six times as many guests and, at opening, was one of the ten largest aquariums in the world.

Before we could open the Grand Aquarium, though, we had to conduct one of the most ambitious fish migrations ever attempted. Excuse the hyperbole, but moves of this difficulty had only been done in Japan and South Africa. Our existing aquarium, Atoll Reef, was located on a mountain ridge; the Grand Aquarium at its base. We had to safely move 2000 fish, including several rare species. We built a special container with a glass window so that park staff could monitor the fish en route. The migration took nearly one month to complete and I'm happy to say that all of Atoll Reef's residents made it safe and sound to their new home.

Inside the Grand Aquarium, we also opened Ocean Park's first high-end dining experience, a restaurant called Neptune's, which offers stunning views of the marine animals as well as sustainably sourced seafood. Behind the scenes, we added new office space, upgraded the maintenance shop, created new infrastructure and expanded the warehouse.

Within the first six months of opening, Aqua City increased the average visitor's length of stay and per capita spending on retail, food and drinks by about 33% each. This was better than anticipated; we were expecting the new offerings to increase revenue by ten percent.

Back in 2010, though, when this entire area was still under construction, I walked the park with members of my GO Team. Before every big opening, I led a process that we called GO, for Grand Opening. Every discipline of the company was represented, so that we could jointly review the progress and see how each division — Food & Beverage, Merchandise, Operational Readiness, Marketing, etc. — could support each other.

It was during one of these walks that the magnitude of Aqua City really struck me. This was going to *disrupt* multiple aspects of the park experience for both guests and staff, from the moment they arrived in the park until they left at the end of the day. So when I saw the first marketing and publicity plans for Aqua City, I realised that my team wasn't thinking big enough.

They were approaching Aqua City as just another launch event. This didn't match the size of our capital investment or the significance it posed for the company. I actually sent them back to the drawing board, though first I began to list all the superlatives of the area and the ways this would be differential for us.

"This is going to be a real exclamation point on our redevelopment, particularly as it positions us against Disney. We need to think bigger than anything we've ever done before," I told the team. "Aqua City is going to disrupt the market. It's disruptive by nature. Our marketing and publicity needs to be disruptive too."

So what does it mean to be Disruptive by Nature?

When I first used the phrase "Be Disruptive by Nature," I was being slightly tongue-in-cheek. After all, Ocean Park's business is centred around nature, and nature can be a hugely disruptive force. At the same time, how could our business — by its very nature — be disruptive? How could it garner consumer attention and market share?

There are two aspects to being disruptive by nature that hold true regardless of the nature of your business. It doesn't matter whether you are developing widgets, selling tacos, or running a theme park.

First, there is the design and function of your product or service.

What is your company's impact on the market? How can you set yourself apart?

When Steve Jobs stood on stage to unveil the first iPhone in 2007, he shared a slide with images of the most popular smartphones on the market: Blackberry, Palm Trio, Moto Q and Nokia E62. Roughly half the space on each phone was taken up by a keypad. The iPhone changed that (and we all know what happened to its predecessors). Similarly, companies like Airbnb, Netflix and Uber are altering how consumers travel and consume media; they've broken the mold when it comes to taxis, television and hotels. These companies not only make use of new technologies, they upend conventional practice and wisdom to stand out from their competition.

While not every company is Apple, we can all use trends and technology to improve, or even transform, our products and services so that they attract new customers and generate repeat business.

Second, there is the manner in which your company communicates with the public.

What can you do to make your product, programme or service stand out? Are you getting the attention of a market that otherwise wouldn't notice you? Consider first your differential values, then what you can do within this space to ensure that consumers take notice. Are there innovative technologies or creative concepts that will grab people's attention, provoke conversations, and generate interest in your brand and products?

Of late, it's been in vogue to talk about viral communications and viral videos. Disruptive Marketing might use social media, but it could just as easily be below the line. What's important is not the medium, but the impact — and to achieve impact, originality and innovation go a long way.

Disruptive Marketing

After walking through the Aqua City construction zone with my GO Team in the summer of 2010, I put the challenge to them to be as disruptive as they could, in a constructive way. We were completely changing the entrance to Ocean Park and modernising one of its core attractions, while retaining many of the familiar connection points guests enjoyed inside the park.

I asked the creative team and ad agency to put their heads together and brainstorm a publicity campaign that would absolutely blow the market away. I also suggested a few elements that this campaign might include: a signature song, a viral video and a big PR stunt for Aqua City's grand opening.

The campaign really made waves.

The first piece was the video. It made no mention of Ocean Park, nor was it clear that we were the ones who placed it on YouTube. The 20 second video, which looks like it was shot with a phone, starts with a view of Hong Kong's Victoria Harbour. The camera makes a rough pan to a whirlpool in the water. The water then begins to sink, almost like a biblical parting of the waves or a waterfall forming right in the middle of the harbour.

It didn't take long for people to start commenting and sharing the clip. Viewers debated whether it was a real phenomenon or a digital trick (the latter was true). Quite a few commenters wrote that they had seen it happen; others offered scientific explanations. The video went has been viewed more than 2 million times and still attracts comments, years later.

The video was intended to create a talking point before introducing the commercial, which featured a similar parting of the waters. Only later would we publicly link the two.

The commercial begins with a scene of a father and son on a small fishing boat. The boy yells "Wow!" as the father reels in a fish. As soon as the fish lands on the front of the boat, it stands up and says "Surprise!!!!". The water surrounding their fishing boat separates, this time on a much larger scale than in the YouTube video. The father and son are then walking on the Harbour's floor, crabs scurrying away from their feet, as the shadow of a large manta ray swims overhead. The duo stick their heads through a wall of water and are immersed in the aquarium.

The bilingual English/Cantonese theme song starts to play, "Happy Fish, Many Happy Fish . . . Yeah, Yeah, Yeah!" and soon we're looking at images of Ocean Park and the new *Symbio!* night show. The voice-over describes Ocean Park as being a whole new park from sea floor to sea shore with the opening of Aqua City.

Happy Fish might sound cheesy, but it became the Number 1 downloaded ringtone in Hong Kong for the next six months. The commercial was the most watched video on YouTube for more than a month, and won a slew of awards. It's particularly significant that we were able to sustain this level of attention, for as long as we did, in a market as dynamic, fast-paced and constantly-changing as Hong Kong.

The viral video, ringtone and commercial succeeded in disrupting the market and drawing attention to Aqua City's opening. Now it was time to make a statement at the launch event . . . and for that, we turned to my boss, Ocean Park chairman, Allan Zeman.

❖

Allan was initially reluctant to have anything to do with Ocean Park. Several years after Hong Kong signed the deal with Disney, Hong Kong Chief Executive Tung Chee-hwa asked Allan if he would lead Ocean Park's board. At the time, the attraction was in freefall.

Born in Germany, raised in Montreal, Allan moved to Hong Kong in 1975. He started his career exporting textiles to Canada, and while he created a very successful business, he made his name in property. In the 1980s, Allan bought a building on a steep narrow street called Lan Kwai Fong and turned the street into one of the city's most popular dining and entertainment districts.

Tung Chee-hwa had to call Allan at least half a dozen times, I'm told, before he would even agree to visit Ocean Park. Allan had never been there before. From the moment he rode the cable car, though, he fell in love with the park and agreed to join the board as chairman, setting in motion the steps that led me to join the company.

Some people describe Allan as flamboyant. He's certainly not shy. He's an astute, successful businessman who doesn't hesitate to speak his mind and is bold in his approach to opportunities, characteristics that have made him a popular go-to source for the media.

In 2007, seventeen months after Hong Kong Disneyland's opening, Forbes magazine dubbed Allan the 'Mouse Killer' for his role in Ocean Park's domination of Disney. Over the years, Allan has dressed like a giant jellyfish, a Neanderthal, a ghost, a construction worker, and has even danced in high heels and fishnet stockings — all to support Ocean Park.

For the opening of Aqua City, Allan didn't need to do anything quite so dramatic. Instead, we contacted a stunt man I knew from my days at Marine World in California. Dan Schlund, also known as the Rocketman, was a daredevil accustomed to taking flight. For the Aqua City launch, he wore a bright yellow and red jumpsuit, along with a harness and jetpack. From the podium, he took off straight into the air, flew around overhead above the crowd, landed, and walked backstage. Allan was dressed just like the Rocketman; he entered the venue moments later. To this day, a lot of people still believe that Allan was the stuntman flying overhead; these high-profile stunts, or 'antics' as the media like to call them, feed Allan's 'mouse killer' persona.

The Aqua City disruptive marketing campaign — the viral YouTube video, award-winning commercial, popular ringtone and a media stunt that leveraged on our chairman's celebrity — was not only innovative and tremendously creative, it also built on the very significant improvements that were being launched in the park. We wanted the public to take note and think, "Wow, here they come again!". The result was even better. In 2011, Ocean Park's attendance leapt from 5.9 to 7.1 million people.

❖

You don't have to build a new aquarium to create disruptive communications. Several years earlier, when Hong Kong Disneyland was entering its second year, I challenged the Ocean Park marketing team to come up with an ad campaign that would cut through the noise. I wanted them to make use of new technology and focus on Ocean Park's differential values.

The campaign would be called "Love Animals, Love Ocean Park". The team came up with a brilliant creative idea. We would create three commercials in which a human surprisingly (you might say, shockingly) mimics an animal behaviour. We then asked viewers a question, and asked them to text their answers for a chance to win free tickets or an annual pass. It might seem like ancient technology, but in 2006, interactive SMS marketing — where you asked potential customers to message you — was still relatively new, but familiar enough for the public to readily engage.

In the first commercial of the series, a woman in a red cocktail dress is sitting at a table in a fine dining restaurant. The waiter walks up, pours a glass of red wine, presents it to her and says, 'Enjoy your wine, madam'. Suddenly, the woman dips her foot into the glass. The soundtrack consists of sniffing and slurping noises. "Which animal tastes with its feet?" the narrator asks. Viewers were given four options — a flamingo, crocodile, butterfly or panda. (The correct answer: butterfly!)

The ad ran for just one week. In that time, we received 30,000 SMS responses. Each of the subsequent ads — featuring a woman whose head rotated more than it should and a man hunched over, carrying a bunch of identically-dressed women on his back — also ran for one week. In week two, we received 60,000 text messages. In week three, 120,000. It was unbelievable to see this type of public response. The campaign got people talking and showed the power of a limited budget, when there is an innovative team behind it.

Trends

Let's return now to the design and function of a company's products and services. What can you do to stay ahead of the curve and be disruptive?

Like many executives, I attend a fair number of industry trade shows — at least two a year. While there, I make a point to watch for what new technologies vendors are hawking, then consider whether their offerings are (a) potentially disruptive, and (b) ready for the market.

The hot ticket in the attractions industry is currently virtual and augmented reality. Six Flags in the United States is probably the most famous adopter of this, having deployed virtual reality to several of its roller coasters. I'm not sure the technology is there yet. For one thing, it's increasing wait times and reducing ride throughput, which cuts into a park's capacity to entertain visitors. It's also still difficult to sync virtual adventures with the twists, turns, wind and noise of real-world coasters. On top of that, virtual reality can have an unsettling experience on some stomachs!

Following the trends in my own sector is a start, but I believe effective leaders must do more than that if they expect their company to be disruptive. It's important to monitor trends in other industries as well.

Throughout the year, I make time to go online and research consumer and business trends. I look for consistent tendencies in food, education, entertainment, technology, and more. I also review the writings of futurists — people who make their living thinking about these sort of things — to see what they have to say about changes in human behaviour, education and entertainment. In my notes, I track which trends continue to receive attention over time, as well as their perceived value.

Several months before my company's annual Strategic Offsite meeting, I compile a list of key trends that I think may impact our industry. I also note whether, and how, Ocean Park is already engaging on each point. My team and I separate short-term fads from important trends, then consider if there are items that should be integrated into the company's three and five year plans.

Here, for example, are a few of the trends I noted for 2016:

1. **Value Drives the Search.** This is particularly true in China, where consumers spent US$17.7 billion shopping online on 'Singles Day 11-11', more than US retail sales on Black Friday and Cyber Monday combined. This rose to $25 billion in 2017.
2. **Cautious Approach to Credit**
3. **Power to the People.** Social media platforms like Trip Advisor, Twitter, and Hong Kong's Openrice have a strong influence on consumer decisions, while crowdsourcing is providing funds for all sorts of projects.

4. **Watching the Waistline**. Focus on healthy foods and fitness, as well as business opportunities to meet the needs of plus-size people.
5. **Age is Only a Number**. Boundaries are blurring as people 'postpone' old age.

Sometimes, after identifying a potentially disruptive technology or trend, we'll experiment before making a major commitment. For example, about six years ago, we introduced augmented reality — the technology behind the 2016 Pokemon Go craze — into the Ocean Park Halloween Bash. Imagine approaching a flat screen TV. Above, you can see a camera filming you and your image on the TV. Following instructions, you hold up a pamphlet perpendicular to the screen. Next thing you know, when you look in the monitor, not only do you see yourself, but also a zombie dancing on your pamphlet. We turned this into a game, with augmented reality characters providing clues about where guests should go next. The augmented reality kiosks were a fun addition to the haunted houses, even if the technology in 2010 was not as advanced as it is now.

❖

Perhaps the most important trend of the past few years has been the widespread proliferation of smartphones and increased use of mobile apps. Unsurprisingly, just about everyone who visits Ocean Park has a smartphone. Our visitors, particularly those from overseas, demand wifi so they can go online without incurring data charges.

Linked to this question of connectivity is an issue that may not be readily apparent at first: how can companies interact better with their clients? Most consumer-oriented companies now offer mobile apps, but is this the best solution?

Disney didn't think so. Instead, it invested US$1 billion in something it calls the MagicBand, a colourful digital wristband that acts like your ticket and charge card. Disney sells the bands online and in stores inside

Walt Disney World for US$13–23. It also gives the bands to season pass holders and guests who stay in Disney hotels. The MagicBands have embedded radio frequency chips, which enable Disney to track where visitors go in the park and anticipate their preferences. It can also be used to make purchases and enter rides, if you've made a reservation in advance.

Let me repeat, they spent US$1 billion — and had a team of more than 1000 people — work on this. Not every visitor gets one; most guests need to buy it. Plus, it comes in packaging that is an absolute environmental disaster. It's like Russian nesting dolls, with three different casings, one lodged inside the other. After you get through the plastic, you still need to activate the device and set up a Disney account if you haven't already done so.

As I watched Disney roll out the MagicBands in Florida, I was shocked by how much they spent. But like Disney, we wanted to know where guests were in the park, so we could quickly gauge and broadcast waiting times, direct visitors to areas that are not crowded, share discount promotions, personalise maps and even offer virtual guided tours. On the back-end, we wanted real-time information to make decisions about manpower, the frequency of shows and other guest services. I thought to myself, there's got to be a better way to do this.

So I challenged my team yet again.

"How can we use existing, off-the-shelf technology to count people in the park," I asked them, "and then use that information to populate a guest interface system?" In plainer English, I wanted a low-cost solution that would provide both our management team and the park's guests with the information needed to ensure that every visitor has a great day.

It was clear from the beginning that we would make use of the device in everyone's pockets, though we weren't quite sure how. To my team's credit, a young guy named Cyrus Wong did a phenomenal job of examining the problem, looking at the analytics and realizing that we could place infrared scanners — the same sort of technology that reads barcodes in a supermarket checkout lane — throughout the park to gather the data we needed.

We developed two applications — a front-end mobile app for consumers and a proprietary back-end management tool called Pflow that measures the flow of people in the park. Pflow provides real-time data about projected and actual guest capacity, wait times for every ride and exhibit in the park, visitors' length of stay, the number of people who have enjoyed a specific ride within the last hour, the breakdown between group tours and individual visits, daily showtimes, maintenance schedules, weather reports and much more. Managers have easy, immediate access to updates on their smartphones. (Remember Principle 3: if you can measure it, you can manage it!)

On the guest side, we installed free high-speed wireless wifi throughout the park. (Hong Kong Disneyland only offers wifi in select areas.)

With the Ocean Park app, visitors can find out about showtimes and wait times, and schedule their day by reserving a place in line on popular rides. There are virtual tours, coupons and customised maps — like Google Maps — that show the best walking route from where they're standing in the park to where they'd like to go, as well as how long it will take. At the same time, if we know that Neptune's Restaurant is crowded while there's space in Tuxedo's restaurant, we cannot only share this information with visitors, we can also offer a promotion to go to Tuxedo's, allowing us to distribute people more evenly throughout the park.

While the PFlow app is still in its infancy, I'm extremely proud of my team. Collecting on-the-spot information will continue to evolve with time, providing guests with information to help them better plan and manage their day in the park. From start to finish, Cyrus and the I.T. team only took about one year to put this cutting-edge application together. To my knowledge, no other attraction has developed a tool like this . . . and we did it all for US$1 million, or about 1/10th of 1% of what Disney spent.

Ocean Park wouldn't have started down this road if we hadn't first been attuned to trends and consumer demands.

Disney, by the way, is not rolling out MagicBands in its other parks. You'll only find them in Orlando. The company's newest resort, Shanghai Disney, is taking a mobile approach instead, relying on its guests' smartphones instead of a bracelet that they need to buy. Sound familiar?

Dominating Disney: Be Disruptive By Nature

While Ocean Park was working on its Master Redevelopment Plan and preparing to roll out Aqua City, Hong Kong Disneyland was not sitting still. In 2009, Disney negotiated a US$450 million deal with the Hong Kong government to expand Hong Kong Disneyland and open three new themed areas: Toy Story Land, Grizzly Gulch and Mystic Point.

Hong Kong Disneyland's critics had always noted that the Hong Kong resort was Disney's smallest, and that many of the attractions did not appeal to Chinese visitors who had not grown up with Disney characters.

The expansion would increase the park's footprint by more than twenty percent, while Disney promised that the additions would feature 'universally understood' content. The first of the three additions — based on the multi-billion dollar Toy Story movie franchise — opened in 2011, about ten months after Aqua City. Grizzly Gulch, which has a Wild West mining theme, followed in July 2012. Mystic Point opened in 2013.

Disney marketed aggressively during this period and after five years of being in the red, 2011 was the first year that Hong Kong Disneyland made a profit. The additions to the park helped Disney stay in the black for four consecutive years, and yet throughout this period, Ocean Park soundly beat Disney, both in visitor numbers and profitability. We not only maintained our place as Hong Kong's premier attraction, we actually took a huge leap above Disney, despite their introduction of new rides and themed areas.

Being disruptive by nature was a key for us, in terms of the design of Aqua City and how we communicated it to the public. Aqua City's launch attracted an additional 1.2 million guests to Ocean Park in 2011, up 20% from a year earlier to 7.1 million people. That's truly remarkable growth. And through it all, Ocean Park stayed true to its core values, by promoting education, conservation and respect for people, community and animals.

When I reflect back on the half-year before Ocean Park opened Aqua City, it's clear that the planning pushed our team to be better. Our marketing team was challenged to deliver disruptive communications; the entertainment team was challenged to come up with a breathtaking stunt that would ensure extensive media coverage; the food team was pushed to make sure the new restaurant was world-class; the retail team was pushed to offer unique, affordable souvenirs that every guest would want. The projects team was challenged to ensure that the aquarium not only set records, but would be the best possible experience. The disruptive nature of the project and associated tasks extended throughout the company.

During this time, it became clear to the Ocean Park team that you don't need a Disney-sized budget to do amazing things. Ocean Park has been able to dominate Disney by being more agile, more creative and more economical. The introduction of attraction-wide wifi and the PFlow management tool is a case in point. To this day, Hong Kong Disneyland is lagging behind in this area, despite a billion dollar expenditure by its parent company, while Ocean Park spent a tiny fraction of that amount and was able to roll out the project within just one year.

Given what Disney is working with — tremendous intellectual property, blockbuster movies, an iconic brand, and over sixty years of theme park experience — each and every one of its new roll-outs should be disruptive by nature. But Disney makes a common mistake: it regularly over-promises and under-delivers.

Take the case of its 2011–2013 expansion. Disney promised that the three new 'lands' would be unique and exclusive to Hong Kong for the first five years. It said the expansion would significantly increase the park's entertainment offerings, while being world-class and living up to the quality and mystique of the Disney name.

Let's look at those three propositions.

Disney largely kept its part of the bargain on the first point. Toy Story Land, Grizzly Gulch, and Mystic Point were new among its parks, though smaller than themed areas in the US, Europe and Japan. To an industry insider, though, the Grizzly Gulch Ghost Town looks to be a rip off of Knott's Berry Farm.

On the second point, Disney said that the expansion would increase the number of 'attractions, entertainment, and interactive experiences' at the resort by 50% to more than 100. Yet if you look at the new areas, Disney actually only introduced five new rides plus a few other small features — the walk-through ghost town, an outside show area with limited standing room, a couple of food kiosks, and some photo-taking areas. The public was disappointed with the small number of new rides as well as the lack of shelter, food and retail in those areas.

Of the new attractions, Mystic Manor is the best. It's an indoor ride that makes great use of animation and special effects. It features an innovative trackless ride technology that keeps riders guessing about which direction they're headed in next.

On the surface, Mystic Manor seems to meet the promise of being world-class, but when it first opened, the ride experienced a tremendous amount of downtime. Disney blamed this on teething issues associated with a sophisticated safety and control system. The park faced a similar issue (minus the new technology) when the Parachute Drop ride opened in Toy Story Land two years earlier. You would think Disney would sort out technical issues like these before launching new rides. But it didn't. As you can imagine, consumers who bought tickets expecting new thrills were not pleased.

Another problem initially was that the voices and graphics inside Mystic Manor were in only one language: English. The mother tongue of Hong Kongers, Cantonese, was only added later.

These were not the only issues. The food on offer in Toy Story Land and Grizzly Gulch — prior to the Mystic Point opening — was underwhelming. The variety was not up to standard, there was limited cover and no air conditioning, all of which attracted complaints because they didn't meet the public's expectations.

Fast forward to 2016 and The Walt Disney Co. does not appear to have learned its lesson. Several months after the high-profile launch of Shanghai Disney, significantly fewer people than expected are visiting the US$5.5 billion resort. Long lines and an expensive ticket price are to blame. Attractions have shut down during park hours, officially for maintenance reasons.

Shaun Rein of China Market Research told the South China Morning Post that "people [appear to] want to wait six months, twelve months, and even longer until the issues are ironed out," adding that "Disney made 'a big mistake' in not better handling long queues.[53]"

Irate visitors meanwhile are airing their grievances on social media, with many saying that a visit to the theme park is not worth the ticket price.

No attraction has received a bigger build-up in domestic and global publicity than Shanghai Disney. Long before Hong Kong Disneyland opened, Chinese and Disney officials were publicly talking about building a park in Shanghai. Throughout the construction and launch

---

53 "Disney still to find its magic in Shanghai," Sarah Zheng, South China Morning Post, 4 October 2016.

process, Disney officials highlighted the groundbreaking nature of the 'Authentically Disney, Distinctly Chinese' resort. Details of the project were strategically shared — and kept secret — to stoke public interest.

But just as in Hong Kong, Disney's Shanghai offerings have not matched the hype. There are not enough rides and attractions to meet demand, even though the crowds are smaller than expected.

❖

Back in Hong Kong, much of the local media coverage surrounding Disney is not focused on the park's offerings, but rather on the company's performance and impact on the local economy. After all, the Hong Kong government has a more direct interest in Hong Kong Disneyland's performance than you might suspect. As part of the deal to attract Disney, it invested a substantial sum of public money in the resort, as well as infrastructure projects to support it.

Hong Kong provided the bulk of the US$450 million capital investment to build Hong Kong Disneyland; it also spent a similar sum to develop Penny's Bay, the site on Lantau Island where the park was built. The government originally owned 57% of Hong Kong Disneyland; this was reduced to 52% after the expansion. But with the park losing money most years, the government regularly received no direct return on its investment.

Disney, on the other hand, has always been assured of receiving licensing, management, and other fees. Disney's lawyers are a smart group and they write very good deals for the Burbank-based company. When Disney enters a new market to build a theme park — which is not often — local partners are so enthusiastic and committed to Mickey and the gang, Disney practically dictates the terms of the agreement. Others pay most of the capital expenses, while Disney minimizes its out-of-pocket costs.

If a park does not perform — as has been the case in Europe, Hong Kong and quite possibly Shanghai — there are mechanisms in the contracts that enable Disney to show its commitment, while actually increasing its long-term profits at the expense of local partners. This strategy essentially has two parts:

1. Subordinate the collection of management, licensing and other fees; and
2. Convert debt to equity.

When times are bad, Disney suspends the collection of its fees. While it appears generous for doing so, the unpaid bills accrue interest. The interest adds up and becomes a very significant number over time. Disney can then offer to help balance its subsidiary's books by exchanging the theme park's debt for an increase in its ownership stake. Alternatively, it can collect the debt and use the funds to offset its own additional investment in the property.

This move caught France by surprise. Hong Kong was more prepared, but the negotiations around Hong Kong Disneyland's expansion still saw the government taking a 5% cut in its equity share.

At the same time, theme parks are only one part of Disney's business. The company leverages its resorts to promote Disney brands and expand the sale of consumer products, home videos and movies.

Applying Disruption to Your Business

In a competitive marketplace, the ability to stand out — to be disruptive by nature — can be the difference between success and irrelevance.

There are three key steps to ensuring that your business is disruptive by nature:

1. Design & Discern
2. Communicate
3. Execute

As you **design** new products and services or evaluate existing ones, make it a habit to **discern** the answers to these questions:

- Is your new product or service consistent with your company's Differential Values?
- Is it distinctive? Will it stand out in the market?
- Will it change the customer experience?
- Will it make an impact on how your employees fulfill the corporate mission?
- What superlatives can you associate with it?
- Have you identified the consumer and market trends that will be important for your company?
- Does your product/service meet a demand that is consistent with those trends?

If your product is distinctive, differential or unique, the next step is to consider how to **communicate** this in a way that will resonate with your target market and reinforce your message. The challenge is to create disruptive communications that will cut through the noise. Be creative.

Two words of warning:

1. Do not create false superlatives. Do not over-promise and under-deliver.

There must be no mistake about what you are offering consumers. They will quickly figure out the truth, to the detriment of your brand and market share.

2. Just because you can, doesn't mean you should.

The media or industry colleagues might be extremely excited about a new technology — bitcoins, GoPro cameras, virtual reality — but that doesn't mean they're ready for widespread adoption or right for your company. Before adopting a new technology, ask yourself whether it will provide a truly differential experience for your customers, if it supports your objectives and goals, and if it will make a difference in your (triple) bottom line.

This brings us to the third step: **execute**. As any good salesperson will tell you, it's always better to over-deliver. The challenge that Ocean Park faced — and which you may as well, if you follow this strategy — is that our ad campaigns made huge promises to the public.

As I pushed our marketing team to communicate the superlative elements of Aqua City, the rest of the team realised that they had to step up their game to match the communication level. They had to superbly execute each element of the project to ensure that it would, in fact, disrupt the market.

📌 Remember This

1. Be Disruptive by Nature.
2. Design differential products and services.
3. Create communications that capture the imagination.
4. Use new technologies and ideas to cut through the noise.
5. Ensure that your delivery matches the message.
6. Challenge your team.
7. Under-promise, over-deliver, not the other way around.
8. Monitor consumer and business trends.
9. You don't need to spend like a giant, to beat one.
10. Just because you can, doesn't mean you should.

Be Genuine

Be Genuine, Not Just Generous

Punctuated by the loud, steady beat of Korean drums, more than ten thousand protesters from across Asia gathered in the streets of Wanchai in December 2005 to demonstrate against global trade as members of the World Trade Organization deliberated inside the Hong Kong Convention and Exhibition Centre — the iconic glass and steel structure by the water, whose roof mimics the waves of Victoria Harbour.

Among the demonstrators was one of Hong Kong's most famous activists, Leung Kwok-hung. More commonly known as "Cheung Mo" — "Long Hair" in English — he is a passionate voice for universal suffrage, workers' rights, and a social safety net. Elected to Hong Kong's Legislative Council a year earlier, Long Hair is hardly your typical politician. He still wears Che Guevara t-shirts and is known to carry his protests from the streets into the legislature, as he would on this day.

Security at the Legislative Council, a little over a mile away, was tight due to the demonstrations, as I entered to seek government approval for Ocean Park's redevelopment plans. With me to testify before the Finance Committee were my chairman Allan Zeman, deputy Matthias Li and the Commissioner of Tourism Eva Cheng.

Overall, the committee members gave us a warm reception. Several legislators, including Dr. Kwok Ka-ki and Bernard Chan, told us that they enjoyed visiting Ocean Park with their families. They were pleased to hear that we planned to develop Ocean Park as "Hong Kong's People's Park" and were generally supportive of our request for government approval of subordinated and guaranteed loans.

While I was presenting to the committee, Long Hair entered the room. His late arrival caused a ruckus. After making his way to his seat, he straight away pressed a button to activate the microphone on the table, triggering a red light indicating that he wanted to speak. When his turn came, Long Hair launched into us.

"I know what you're going to do!" he exclaimed accusingly. "You're going to give contracts to all your friends!" We assured him that Ocean Park was following a transparent tendering process. The guidelines had, in fact, been prepared with the assistance of Hong Kong's Independent Commission Against Corruption. The Commissioner for Tourism, Eva Cheng, backed us up.

Long Hair let that point go, but then challenged us on a second issue.

"You call yourself 'Hong Kong People's Park'," he said, "but if that was really true, you would let every Hong Kong citizen in for free."

"We could do that," Allan replied, "but without admission fees, we wouldn't be in business for long. Pretty soon we'd have to shut the place down. Either that or we'd become a burden to taxpayers."

While this was true, Long Hair's question got me thinking. He was challenging us on the genuineness of Ocean Park's brand. What if, I wondered, we took him at his word and let people in for free. How could we do this? How could we give every Hong Konger a chance to enjoy Ocean Park without paying?

I gathered my team, we talked it through, and a new idea was born. We would offer free admission to every Hong Kong resident on their birthday. In this way, we could meet Long Hair's challenge while managing the demand and impact on the company's resources.

Ocean Park launched the promotion in January 2006, just weeks after the LegCo Finance Committee meeting. On average, about three thousand people take advantage of this offer every week. Rather than being a drain on revenue, it actually increases ticket sales. Few people go to a theme park alone on their birthday; most are accompanied by family and friends. For every ticket given away, we're selling three to four more.

At first we announced that the birthday giveaway would run for one year, but then I decided we should make it a perpetual offering, a part of Ocean Park's culture, because it's a genuine community give-back that also encourages more visitation from the local market.

A couple years later, while attending an international trade association meeting of the attractions industry in Orlando, I received a big surprise when Disney announced a new high-profile promotion: free admission to U.S. park-goers on their birthday. "Wow," I thought, "that's quite a compliment, when Disney copies you."

❖

In 2008, an IBM researcher met me at Ocean Park to pose questions about our business and future plans. What sort of external factors are having the greatest impact on the company? In what areas are you investing? How are the internet and other new technologies affecting your corporate strategy? How important are transparency and community initiatives?

My answers would contribute to IBM's biannual CEO survey. The computing giant, with assistance from the Economist Intelligence Unit, conducted interviews about business trends and decision-making processes with more than eleven-hundred corporate and public sector leaders from forty countries. The end result was a 78-page booklet, "The Enterprise of the Future".

When I received my copy of the publication, I was struck by several of the chapter headings, including one entitled *Genuine, Not Just Generous*. "This is us!" I thought. "This is what Ocean Park is all about!" I started incorporating the phrase into my daily lexicon, adding it to speeches and presentations, because it fits so perfectly and helps encapsulate Ocean Park's strategy and place in the community. It also highlights, I believe, a key differentiator between Ocean Park and Disney.

So what does it mean to be genuine and not just generous?

"The Enterprise of the Future goes beyond philanthropy and compliance and reflects genuine concern for society in all actions and decisions," IBM wrote in its executive summary. "The next generation of socially-minded customers, workers, and investors is watching every move a company makes. CEOs recognize this and corporate social responsibility (CSR) is climbing higher on the agenda."

Yet, in my view, "Being Genuine, Not Just Generous" goes far beyond CSR. It starts with a fundamental question, "What do you, as a company, stand for?". As you start down the path of answering this question, others that are likely to follow include, "Does your company better society? Does it make the world a better place? Does it contribute to the community? If not, why?"

Being Genuine means doing what you say you are going to do. Are your actions aligned with your words? Being Genuine fosters credibility, validates your company's vision and mission, and provides a connection with the community. Generosity becomes a supporting detail. While giving away money is a part of being generous, true generosity requires being generous with your time, resources, and influence as well.

When I first arrived at Ocean Park, CSR was largely defined by what happened at the gate. How many people did we let in without charging? The company had a good Community Access Programme — free admission for seniors and people with disabilities, plus half-price tickets for their care providers — which we have built on over time. Today, we have a dozen ticketing initiatives, including complimentary admission and free animal encounters for charity groups, and steep discounts for low-income individuals. During the 2015–2016 fiscal year, more than 454,000 Hong Kong residents enjoyed complimentary or generously discounted admission to the park. Those programmes cost the company over US$19 million annually in foregone revenue.

While I am proud of these initiatives, genuine social responsibility requires significantly more than free tickets. It must be integrated throughout the company's daily operations. How are we delivering on our mission to promote conservation, encourage life-long learning and be an employer of choice?

We realised that CSR at Ocean Park was organic. We have a variety of programmes that I'll discuss in more detail in the next section. It was never a conscious effort, though. It just seemed like the right thing to do, so we did it. Now, the company is in the process of codifying those efforts, putting policy and process in place, to measure and report on it. A new CSR Report Card tracks targets and objectives, while transparency ensures environmental and community advocates can do the same.

Corporate Social Responsibility, as many proponents will tell you, is not about how you spend your money, but rather how you make it. Being Genuine requires the same focus and attention to supply chains, wages, working conditions and environmental impact. Good business isn't only about the bottom-line. It's what you represent to your community. How does your business affect people and the world around you? Is it a positive or negative effect? When the impact is negative, what are you doing to genuinely offset it?

Following are some examples of how Ocean Park addresses these issues.

A Dollar from Every Ticket

On Monday, 12 May 2008, an earthquake measuring 7.9 on the Richter scale hit China's Sichuan province. Villages and towns near the epicentre were devastated. Homes, schools, and other buildings were reduced to rubble. More than 87,000 people were killed by the quake; another 4.8 million lost their homes.

As soon as word of the Sichuan calamity reached our shores, Hong Kong jumped into action. There was a huge humanitarian effort to assist the men, women and children affected by the disaster. Ocean Park and its staff joined these efforts by contributing HK$1 million (about US$128,000) to the Hong Kong Red Cross China Relief Fund.

While public attention was rightfully focused on the human aspects of the calamity, scant attention was given to the animal world, which also suffered massive losses.

The Panda Research Centre in Wolong National Nature Reserve was seven miles from the earthquake's epicentre and decimated. The roads in and out of the reserve, as well as offices, field stations and the breeding space were all destroyed. One giant panda — Mao Mao, a playful nine-year old mother of three — was crushed and killed by a fallen wall, while another died from illness. Several other pandas escaped, and were eventually recovered. We don't know how many pandas in the wild died, but more than eighty percent of their habitat — some two hundred square miles — was completely destroyed, cutting off wildlife access to food and one another.

There was an urgent need, as well as an opportunity for Ocean Park to step forward. Ocean Park had a direct link to Wolong. All four of our giant pandas had come from the centre there.

We decided to take action. Through our philanthropic arm, the Ocean Park Conservation Foundation, Ocean Park committed to help restore the Wolong reserve, as well as eleven others in Sichuan province. We started by making a RMB 1 million donation to buy emergency relief supplies, then helped lead a larger effort supported by the Hong Kong government. A Giant Panda Base Rebuilding Fund — funded in part by the sale of commemorative giant panda stamps by Hong Kong Post — raised another million yuan that helped purchase trucks, computers, digital cameras, and more.

We provided human resources to help redesign and rebuild facilities, as well as the reviews and assessments needed for the reserves to get back on their feet. While the relief efforts shined a light on Ocean Park's ties to Wolong, we had actually been collaborating with the Sichuan team for years, ever since China donated pandas from that facility to Hong Kong in 1999. We regularly shared new husbandry techniques, for example, developed by Ocean Park's panda caretakers, who have been trailblazers in finding ways to provide non-invasive veterinarian care. They can conduct ultrasound tests, take a panda's blood pressure and even draw blood, all without anesthesia.

I'm really proud of how Ocean Park responded to the Sichuan earthquake. The donations went a long way to support the staff, who then cared for the animals and restored the reserves. The earthquake relief was by far the Ocean Park Conservation Foundation's largest project to date, expanding the group's work in a way that was directly in line with the company's conservation mission.

❖

The Ocean Park Conservation Foundation (OPCFHK) was established in 1993. Its mission is to promote effective conservation of Asian wildlife, as well as their habitats. The foundation's work focuses primarily on conservation, research and education. It grew substantially in 2005, a year after I joined the park, when we merged it with the Hong Kong Society for Panda Conservation. Since then, the OPCFHK has allocated about HK$60 million to fund more than four hundred research projects.

A key initiative is to monitor and understand the population and habitat of the critically endangered Chinese white dolphin (many of which are actually pink or grey). There are about 2500 of these humpback dolphins in the Pearl River Estuary, but fewer than 100 left in the Eastern Taiwan Strait. From time to time, they end up stranded on Hong Kong's shores. OPCFHK officials investigate each case, free the dolphins when possible, and establish the cause of death when it's not. We also provide genetic samples to local universities and the Chinese White Dolphin DNA Bank in China, with the aim of developing an effective conservation plan.

In addition to projects focused on the white dolphins and giant pandas, OPCFHK supports the conservation of twenty other animals, most of which are on the IUCN Red List of Threatened Species. As a member of the Association of Zoos and Aquariums, and the first accredited member from Asia, the foundation supports a programme called SAFE, Saving Animals from Extinction. We've identified ten animals — including the horseshoe crab, blue-crowned laughingthrush, Chinese white dolphin and the giant panda — and we are committed to ensuring that they do not go extinct on our watch.

While members of the public can donate to the foundation, its primary funding is intricately linked to Ocean Park's business. Since 1999, Ocean Park has earmarked 5% of the proceeds from panda-related retail sales to the foundation. We expanded this to include a percentage of sales from animal interactive programmes and peak day parking surcharges, plus restaurant receipts at Tuxedos restaurant — our eatery overlooking swimming penguins which opened in the Polar Adventure area in 2012. During my time as CEO, I donated all external consultancy fees to OPCFHK. Every year, on our annual Conservation Day, all proceeds from the gate go to the foundation, and most importantly, every single day, one dollar from every paid admissions ticket goes to the foundation.

In the financial year ending June 2016, these combined revenue streams generated HK$11.6 million (US$1.5 million) for the foundation's work.

Education, Orangutans and Horseshoe Crabs

Huge fires on the Indonesian islands of Borneo[54] and Sumatra — fuelled by corporate and small-scale farmers burning vegetation to clear the land for palm oil, pulp and paper plantations — cause a dangerous haze to spread across Southeast Asia on a near-annual basis. The fires are aggravated by the fact that many occur on dry peatland, where flames can burn underground for months and easily spread to other places.

---

54 Borneo — one of the world's largest islands — is divided between three countries: Indonesia, Malaysia and Brunei. The Indonesian section, which is the largest, is known as Kalimantan.

To give you an idea of how bad it is, a reading above 100 on a standard Air Pollutants Index is classified as unhealthy. Anything above 300 is hazardous. In the fire zones, API readings have topped 2000.

The 2015 fires were the worst on record, destroying some 10,000 square miles of forest, decimating natural habitats, and causing an estimated US$16 billion in economic losses.

The Indonesian forests are home to one of mankind's closest relatives, the orangutan. These 'people of the forest' (as the Malay word 'orangutan' translates into English) are unfortunately a threatened species, even without the fires. The Borneo orangutan population dropped by more than 60% between 1950 and 2010, and is expected to fall a further 22% by 2025. The 2015 fires are known to have killed at least nine orangutan and dislocated one hundred more, who were found wandering near villages.

To help address this crisis, OPCFHK is providing multi-year funding for a variety of initiatives, including community forest patrols that fight illegal logging and fires, damming drainage channels to make it harder for peatlands to burn, and efforts to restore the forest. In addition, we're helping another organization that provides medical care to rescued orangutans, and helps rehabilitate and return them to the wild.

In May 2016, three Hong Kong university students — Anson Wong, Marcus Shum, and Ben Tsoi — travelled to Sumatra, where they worked with Indonesian professionals to respond to reports of human-orangutan conflicts. They were there with the support of Ocean Park's foundation. Over six days they responded to several calls from local villagers who had encountered orangutans on their plantations. They spent hours in the field, tracking the orangutans over rough terrain, looking for tell-tale swinging branches or their nests perched high up in the trees.

The students helped set up nets as the team tranquilised and rescued the creatures, including a mother and baby who were relocated from an isolated habitat to a nearby national park.

"Joining the rescue of two orangutans gave us new perspective on local conservation and the global palm oil issue," the students told us when they returned. "Orangutans are forced to live in a habitat fragmented by palm oil plantations, and the rangers . . . risk their lives tracking and relocating (them)."

The five-man relocation team "has been stretched to its limit," they added. "We must help them by reducing our demand on palm oil, as it is the one major threat that everybody can help mitigate. China and Hong Kong are one of the biggest palm oil importers. We have the power to save forests and orangutans by stopping or reducing consumption of palm oil."

"People often ask 'Why do you care what happens in Indonesia? That's so far away. You don't have to care, you're living in Hong Kong.'" Anson later told RTHK radio presenter, Annalie Chow, during an interview: "But we are not saving the orangutan, we are just saving ourselves from ourselves, because the orangutan helps sustain the ecosystem in Indonesia. So if we can save orangutan in Indonesia, there will be hope for everything else in that forest."

Anson, Marcus and Ben are among more than three hundred Hong Kong university students who have travelled overseas for fieldwork, then returned to Hong Kong to share their experiences, as part of Ocean Park's University Student Sponsorship Programme (USSP). Since we started the programme in 2005, students have participated in more than 130 projects across Asia. We're proud to connect curious, conscientious young people with passionate researchers, giving them the chance to experience how conservation projects are carried out in places with limited resources and accessibility.

In addition to the orangutans, a partial list of USSP projects conducted in recent years includes restoring coral reefs in Hainan, China, and studying the local coral craft market there; population surveys of Bengal tigers in Nepal, red-crowned roofed turtles in a Rajasthani river, and Chinese white dolphins in the Formosa Strait; and a review of the long-term strategy for conserving whale sharks and marine mammals in The Philippines' Northern Bohol Sea.

Beyond raising awareness and fostering an appreciation of nature, Ocean Park aims to inspire the next generation of conservationists. That's one reason why educational outreach is a major thrust of the foundation's work. The university programme is a key component. More than half of its alumni now work or study in conservation-related fields; many have become mentors to new participants.

The USSP initiative was made possible by Dr. Allan Zeman. Throughout his tenure as chairman of Ocean Park, he donated HK$300,000 (US$38,500) annually from his personal funds to finance the programme.

❖

Horseshoe crabs have been around for more than 475 million years. These primordial looking sea creatures first appeared on Earth some 200 million years before the dinosaur. Over the last century, they've been exploited by humans — first as fertilizer, then as bait for catching large snails, and more recently for modern medicine.

Their blood, which interestingly enough is baby blue in colour, contains a chemical that can detect and immobilise faint traces of bacteria. Pharmaceutical companies use horseshoe crab blood in a procedure required by the US Food and Drug Administration to certify new drugs and vaccines. As Alexis Madrigal writes in The Atlantic, "every single person in America who has ever had an injection has been protected because we harvest the blood of a . . . sea creature with a hidden chemical superpower.[55]"

The blood-giving horseshoe crabs are released back into the oceans after being given apple juice and crackers. But they're now spawning less. So while harvesting their blood may be good for public health, it's not so good for crab populations. Taken together with habitat loss caused by urbanisation, pollution and entanglement in fishing nets, the crabs are at risk. In Hong Kong, the population of these 'living fossils' has dropped 90% in the past decade.

---

55 Alexis Madrigal, "The Blood Harvest", The Atlantic, 26 Feb 2014.

Ocean Park began working with the City University of Hong Kong in 2006, on an artificial breeding programme for this unique local species. Over time, CityU has successfully refined the techniques and improved the survival rate of Chinese horseshoe crabs bred under human care. We've also conducted population surveys to better understand the situation in the wild.

While research provides critical information about animals and their natural habitats, we strongly believe that public awareness and community education are essential for conservation, which is why the foundation works with students and schools across Hong Kong, as well as in China.

A prime example is the Juvenile Horseshoe Crab Rearing Programme, which OPCFHK and CityU founded in 2009. Secondary school students nurture and monitor baby horseshoe crabs for half a year. Then they visit a mudflat like the one at Ha Pak Nai, on the northwest coast of Hong Kong. After picking up trash, the students release the crabs into their natural habitat. Some of the larger crabs are tagged with microchips, so researchers can monitor their growth.

Over the course of the project, the students organise public events to talk about the work they're doing. They advise Hong Kongers not to catch razor clams — a popular dish — from the mudflats, because this harms the horseshoe crabs' habitat. Meanwhile, Ocean Park, in partnership with Hong Kong Land, held a conservation awareness video competition. The winning team from the Diocesan Girls' School — which created a great 90-second animated video about Hong Kong's 'last horseshoe crab' and ways the tragedy could have been prevented[56] — won a trip to Guangxi, home to China's largest horseshoe crab population. We run a similar programme in China, where Guangxi students ask local residents to stop eating horseshoe crabs and to release them when they become entangled in fishing nets.

---

56 You can view the winning videos at facebook.com/OPCFHK/app/569460346543498

Since the start of this educational initiative, more than 3200 Hong Kong students have participated, sharing their message with 150,000 members of the public. Thirteen hundred juvenile horseshoe crabs have been released into the wild.

Carbon Footprint

As a socially responsible company — one that wants to be genuine, not just generous — it was clear that we needed to do more than support conservation and community projects. We had to look at our environmental impact as well.

In 2008, we hired a consultancy called Carbon Care Asia to conduct a carbon audit of Ocean Park and help us devise a plan to reduce the park's carbon footprint. The process took four years and at the end of it, Carbon Care determined that Ocean Park was emitting 56,906 tonnes of carbon annually.[57] That's equivalent to the carbon emitted by burning 200 million pounds of coal, or the greenhouse impact of driving 450 million miles in a passenger car. Alternatively, it's about the same as the carbon emitted by 20,000 homes.[58]

How could Ocean Park address this?

At the time, a lot of companies were setting 'zero carbon' goals. However, the reality is that there are no truly zero-carbon companies. Companies that talk about zero carbon emissions are likely doing one of two things: (a) limiting *the increase* in their emissions to zero percent, as compared with a baseline measurement, or (b) purchasing carbon credits to offset emissions. In my view, the former is insufficient and the latter, disingenuous.

---

57 This figure is the amount of carbon emitted in 2011/12, which was chosen as the base year for future comparisons.

58 These comparisons are based on a calculator developed by the US Environmental Protection Agency. See www.epa.gov/energy/greenhouse-gas-equivalencies-calculator.

Buying carbon credits is simply cheating that enables companies to continue business as usual. As The Guardian and author, George Monbiot, point out, carbon offsets are like "the ancient Catholic church's practice of selling indulgences: absolution from sins and reduced time in purgatory in return for financial donations to the church".[59] Moral implications aside, there's a debate as to whether these offsets — which in theory help finance renewable energy projects — are actually effective.

If a company is committed to reducing its carbon footprint, it should find ways to do so within the business. This challenge becomes even greater for a business that is expanding. Then, as now, Ocean Park was investing capital, adding attractions and preparing to welcome an increasing number of visitors every year. By its very nature, the growth would increase, not decrease, the company's carbon footprint.

In the end, Ocean Park set two goals as part of a ten-year carbon footprint plan: (1) reduce the company's absolute carbon emissions by ten percent, and (2) reduce its 'carbon intensity' (or carbon output per guest) by 25%.

When these targets were announced in 2012, we also committed to spend HK$50 million (US$6.4 million) on carbon reduction programmes. We expected this investment to yield savings of HK$70 million in utility costs.

"Ocean Park's commitment to reduce its overall carbon emissions by ten percent is quite ambitious and could help set new industry standards," said Trini Leung Wing-yue, Carbon Care Asia's executive director, when we announced the plans. "Other theme parks around the world, such as Disneyland, also have carbon reduction targets, but they're often selective, focusing on only cutting fuel emissions, for example."

We've had to examine every animal habitat, every ride, every attraction, street lights, and more, both in the park and backstage.

We redesigned the animal habitats and developed new energy-efficient life support systems for them. This meant changing refrigerants, rerouting pipes

---

59 Duncan Clark, "A Complete Guide to Carbon Offsetting", The Guardian, 16 September 2011.

to create more efficient water circulation systems, strengthening insulation, switching to water-cooled chillers and introducing real-time computer monitoring to adjust the inflow of fresh air and water. At the same time, we were always conscious that the animals' living conditions must be within the normal ranges of their natural habitats as their health and welfare comes first.

We installed solar panels on the electric carts used to transport materials and mascots, and set up a mechanism to convert food waste into animal feed. Like many companies, Ocean Park also reset thermostats and changed lighting fixtures.

When it came to new developments, we made it a policy to look at life-cycle costs, not just the price tag of initial investment. For example, when we renovated the Administration Building, we sourced recycled plastic materials to use in the construction, and built a 'green wall' and sun shading devices to reduce the need for air conditioning.

When we built the Polar Adventure attractions — which are home to pacific walruses, spotted seals, northern sea lions, snowy owls, arctic fox, and hundreds of Gentoo, King, and Rockhopper penguins — we created a fully enclosed, insulated space to reduce heat exchange and energy loss. As you can imagine, these animals require cool temperatures (8–10 degrees Celsius for the South Pole Encounter, 15–17°C in the North Pole Encounter), but we used the latest environmental technologies to minimise the attraction's carbon footprint.

Educating staff and the public is a key part of the programme. Remind staff to switch off lights, air conditioning units and other appliances before leaving a room. Educate visitors about the impact of climate change and ways to adopt a low-carbon lifestyle.

So, how are we doing?

The investments are paying off. Four years in, Ocean Park is well on its way to achieving its first goal. Absolute carbon output during the 2015/16 fiscal year was 7.9 percent less than at the start of the programme. However, due to a drop in attendance (more about that in the Epilogue), the park's carbon intensity was 8.2 percent higher than the base year, at

8.7 tonnes per 1000 visitors. I fully expect the carbon output per guest to fall back into line as park attendance rebounds. Every year, Ocean Park publishes these numbers in a Sustainability Report so the public can hold us accountable to our goals.

Meanwhile, in Tuxedos restaurant, overlooking the penguins, Ocean Park introduced a Low Carbon Menu. Low carbon — not to be confused with low-carb — dishes feature local produce to minimise the need for long-distance transport and meats from smaller animals, like free-range chickens, that have a low carbon footprint. Five percent of the restaurant's proceeds goes to carbon care research to further help Ocean Park reduce its footprint.

Ocean Park's restaurants only sell seafood purchased from suppliers who employ sustainable fishing methods, and the park has a comprehensive waste management programme to recycle and reuse paper, metals, plastics, glass, cooking oil, and rechargeable batteries as well as seasonal items like mooncake boxes, calendars and 'red packets' (which are given to friends and family during Chinese New Year).

Special Training and Employment Opportunities

Ocean Park has a dozen different initiatives to provide free or discounted tickets to members of the community. For example, throughout the year, people with disabilities can enter the park for free, while a care provider pays half-price. Then on the International Day of Disabled Persons (3 December), we extend complimentary admission to the families of people with disabilities; typically, at least 6000 people with disabilities, plus their families, take advantage of this promotion to enjoy Ocean Park.

Yet, as I explained earlier, genuine social responsibility must go beyond the entry gate.

Even before I joined the company, Ocean Park had a focus on *employing* people with disabilities as well, particularly individuals who might not be hired elsewhere. At the time, we worked with a charity called St. James Settlement. A number of people with disabilities who lived there arrived each morning on a bus, along with a case worker. They would work throughout the day, then return to St. James Settlement at night.

A few years ago, we began looking at how to expand this programme. About the same time, a couple of Hong Kong legislators criticised Ocean Park in the press, saying that we should be doing more for the disabled. We were actually quite offended by the comments, so we invited the lawmakers to visit Ocean Park to review our programmes for themselves.

When Regina Ip and Fernando Cheung arrived, they attacked us again. "As a statutory body, Ocean Park should be setting an example for other companies," they said. "But what are you doing? Nothing!"

"Now wait just a second," I told them. "Did you know we employ more people with disabilities than the government, in percentage terms? The percentage of people with disabilities in Ocean Park's workforce is also higher than the percentage in the overall Hong Kong population. We feel we're doing pretty darn well."

Regina and Fernando started to listen. We went down a list with them, not just of statistics, but also of people. We highlighted that we put individuals in roles that match their skill sets and where their disabilities would not disadvantage them. I introduced four employees, including a young woman from The Philippines who works in the kitchen and is deaf. While no one in her department speaks Tagalog, it doesn't matter; she has trouble speaking it as well, due to her hearing impairment. A chef is assigned to look after her, and they have a great working relationship.

The legislators asked me to leave the room, so that they could interview her and the others separately, to be sure that this wasn't staged. I was happy to comply. When Regina and Fernando realized Ocean Park already had a job training programme — plus sensitivity, awareness and diversification within our workplace that would allow people with disabilities to come in and get a job — it took the wind out of their sails. The lawmakers had an agenda. They wanted to come in, beat the drum and get publicity for introducing a programme to us. As it was, we were ahead of them, so we just became an outlet for the initiative they were promoting.

One difference we had with the legislators was that I felt they were putting the disabilities first. "We hire the person, not the disability. Let's change the thought process," I suggested. "Don't look at the disability, but at individuals, their skills and how they can best use these skills in the workplace."

We continued to talk with members of the Legislative Council and, taking their inputs on-board, we developed an expanded Selective Placement Training Programme (SPTP) to recruit and train people with disabilities. After finishing the nine month programme, some participants are hired directly by Ocean Park, while others take the skills they've learned — along with a graduation certificate and reference from Ocean Park — and apply for jobs elsewhere.

We have differently-abled people working in housekeeping, kitchen jobs, front-of-house positions and other departments. In a sense, the training is no different than that given to other employees, except there are additional resources and participants have more time, if needed, to learn the skills required for a job. When training is complete and the trainee starts working, a co-worker shadows and is on call to assist. We want to ensure that the work experience is positive for them. We also ensure that the trainee is placed in a role where disability does not potentially impact safety. For example, in the case of the sous-chef who is deaf, she is working in a place where it doesn't matter that she can't hear.

One graduate of the SPTP is Jacky Chan Yap Fai, who was hired by Ocean Park's ticketing department. The training programme was a game-changer for Jacky. Before joining the company, he graduated from the Hong Kong Institute of Vocational Education. Jacky sent out over one thousand cover letters and was invited to thirty interviews. For three years, no one would hire him. He suffers from severe hearing and sight problems. Now, Jacky is responsible for data entry and assisting visitors through the entry turnstiles.

"Joining the programme broadened my horizon," he explains. "I was able to meet a range of people. My supervisors gave me a lot of freedom and guidance, which helped me settle into the working environment and increased my confidence.[60]"

During the 2015/16 fiscal year, eleven differently-abled people participated in the SPTP. Overall, Ocean Park employs more than fifty people with disabilities, or 2.6% of our entire workforce.

Creative Employee Engagement

On 24 May 2016, at an annual employee gathering, thirty-two teams from every division of Ocean Park compete in a Jeopardy-like challenge for cash and prizes. The contestants spend hours cramming details into their heads so they can be the first to beep in after a question is read. The categories do not consist of general interest information or current affairs, nor are there queries about world history or sports. Instead, the contest centres on environmental issues and safety related ordinances, such as:

1. *When is Earth Day: 5 June, 22 April, or 12 April?*
2. *What is the percentage of drinkable water on the Earth: (a) 20%, (b) 10%, or (c) less than 1%?*
3. *What measure(s) could we take to reduce solid waste: (a) bring your own meal-box to the canteen for buying your meal, (b) request only the portion of the meal you need, or (c) all of the above?*
4. *Which of the following factor(s) affect the life of the Humphead wrasse: (a) damaged habitat, (b) overfishing, or (c) habitat pollution?*
5. *According to the World Wide Fund for Nature's Sustainable Seafood Guide, which of the following species belongs to the 'Recommended' category: Australia Abalone, Golden Threadfin Bream, or Sabah Grouper?*

---

60 See Ocean Park Media Release, 20 August 2014.

While quiz night might seem like just an innovative training exercise, it's actually much more than that. It's a way for Ocean Park to ingrain genuine CSR into the fibre of our workforce. To truly be successful, community and environmental messages require the support of everyone in the company, not just top management. These are big programmes that teams from across the park are in charge of implementing. Plus we're welcoming millions of guests every year to the park and trying to get them to be advocates as well — a mission that is only possible if Ocean Park's team has internalised the message too.

Without being overbearing or giving a lecture, we've set up a platform to show visitors how they can make a difference too. Information is shared in a way that's engaging and easy-to-understand, so the company's employees and guests both become conservation evangelists.[61]

By the way, if you're wondering about the answers to the questions on the previous page:

- Earth Day is 22 April.
- Less than one percent of the Earth's water is drinkable.
- You can reduce solid waste by both bringing your own meal-box and only ordering what you will eat.
- All three factors affect the life of Humphead Wrasse.
- Australia Abalone is sustainable, Golden threadfin bream are overfished, and the Sabah grouper is a non-indigenous hybrid carnivore that threatens Hong Kong's local marine ecosystem.

---

61 A previous version of this section was published in Funworld Magazine. See "Corporate Social Responsibility in Asia's Theme Parks," by Michael Switow, November 2015.

Dominating Disney: Be Genuine, Not Just Generous

Workers like Qin Renfang at the Mizutani toy factory in Shenzhen, China — just across the border from Hong Kong — sewed the seams of plush Mickey and Minnie Mouse stuffed animals for Tokyo Disneyland, until Mizutani shut the factory down and shifted operations to The Philippines. While plant closures may be common, Mizutani failed to provide sufficient termination notice or compensation. Worse yet, the company failed to set up pension plans for its employees, as it was required to do by law, according to Shenzhen officials.

To what extent is Disney responsible?

Globally, The Walt Disney Company has a fairly comprehensive corporate citizenship programme, and its website details policies related to supply chains, human rights, recycling, live animals, nutrition, and more. But Disney initially disclaimed responsibility because Tokyo Disneyland is a franchise, operated by The Oriental Land Company.

Never mind that Disney receives royalties from Tokyo Disneyland every year, that its code of conduct requires suppliers to abide by local laws, and a Chinese-language version of Disney's 'Code of Conduct for Manufacturers' was displayed on the shop floor of the factory.

"We definitely take these cases seriously," Marcus Wong, a Disney spokesperson based in Hong Kong, told the Los Angeles Times. "Disney's role is that of a mediator to facilitate the discussion between the workers and the factory. We're assisting in bringing this to a resolution.[62]"

The amount owed the workers is reportedly US$1.5 million. In February 2016, some eight months after the factory's closure, Mizutani started negotiations with the workers' representatives. It offered less than 10% of what was owed. The workers rejected this.[63] As of mid-2016, the dispute was unresolved, but Mizutani is still a Disney supplier.

A civil society organization called China Labor Watch regularly dialogues with Disney. CLW has documented numerous problems in Disney's supply chain, including workers who are exposed to toxic chemicals without being provided protective gear or training in how to handle them. In an open letter, CLW writes that "Disney lack(s) sincerity" when it comes to addressing labour issues in China.[64]

❖

To Disney's credit, the company is transparent about its policies. Not many businesses publish a Code of Conduct for Manufacturers on their website,

---

62 Violet Law, "Chinese toy factory workers seek missing pension funds from employer and Disney," Los Angeles Times, 19 December 2015.

63 "The development of the labour dispute in Mizutani, Disney's Supplier," Hong Kong Confederation of Trade Unions, http://en.hkctu.org.hk/mainland-china/labour-news/the-development-of-the-labour-dispute-in-mizutani-disneys-supplier. See also "Amidst Shanghai Disneyland opening, Disney toy workers protest unfair treatment", Open Democracy Network, 16 June 2016. www.opendemocracy.net/beyondslavery/au-lap-hang-kevin-lin-liana-foxvog/amidst-shanghai-disneyland-opening-disney-toy-worke.

64 "The Dark World of Disney," Li Qiang's Open Letter, 13 June 2016, www.chinalaborwatch.org/report/117.

or policies about conflict minerals and the rights of children. Disney also has a number of community service and environmental projects.

Yet it seems Disney is often more interested in the communications value of these initiatives than anything else, and driven by perceptions rather than real impact. When it comes to supply chain issues, action only appears to be taken when grievances are made public, and sometimes not even then. While we do not know everything that goes on behind the scenes, it appears clear that the company reacts more to hot topics and pressure, rather than taking a holistic approach to social responsibility and ensuring proper implementation.

When Hong Kong Disneyland first opened, the resort did not have a coherent community or environmental plan. It took a couple years before they realised it needed to change. To meet the demands of Hong Kong and Chinese families, Disney began to roll out education-based programming, like a well-publicised 'Youth Education Series' in 2007 and a 'Jiminy Cricket Environmentality Challenge'.

As the park's attendance continued to suffer, Disney shook up the Hong Kong management team. It brought in a local Hong Konger — the deputy general manager of Coca-Cola China, Andrew Kam, to be the resort's managing director in August 2008, replacing Bill Ernest from the home office. With Andrew as the public face of Hong Kong Disney, his team started looking at more community initiatives. They also hired away members of Ocean Park's education team. Imitation is flattery, though many of Disney's initiatives still have an ad hoc or PR feel to them.

Consider for example Disney's '10K Weekend' in September 2016, a series of races organised in partnership with AIA Vitality, a wellness company that's a unit of the insurer, AIA. Disney promoted the run as a 'green' event because it's carbon neutral. It purchased carbon credits to offset the event's footprint. The public doesn't know what Hong Kong Disney is doing, though, in its day-to-day operations to be environmentally responsible.

Globally, Disney has set a goal to 'reduce its emissions' by 50% by 2020. Again, the primary tool to do this is the purchase of carbon credits, so it's not exactly cutting emissions by the stated goal. Disney also does not release detailed emission numbers — so we don't know how Hong Kong Disneyland is doing — nor has it set an impact target of emissions per visitor.

❖

The years following the 2014 Umbrella Revolution have been a challenging time for attractions and tourist-related business in Hong Kong. In April 2016, word leaked out that Hong Kong Disneyland was laying off one hundred employees; some of the people losing their jobs had been with Disney for more than ten years.

Ocean Park has also been affected by the economic slowdown. But during my twelve year tenure at the company — and in the time since — Ocean Park has never retrenched workers. As a government owned, not-for-profit, statutory body and public trust, we felt an obligation to sustain employment — even if the bottom line was impacted.

Admittedly, some companies may find it more challenging than others to take this approach, but the public does take note, even more so when there is a sharp contrast between you and your competitors.

❖

Ask any Hong Konger whether they have visited Ocean Park, and the odds are they'll say 'yes'. I dare say that close to 100% of the local community has passed through our gates and has a connection with good memories of the park. Yet, more than a decade after its opening, I run into people all the time who have yet to visit Hong Kong Disneyland, and have no intention of going.

The difference, I believe, is Ocean Park's genuine connection to the community. Being 'Hong Kong's People's Park' is much more than a slogan. We have a generational connection with both old and young. Our admissions programmes ensure that the park is accessible to people from every income bracket, and free at least once a year. Our community and environmental programmes are intricately linked to the company's strategy and operations. All these factors put Disney on its heels, particularly when it was a newcomer to the market. It has had to work very hard to re-establish itself, and it's still working on it.

Being Genuine in Your Business

Whether you are entering a new leadership role, or simply wish to revisit your company's place in the community, start by returning to your corporate mission statement and core values. Do they represent what your company stands for? Are they genuine and do they link to your company's CSR initiatives? If not, work to align them.

Next, take a fresh look at your corporate strategy. Does it connect to your community goals? Being Genuine will require you to think more deeply about the strategy. You will likely add layers to ensure that you satisfy all your company's goals, not just the profit and loss statement.

Once you do this, you'll find that being genuine provides credibility and, a better connection with the public.

Ocean Park is a government-owned, not-for-profit, statutory body. Some readers might argue that it's easier for Ocean Park to work towards a triple bottom line, one that reflects social and environmental goals, as well as financial ones. But there are a number of prominent companies that also take this approach.

TOMS Shoes helped pioneer the Buy 1, Give 1 model. Buy a pair of shoes and the company will give another pair to a child in need. So far, it's given away sixty million pairs of shoes in more than seventy countries. Beyond that, TOMS has sales-linked initiatives to support clean water, eye sight, safe birth, and anti-bullying initiatives.

Patagonia has developed a reputation for ensuring that workers throughout its supply chain are treated fairly and that its manufacturers manage their environmental impact. Hiring practices are audited, employees must be able to file grievances, and many of its products are certified to be Fair Trade.

McDonald's may not have the best nutritional record, but the Ronald McDonald House is a fantastic, genuine community initiative that helps seven million seriously ill children and their families, every year in more than sixty countries. Ronald McDonald Houses provide a place for families to stay near a hospitalised child at little or no cost. Mobile units provide customised pediatric services like dental and eye care in Thailand and immunisations in New Orleans. McDonald's community efforts link directly to its stated ambition to be 'a good neighbour', 'champion happy, healthy kids' and 'keep families together'.

Being 'Genuine, Not Just Generous' is much more than just setting up a new programme. A company's social and environmental efforts need to be consistent with the rest of its business. Otherwise, it's little more than PR spin. Consider BP's 'Beyond Petroleum' push or Shell's 'green investments'. Oil giants run emotional ad campaigns showcasing their environmental initiatives, but the projects look insubstantial or unbelievable, because they're not in sync with the companies' business. Shell even tries to redefine sustainability as 'providing essential energy for a growing population'. Plus, the green funds pale in comparison to the companies' environmental impact. If Shell wanted to make a genuine statement, it would pledge that all (or a majority) of its energy production would be green by a target date. But that would require transforming its business. Until then, the public will see through these companies' efforts.

Being Genuine — and Generous — is good business. It will enhance your brand, build customer loyalty and boost employee pride. At the end of the day, though, it's not about the bottom line, or even the triple bottom line. It's just the right thing to do.

📌 Remember This

1. Be Genuine, Not Just Generous. Why? It's the right thing to do.
2. Ask yourself, "What do you, as a company, stand for?"
3. Do what you say you are going to do; ensure that your company's actions are aligned with its words.
4. Be generous with your time, resources and influence, as well as your money.
5. CSR is not just how you spend your money, it's how you make it.
6. Genuine social responsibility is integrated throughout a company's strategy and daily operations.
7. Dedicate a portion of corporate sales directly to community and environmental initiatives.
8. Be sustainable. Develop and implement a comprehensive plan to reduce carbon emissions, recycle waste and address other environmental issues like water shortages and clean air.
9. Engage and educate employees so they become full partners, possibly even evangelists, of your company's community efforts.
10. Be transparent. Set goals, track your progress and share the results with the public.

Aspire,
Then Expect

Make the Expectations Transition

And the winner is . . . "

My colleagues and I waited anxiously for Andreas Anderson, president and CEO of Sweden's Liseberg Group and chair of the Applause Award Board of Governors, to finish his sentence.

Ocean Park was one of three finalists nominated for the theme park industry's highest award. Presented biannually, the accolade is the Academy Award of the attractions industry. It honours a park "whose management, operations and creative accomplishments have inspired the industry with foresight, originality, and sound business development". The list of Applause Award winners reads like a Who's Who of theme parks. Disney's Magic Kingdom was the inaugural champ in 1980. Other recipients include Opryland, Universal Studios Florida, Dollywood, and Epcot Centre. In 1988, I was incredibly proud when my employer, Knott's Berry Farm, earned this recognition.

The award itself looks like an antique brass sculpture of two hands clapping. It's heavier than you'd expect, probably 20–25 pounds, and stands about a foot high on a square pedestal. The Liseberg Group presents the trophy at the kickoff of the IAAPA Attractions Expo, a trade show that is usually held at the Orange County Convention Centre in Orlando, Florida. The International Association of Attractions of Amusement Parks and Attractions (IAAPA) includes parks, museums, aquariums, zoos, family entertainment centres and suppliers from nearly 100 countries. To give you an idea of how the industry has grown, when I first travelled to Florida for the Attractions Expo in the mid-1980s, IAAPA lauded the record attendance: 13,500 delegates. Fast forward thirty years and the trade show attracts more than 35,000 people to 578,000 net square feet of exhibit space; it's one of the largest business conventions in the U.S.

In addition to Ocean Park, the other two finalists for the 2012 Applause Award were the Santa Cruz Beach Boardwalk and Puy de Fou. The former is the oldest amusement park in California and a national landmark, the latter a cutting-edge historical attraction with spectacular shows in western France. Each award cycle, some fifteen to twenty attractions apply. After narrowing down the nominees, a team of operators and suppliers visit each finalist. In addition to touring the facilities — both the front and back of house — the adjudication panel asks detailed questions about company finances, visitor trends, community involvement, park maintenance and safety.

One of the judges who visited Ocean Park — Bob Masterson, the former CEO and chairman of Ripley Entertainment — was particularly impressed that we had received accreditation from several international institutions, including the Association of Zoos & Aquariums (AZA), World Zoo Association, and the Alliance of Marine Mammal Parks & Aquariums. "Applying to the AZA was one of the most difficult things Ripley ever attempted," Bob told me, "and our aquariums still didn't get in. For Ocean Park, applying from outside the U.S. had to be that much more difficult. AZA accreditation is a real feather in your cap."

Going into the IAAPA theatre on the trade show floor that November morning, I felt confident, but far from assured. The competition was very strong. After an elongated pause that felt as long as the preceding paragraphs, Andreas Anderson finished his sentence. The winner was Ocean Park!

"Ocean Park has implemented a very courageous strategy, which has paid off with a doubling of attendance over the last few years, and a sound financial development," Anderson told the media after the event. "Ocean Park operates with a strong vision, a high sense of quality and a dedicated leadership, setting a great example for the whole industry." He also commended Ocean Park's 'high-value product' and 'unique base in the local community'.

The award marked the culmination of six years of redevelopment work and eight years for me on the job. Near the beginning of my tenure, my team and I had set a goal: we would win the acknowledgment of our peers; we would win this award. And now we had! We became the first — and so far, the only — attraction not just in Hong Kong, but in Asia, to win the Applause Award.[65]

Aspiring to Success

When I conduct leadership presentations, I often begin by asking participants, "Do you desire success?" Sometimes a lot of hands go up, sometimes only a few. "It's not bad to desire success," I continue, seeking to encourage those still contemplating which answer is the better one to give. "But as a leader, you need to gauge the temperature of your team. As we'll see, there are times to desire success . . . and there are times to expect it."

Back in October 2004, I posed the same question to my leadership team at Ocean Park.

We were gathering for an off-site strategic meeting at a Hong Kong Jockey Club (HKJC) facility in the far north of Hong Kong, fifteen minutes from the mainland border and about as far as you could get from Ocean Park without leaving the territory. The retreat was taking

---

65 Puy de Fou would go on to win the Applause Award two years later, beating out the only other Asian park, to date, to become a finalist, Guangzhou's Chimelong Paradise.

223

place about nine months after I had joined the company. The Master Redevelopment Plan was coming together. We had a better sense about pricing and the underlying metrics. A new design team and storyteller were on board. We were preparing to produce a marketing video to sell the plans to Ocean Park's diverse stakeholders and potential financiers. It was a perfect time to take a step back, evaluate our progress, and ensure that the new redevelopment plans fit within a broader framework of Ocean Park's vision, mission, and values.

The HKJC's Beas River club, where we were gathering, is a beautiful facility with manicured lawns and mountains in the distance. It's popular with wedding planners as well as Hong Kongers looking for an escape from the city. The setting was also significant, because the Hong Kong Jockey Club was Ocean Park's first financier, providing about US$50 million in start-up funds in the 1970s and early 1980s.

In 2004, seven directors reported to me. Matthias Li was my deputy; he also served as Corporate Secretary and Chief Financial Officer. Suzanne Gendron was in charge of Zoological Operations & Education. Alex Chu ran Design & Planning. Paul Pei headed Marketing. George Tso was our chief engineer, Alan Chan ran Operations and Brian Ho oversaw Human Resources.

When I stood before them at the beginning of the two-day retreat and asked, "Who desires success?", Matthias, Suzanne, and Paul said 'me'. The others, perhaps, were trying to figure out if it was a trick question. It wasn't. No one's job was on the line. This team had weathered incredibly difficult times, and I respected them. A number of factors outside their control — the Asian Financial Crisis, Bird Flu and SARS — had plunged the company into the red for six of the seven years before I joined it. But Ocean Park never needed financial support; it never turned to the government for a grant or subsidies. Every person in the room had a key role to play in the company's transformation.

As a new leader stepping into a struggling business and on the verge of embarking on a major project, I wanted to see if they hungered for success.

The previous nine months had been gruelling for everyone — operating the park while also contributing to the new concept designs, and all the related assessments. Were they still ready for the journey ahead? I had confidence in them, but was doing a last 'gut check'.

Asking about the desire for success allowed me to set the tone of the retreat. The team was enthused with the possibilities as we proceeded to develop Ocean Park's vision, mission, and values. The company's vision became aspirational: "Ocean Park aspires to be the world leader in providing excellent guest experiences in a theme park environment connecting people with nature." As we refined the corporate mission, we discussed what success would look like, and then set our targets accordingly. We aimed to welcome five million[66] guests a year — 33% above our attendance at the time — and to redevelop the park over a six-year period. We also set our sights on the Applause Award. While these were stretch targets, we believed they were achievable.

Once the directors were on-board, we needed to spread the word. We wanted every member of the company, from managers to line-level staff, to understand and support the new goals. On the lower floor of the cable car building at the Summit, we converted a 10,000 sq. ft. space into a showroom for the redevelopment plan. Today, this area houses the Sea Jelly Spectacular, but at the time, we placed a large model of the future Ocean Park there, as well as artist renderings. Throughout the first quarter of 2005, I regularly presented the MRP here to employees, so they could get a sense of what was coming.

During these presentations — as well as in every company newsletter and every departmental discussion over the next six months — I seized the opportunity to pose the same question: 'Do you desire success?'. It became like a mantra, not just for me, but for the entire team. You could see the change; everyone was getting sincerely excited.

---

66 As discussed in Chapter 1, we hit this target well ahead of schedule, in 2006, while attendance topped 7 million by the time the Master Redevelopment Plan was completed in 2012.

Who Expects Success?

When we brought the Applause Award back to Ocean Park, we made sure that it made its way around the park, to every departmental and division meeting, before mounting it by the reception desk of the Administration building. We changed the corporate letterhead and company description to reference the award, and created pins that every staff member could wear on their lanyards. The award became like a seal of Good Housekeeping, showing that the company had been acknowledged as one of the best theme parks in the world.

The moment you start publicising this, though it doesn't take long for some guests to say, "Oh, really? Are you *really* that good?" While compliments outnumbered gripes, the complaint letters would begin with, "You say you're the best . . . You call yourself an award-winning park. . . Let me tell you about my experience . . ."

Expectations had changed. Before, we could *aspire* to be a world-class park. Now, the public expected it. Every single day that we opened our gates, every guest, every employee, every vendor would hold the company to a higher standard of excellence. They expected us to be the best park in the world, and they would not hesitate to let us know if we fell short.

"Winning the Applause Award is the culmination of seven years of hard work," I told my team. "We set a goal to be the best, and we achieved it. We should be proud. Before we won the award, the public viewed us as a local park. From the moment we announced the Applause Award, we entered a whole new category. We have to demand more of ourselves. Just meeting visitor expectations is no longer enough. We are going to have to exceed their expectations in everything we do."

❖

Every year, before the annual strategic planning meeting, usually on a weekend when things were quiet at the office, I habitually revisited Ocean Park's core

226

documents. Reflecting on the experiences of the previous twelve months, I would examine the vision, mission and values to see if they still held true. Usually, they did, but from time to time I would highlight a word or two, plug in replacements, then ask the team which phrasing seemed best.

As I did this, preparing for the company's 2013 Strategic Meeting, I had an Aha! moment. I realised that Ocean Park had achieved everything we had aspired to eight years earlier. We more than exceeded our attendance and revenue targets. We built up the company's cash reserves. We completed the Master Redevelopment Plan on time, on budget and at a quality-level even higher than expected. And now we had even won the Applause Award. I sat there, as I looked at my papers, and thought, 'Geez, we've really hit all the key markers.'

As I did every year, I started the March 2013 strategic meeting with an overview of the lifestyle trends that could impact our industry. Then, I looked directly at the crowd — which was composed of 120 Ocean Park leaders, all staff who held the post of Assistant Executive or higher — and posed a variation of the question that had permeated our company some eight years earlier.

Only this time, I asked: "How many of you *expect* success?"

Hands began to rise.

This was a tectonic shift. Instead of desiring success, instead of aspiring to succeed, we now expected it.

When we revisited the company vision, it no longer seemed appropriate to say that "Ocean Park *aspires to be* the world leader in providing excellent guest experiences in a theme park environment connecting people with nature." We debated how to change the wording, and decided that the only phrase needing amendment was the aspirational portion, 'aspires to be'. We considered stating that "Ocean Park *is* the world leader . . .", but that seemed too definitive, as if the journey stops there. In the end, we wrote that "Ocean Park *will be* the world leader . . .". The team collectively agreed to change just those two words, 'aspires to', which is pretty phenomenal in a discussion with over a hundred participants.

With the Applause Award, guest expectations rose. Now our staff's expectations were rising as well.

We were making the shift from an aspirational to an expectational business.

❖

In addition to impacting attitudes and goals, expecting success had another profound impact on Ocean Park's operations. It required the team to become significantly more proactive.

When I first joined Ocean Park, I had never seen a team that was so good at reacting to a situation. They were impeccable. We went through a number of years where surprises were the rule and expectations hadn't caught up. If 20,000 guests walked through the gates on a day when we were anticipating half that number, they could quickly respond to ensure that every guest's experience that day was still first-rate.

It got to a point where the operations team was fully staffing the park every day, just in case the number of guests surpassed expectations. As you can imagine, this was less efficient and more expensive than proper planning. I'd rather be a firefighter only when necessary and not every day.

Once we began to expect success, the team's mindset changed and they became more adept at using situational models to project staffing and other needs. Surprises became the exception, rather than the rule.

What does it mean to Aspire, then Expect?

At the start of a new venture, or a moment when a company sets goals that are unprecedented, at least when measured against recent experience, that company is setting down the path of aspirations. It aspires to achieve, while its employees desire success.

Once those goals are reached, the company enters a new space, that of an expectations-based business.

228

Each space has a different mentality that drives the planning and goal-setting process. As you shift from one to another, the company's vocabulary needs to change. From vision and mission statements to the crafting of strategies and KPIs, the language you use to set goals needs to reflect your new reality.

For example, an aspirations-based mission is driven by hope, while an expectations-based mission is fuelled by confidence. In an aspirations-based business, staff endeavour to achieve their commitments. In an expectations-based situation, staff promise to achieve their commitment (and will work harder, if needed, to keep their word). Expectations-based terminology is more affirmative, more definitive, and less speculative. The following table provides more examples.

Table 5	ASPIRATIONS	EXPECTATIONS
Vision	Desire	Believe
Mission	Hope	Confidence
Appeals to	Ambition	Reliance
Approach	Theory	Practice
Commitment	Endeavour	Promise
Decisions	Wishes	Trust
Energy	Pursuit	Presumption
Essence	Dream	Purpose
Focus	Passion	Motive
Form	Prediction	Plan
Have	Inclination	Intention
Journey	Uncertainty	Clarity
Motivation	Yearning	Fire in belly
Orientation	Outcome	Results
Outlook	Destiny	Success

Table 5	ASPIRATIONS	EXPECTATIONS
Power	Possible	Probable
Quest	Longing	Assurance
Truth	Anticipation	Likelihood
Value	Horizon	Bottom-line

Warren Bennis often said that a manager has his eye on the bottom line, while a leader has his eye on the horizon. It's true that leaders tend to be aspirational, while their managers may focus on what they expect to be true for the year or financial quarter. Both characteristics can be productive, but it also depends on where the company is situated on the aspirations-to-expectations spectrum.

❖

A company's journey does not simply begin with Aspirations and end with Expectations. The route is cyclical and often returns to Aspirations again.

When a company has achieved its initial set of goals, it may be content for some time to work at the same level. Perhaps that's all the market can sustain. However, it's not unusual for leaders to enhance the vision and set new targets. When this happens, one portion of the company may be working on expectations based on previous success, while another has returned to the aspirational space.

In the case of Ocean Park, we wanted to continue to grow the business and began to aspire to be more than a world-class attraction. We set our sights on becoming a world-class destination resort. The difference, in our industry, is that consumers generally spend one day (or less) at an attraction, while they spend two or more days and nights in a resort. The switch from an attraction to a destination resort will affect guest profiles, target markets and the way in which the park is presented.

To become a resort, Ocean Park is building a new, all-weather, indoor-outdoor water park and two hotels. More about that later, but for the purpose of this discussion, the important point here is two-fold:

- One, in daily operations, we expect success every single day, while
- Two, for the water park and resort, which are uncharted terrain for the company and still under development, we aspire to success and are setting aspirational targets for their opening.

Similar cycles play out in other companies as well. When you are setting goals and writing KPIs, consider where in the cycle your company or department is situated.

Dominating Disney: Aspire, Then Expect

Aspiring for Success set the tone for Ocean Park's massive redevelopment.

It provided a common vision that motivated employees throughout the company and pulled them in the same direction. When I first arrived at Ocean Park, there was a silo mentality. Operations looked after operations. Zoology focused solely on the animals. People weren't talking to each other; they were just doing their jobs.

At this point, though, our team understood that we were building a park for the future. They realised that the crowds would grow, and we would have to adapt to serve them. We anticipated the company's needs based on good market intelligence, and identified which business segments would be productive.

As Ocean Park's aspirations became reality, I wanted our team to realise that we could continue beating Disney. We simply needed to Expect Success. Making the Expectations Transition would ensure that we maintained our focus on the basics — living up to the company's core and differential values, and offering a culturally-relevant, world-class product — factors that had contributed to our success in the first place.

Winning the Applause Award in 2012 provided validation. More than that, it gave everyone on the team the knowledge that Ocean Park had reached a pinnacle unattained by Hong Kong Disneyland. It provided the confidence to strive even further.

Expecting Success led the team to set more aggressive targets, which in turn set expectations about what we should achieve. As we adopted this mindset and pushed the envelope, our sales team approached new markets and our operations team was driven to ensure an even more positive experience for visitors to the park.

Aspire, Then Expect provided a critical framework for the team, which in turn enabled us to dominate Disney year after year. As Ocean Park re-enters an aspirational environment and strives to become a world-class destination resort, I'm convinced that this success framework will help the company achieve its goals and once again set it apart from its competitors.

Applying Aspirations and Expectations to Your Business

Part 1: Aspirations

When a company or a business unit plans a move into uncharted territory — perhaps due to an expansion of existing services or the introduction of new product lines — it is entering an aspirational space.

You have identified an opportunity, set targets based on all available information, and are aspiring to achieve a goal. Aspiring, though, should not be confused with hope. As I shared in Chapter 1, hope is not a management principle. The belief that you can achieve a goal is based on facts, market research and trends.

To start your aspirational journey, I recommend beginning with a variant of the same question that I posed at the beginning of this chapter. Meet with your team and ask, "How many of you desire success?" Then describe what success for the company looks like to you. This is important because, often, people think about success in terms of personal achievements or departmental goals, without linking back to the big picture. As a leader, your role is to ensure that team members share a common, overarching view of corporate success, then break this down into departmental and individual successes to show how they are linked.

You want every person to have a vested interest in the outcome and feel that he or she has an important role to play. Every employee should believe in the aspiration and feel a part of it, rather than thinking that is something far removed from themselves.

Setting Aspirational Goals

As you set goals and targets, they may be a stretch, but they still must be measurable, practical and achievable.

Particularly if you are new to a company, I recommend a five-pronged methodical approach to understand where you are, where you could go and how to get there:

233

1. Review historical performance.
2. Consider the Board of Directors' view on the company's potential.
3. Solicit the input of your leadership team.
4. Meet with the front-line and back-office employees who actually implement the corporate strategies.
5. Examine what gaps, if any, exist between these perspectives, then determine ways to address them.

Essentially, you need to apply Principle 1: Seek First to Understand, Then to Be Understood. Note that some aspirational targets and goals will be part of a long-term strategy such as a three-year, five-year or even ten-year plan, while others will be more immediate. Longer-term goals still need to be revisited and tested every year, taking current market conditions into account.

There are two pitfalls to avoid when embarking on an aspirational journey:

1. *Setting unrealistic aspirations.* Many companies set a goal or vision to be 'the world's best' at what they do. Obviously, not everyone can be 'the best', though every business can strive to be 'world-class'. If Ocean Park had targeted twenty million visitors a year — up from a base of three million — neither our employees nor other stakeholders would have bought into the plan. Your aspirations — as well as the related concepts, vision, mission and goals — must be rooted in reality.

2. *Enabling a culture where team members do not take the goals seriously.* In these cases, employees believe that targets are flexible and it's OK if they don't achieve them. As a leader, you have to ensure that people are not simply hoping to reach a goal, but are driven to achieve it. Every member of the team needs to commit to this. Success is not a one-person job; a company will not fulfil its vision with the CEO alone.

There may be times when members of your team think an aspiration is too hard to achieve. In these moments, I'm reminded of something I used to tell my children — and which they still hate to this day: "If you believe you can't, then you're right."

At the end of the day, you have to believe in what you're doing.

In the case of Ocean Park, we knew that tourism to Hong Kong was on the rise and Hong Kong Disneyland's launch would further expand the market. We structured our redevelopment to ensure that our offering was relevant to consumers and different from our main competitor. The opportunity was within reach; it was not a dream.

As you work towards your new goals, you may need to make changes in the plan along the way. In our case, for example, if I look back at the initial artwork we approved as part of Ocean Park's Master Redevelopment Plan, I see elements that do not appear in the park today: beluga whales, killer whales, a Cinderella-like castle, a massive, curved LED screen immersing the entryway with images of animated ocean animals. As we commenced the redevelopment, we realised that those features did not belong in the park. Dropping them did not mean backing off of our goals. Rather, the MRP was about an overall product offering, not a specific attraction, ride or animal. We needed to keep our focus on the big picture.

Part 2: Expectations

Take the time to periodically and strategically meet with your leadership team, to evaluate the aspirational goals that have been set over prior years. Examine your corporate vision and mission statements too. As you reflect and take stock, evaluate the following questions:

- How has our business evolved?
- Have we achieved our initial goals?
- If so, what's next?
- How far have we progressed towards the corporate vision and mission?
- Should we adjust or reset these key statements?

It may be time to make the shift from aspirations to expectations if:

- You have achieved some or all of your macro goals.
- You conclude that your company's vision and mission statements need to be updated to reflect success.

Think about where your company is on the Aspirations-Expectations continuum. If you and your colleagues conclude that your company now expects success — based on past achievements and the outlook for future business — rather than simply desiring it, it is time to set your goals differently and use expectations-based terminology.

Beware. If your company does not make the Expectations Transition, it runs the risk of complacency, which in turn can lead to mediocrity and decline. Not only will your business fail to achieve its ultimate potential, it may be surpassed by competitors. Expecting Success is the opposite of complacency; it means that every day you have clarity, intention and confidence to deliver the best. As a leader, you need to foster a culture where employees are driven and continually looking for better ways of doing things. Consider companies like Blackberry, Kodak and Nokia, which were once dominant in their fields. If you could look into their boardrooms, you'd probably find that their management teams thought the companies were doing fine. They were at the top of the market, and nobody could beat them. Except this wasn't true. Those leaders failed to make a transition — either to Expectations or back again to Aspire.

Part 3: Aspire Again

There will come a time when your company needs to transition back to aspirations. You will know it's time to make this shift if:

- you wish to significantly top your own records.
- a new transformation is needed to further grow the company.
- your competitors are catching up with you.

- factors outside your control — such as a downturn in the economy — have affected your business.

You'll note that the first two scenarios above are quite positive. Business is good, you wish to stay on top and are striving for new successes outside your company's current reality. In the third scenario, your company may still be performing well, but it's time to refocus on what makes it unique. As discussed in Principle 2, you need to seek a 'blue ocean' to once again make competitors irrelevant.[67] In the fourth scenario above, no degree of expectation will change what's happening outside; your company must simply adapt.

Finally, it's important to realise that Aspirations and Expectations are not mutually exclusive. In some dimensions, your company may expect success, while in others, it aspires. In the case of Ocean Park, the company has re-entered an aspirational space as it strives to become a destination resort. At the same time, we expect success in current operations, particularly when it comes to metrics for safety, service and show.

---

67 W. Chan Kim and Renee Mauborgne, "Blue Ocean Strategy", Harvard Business Review Press, 2005.

📌 Remember This

1. Aspiring for Success provides a common vision.
2. This vision needs to inspire and motivate employees.
3. Working to achieve this vision will break down company silos and encourage cross-departmental communication and collaboration.
4. Every employee should feel that they have a vested interest and role to play.
5. Goals and targets should stretch the team, but must still be rooted in reality.
6. Do not confuse Aspirations with Hope; hope is not a management concept.
7. Evaluate your progress, plus the company vision and mission statements, at least once a year.
8. When most of your aspirational targets have been achieved, make the Expectations Transition.
9. Be conscious of language when writing strategic documents and setting KPIs. Some words designate Aspiration, others Expectation.
10. Avoid complacency by Aspiring again.

New Opportunities

Amidst a Changed Landscape

During the last months of my tenure as CEO of Ocean Park, and for some time after that, Hong Kong's economy and tourist arrival numbers headed south, pulling Ocean Park's financial performance down with it. Those drops, though, appear to be blips in a bigger story.

Two point six million fewer people visited Hong Kong in 2016 than a year earlier, a decline that was the sharpest since the 2003 SARS outbreak, and almost entirely attributable to fewer travellers crossing the border from mainland China. Mainland Chinese normally account for about three-quarters of all visitors to the city.

Globally, Chinese are actually travelling overseas now more than ever. They're just not coming to Hong Kong. China had 129 million outbound travellers in 2017, up 55% from four years earlier. Yet 6.7% fewer Chinese visited Hong Kong in 2016 than a year earlier. Cross-border traffic is picking up again and may finally reach 2015 levels in 2018.

The contraction in visitor arrivals placed a big drag on Hong Kong's economy, affecting retail sales, hotel occupancy and the attractions industry. Overall, Hong Kong's Gross Domestic Product grew 1.9% in

2016, which might sound good by U.S. standards, but was actually the worst economic performance since 2012. In 2018, Hong Kong's economy is projected to grow three to four percent.

The impact of these macro-economic forces is being felt at both Ocean Park and Hong Kong Disneyland.

- In 2017, about 5.8 million people visited Ocean Park, a 25% drop from the peak three years earlier. In the fiscal year ending 30 June 2016, Ocean Park dropped into the red losing nearly US$31 million, its biggest loss since 1987. This was the first time an attraction that I've managed has suffered an annual loss. In 2017, Ocean Park recorded another deficit, of almost the same amount, and it's projecting a third consecutive loss for 2018.
- Hong Kong Disneyland lost US$22 million in 2016, 15% more than a year earlier, despite an attempt to ride on the success of the Star Wars movie series with a 'reimagined' Space Mountain ride and other new Star Wars themed attractions. In 2017, HKDL launched 'Iron Man Experience' and a new hotel, the Disney Explorers Lodge. But losses deepened in 2017, rising to US$44 million. The resort has lost money in 9 out of 12 years.

This contraction is not a surprise; we saw it coming, beginning with the 2014 Umbrella Revolution and the negative impact that had on tourism from the mainland. Despite the downturn, I am extremely optimistic about Ocean Park's future and expect that before long, record numbers of visitors will enjoy a day, or two, in the park.

My positive outlook is grounded by several factors:

One, the company is in strong financial shape. Over the previous twelve years, we grew Ocean Park's financial reserves from less than US$13 million (just three months operating capital) to nearly US$300 million, enough to weather a sustained downturn. Unlike the late 1990s and early 2000s, the company does not have to go into crisis mode.

In addition, we have already secured financing for Ocean Park's capital investments.

Two, it's never been easier to reach the park. After more than a year's delay — and a dozen years after the government built a train line to ferry visitors to Hong Kong Disneyland — a new train station opened outside Ocean Park's main gate at the end of December 2016. Commuters now need just four minutes to travel from Admiralty (in the central business district) to Ocean Park; it used to take at least 25 minutes to make the journey by bus, assuming there were no jams in the tunnel along the way. The opening of the South Island Line contributed to a 10% jump in attendance in the first two months of 2017, which is particularly encouraging as we only anticipated a five percent bump. Nearly sixty percent of visitors now arrive by train. Going forward, one of the region's most ambitious infrastructure projects — a 31-mile bridge and tunnel linking Hong Kong, Macau and Zhuhai — should open before the end of 2018 It's the world's longest sea-crossing bridge, and it will make travel between these cities significantly easier. The project is expected to provide a boost to the Pearl River Delta region, and with it, visitors to Ocean Park.

Three, the leadership team that succeeded me is exceptional. Matthias Li has helped guide Ocean Park for some twenty-two years, including more than a decade as my deputy. I have always treasured his counsel and admired his passion for conservation. Matthias embodies Ocean Park's core values, understands its operating culture, and has earned the respect of the company's staff and stakeholders. He has also kept a fantastic management team intact.

Four, the transition from regional attraction to destination resort is firmly underway. In 2018, Ocean Park's first hotel will open, followed by a state-of-the art water park in 2019 and a second hotel in 2020. These capital investments will provide fresh reasons for people to visit Ocean Park, lengthen the time they spend there, increase per capita spending and attract new types of visitors, as families plan getaways and companies take advantage of the meetings and events space.

241

Five, Ocean Park's success has never been about me. It's about the legacies and processes that have been put in place.

In summary, we prepared for the market downturn by building Ocean Park's cash reserves. We pulled back on capital allocations to preserve cash. At the same time, we made sure that major projects went forward. Infrastructure is being installed to accommodate the market recovery, which is expected to occur within the next two years. As long as the Ten Principles are followed, Ocean Parks' future is bright.

Building an International Resort

In November 2015, Ocean Park broke ground on a new water park that will be an integral part of the company's transformation from a regional attraction to an international resort destination. The all-weather, year-round US$335 million facility is expected to open in the second quarter of 2019.

Situated on the mountainous backside of Ocean Park, Tai Shue Wan Water World will feature 27 indoor and outdoor attractions, spread across a series of terraced platforms and wave pools facing the South China Sea. Extensive vegetation and green roofs blend into the natural terrain. The steep gradient of the setting presents construction challenges, but also makes it possible to build gigantic water slides without having to construct extensive supporting structures.

The water park has a generational connection, one of the Differential Values which helps make Ocean Park so special in the eyes of Hong Kongers. Parents with fond memories of Ocean Park water fun from their youth can look forward to bringing their children to the brand new Water World. An eight-lane aqua-twist mat racer is reminiscent of an old crowd favourite, the Rainbow Slide, which used to be near Ocean Park's entrance.

The new Water World will be twice the size and features three times as many attractions as the previous incarnation that closed in 1999.

Several attractions — like an indoor wave pool with a stage and video screen for live performances, as well as a 'surf rider' — another wave pool where enthusiasts can ride the waves — will appear in Hong Kong for the first time.

Like an adrenalin-rush? Thrill-seekers will love the free-fall style speed slides, where riders descend 100 feet — about ten stories — in five seconds. After I ride that one, I expect I'll calm my heart in an inner tube on the lazy river. We're also putting in multi-person water rides — like WhiteWater's Boomerango and ProSlide's Tornado and Mammoth Bowl, all of which will be new to Hong Kong — plus retail stores, eateries and a resort-style cabana area for families and friends to dine and relax together.

Construction of the facility is setting new standards for integrating an attraction with its natural surroundings. Ocean Park has been highly focused on limiting the facility's impact on the natural environment. "We kept the development sufficiently away from the water to avoid the need to modify the existing sea wall, thereby minimising the impact on marine habitats," Ocean Park's executive director for project development explains. "We also minimised the need for excavation and the related disposal of construction waste. Furthermore, to save energy and cut operating costs, the indoor facility uses natural ventilation and a translucent skylight system to maximise the amount of daylight reaching the interior."

Ocean Park is also working with internationally-acclaimed brands to build two new hotels. The three-wing US$526 million Hong Kong Ocean Park Marriott Hotel will be situated in front of the park's main entrance in Aberdeen and is slated to open in the fourth quarter of 2018. Two years later, the US$385 million Ocean Park Fullerton Hotel will open near the Tai Shue Wan water park. Combined, the Marriott and Fullerton will have about one thousand rooms.

Water World will increase the diversity of Hong Kong's tourist facilities and reinforce its status as a premier Asian destination for family travel. We expect many locals to take advantage of the new offerings, as well during 'staycations', particularly given how easy and quick it is to get to the park with the new South Island train line. The hotels and park should prove to be popular venues for corporate meetings and events as well.

Once the new facilities open, I expect annual attendance to rise to at least 8.5 million people and gross revenues to top US$500 million (more than double current levels).

Ten Principles

Ocean Park enjoyed more than a decade of exceptional growth and success. But as it prepares for the future — and adjusts to a more difficult present — the company has entered a new cycle. Faced with a revenue shortfall and decline in attendance, management needs to re-evaluate the company strategy. How can it pick up new markets and make the most of existing ones? How does it ensure consistency so that no one experiences a diminished product? The answer to these questions lies in continued application of the Ten Principles outlined in this book. Here's how I would apply these principles, and how you can do the same in your business during a period of economic downturn or uncertainty.

1. Understand

Seek first to understand the nature of the opportunities facing the company, then seek to be understood. At this juncture in particular, we need to understand the source of current 'challenges'. Are they market-driven or the result of product or management? To find the answer, listen to stakeholders at all levels of the company, as well as input and views from independent economic analysts.

Before I left my role at Ocean Park, I advised the Board, "Let's be careful that we don't look at what's happening in the market and view it as a management or product issue. Ocean Park's product offerings and management are first-class, but the Hong Kong economy, particularly tourist-related sectors, is facing a downturn. Hotel occupancy is off. Retail sales are down. Other attractions are facing a reduction in business. Significantly fewer visitors are arriving from the mainland, despite a large increase in the number of Chinese travelling overseas. The issue is the market."

The question then becomes one of determining how to address the market downturn. The poor sentiment and macroeconomic factors leading mainland tourists to travel elsewhere are systemic issues. Effective actions are likely to surpass those that can be taken by a single company alone. Instead, Ocean Park should work with industry bodies and government agencies, like the Hong Kong Tourism Board and the Hong Kong Tourism Commission, to sway mainland sentiment. At the same time, if Hong Kong's tourism sector is to fully recover and reach its potential, work should be done at home to address social concerns and ensure that Hong Kong is more gracious to mainland visitors.

2. Value

Never forget who you are. Make sure that company values are reflected throughout the actions of management and the entire staff.

At Ocean Park, the Core Values — Fun, Safety, Service, Show Value, Conservation & Education, Respect for Community, People & Animals — continue to provide operational and strategic direction, while Differential Values create a 'Blue Ocean' where the competition is irrelevant.

OPHK's Differential Values have remained relatively consistent over time, though there have been some amendments as competition has widened to include not just Disney, but attractions in Macau and nearby Zhuhai as well. Ocean Park defines its Differential Values as:

- Location in Hong Kong and Cultural Relevance
- Generational connections and memories as Hong Kong's People's Park
- Value for money
- Natural scenic environment
- Internationally accredited
- Iconic attractions and events
- Conservation efforts

The decision to build Tai Shue Wan Water World was driven by differential values. It will be Hong Kong's only water park. There is a generational connection. Built on the side of a mountain with a sweeping view of the South China Sea, it is 'Distinctly Hong Kong', 'Uniquely Ocean Park', and we believe it will quickly become an icon.

3. Measure

If you can measure it, you can manage it.

Measuring is a key part of Understanding. Studying existing metrics will help answer the question of whether the company's performance is a product, management or market issue. Internal metrics — such as guest feedback and surveys — provide intelligence about the product. External data — related to tourism, hotel occupancy, retail sales — reflect the broader market. If tests of the product and market come back as negative, then the remaining issue is management (which you can then narrow down to Anticipation, Communication and Execution).

In the face of a market issue, the challenge becomes how to develop a strategy for what the company can do at the margins, until the economy adjusts.

While no other market in our region is big enough to replace China, you can measure to see who else is coming to town, which markets are beginning to grow and what factors might influence those consumers. With this information, you can then start building new marketing plans to move those markets in a positive direction.

At the same time, data from within the company — about which attractions visitors are frequenting, the wait duration at each attraction, etc. — can be used to adjust the park's offerings. Fewer visitors means that fewer shows and attractions are needed to provide a first-class guest experience. Real-time data and weekly reports can be used to determine which areas can be closed without affecting guests' perceived value of their day in the park.

4. Plan

ACE: Anticipate — Communicate — Execute.

First you need to anticipate that there will not be any change in market conditions overnight. This means the park needs to look more at the local market for immediate returns. Going forward, it's also clear that the company needs to plan beyond the local market. Throughout, maintain a clear vision based on Understanding and Values, and ground your plans with realistic expectations, linked to Measurements.

For Hong Kong attractions, the conversation naturally returns to Chinese travellers, because the current and potential size of this market segment are both so much greater than any other region. The question becomes, 'How do you anticipate where in China growth can potentially come from?' Is it first-tier, second-tier or third-tier cities? Is it tour groups or independent travellers? Are any new direct flights being added or are airlines offering discounts on particular routes? From the information that you gather and measure, you can then target specific campaigns to attract business.

Once you've done the anticipation work, you need to clearly communicate the plan, internally and externally, with appropriate teams and stakeholders. In this case, internal communication would focus on the marketing and sales staff, while external communication would be with tour operators and other travel professionals in your key markets. For the latter, partners need to understand the incentives that are available and how you can support their efforts. Throughout the communication process, there needs to be continual dialogue. Remember that communication is not a one-way affair.

Executing the plan requires a clear set of objectives linked to desired outcomes, so that all participants understand what must be done. Ensure that complacency does not set in, and that plans are implemented on schedule, within budget and to the highest possible quality.

5. Relevance

Once you've identified the key markets and market segments, look at each one and ask, "What would push it over the top?"

Is there a culturally relevant aspect of the market that would entice a greater percentage of people there to travel to Hong Kong and visit Ocean

Park? Is there something we can offer or add that would be relevant to them, that they would feel a need to come to see, within the context of a Hong Kong theme park?"

If, for example, there is tremendous potential from Indonesia — a market segment that rose 12% in 2016 — then Ocean Park could increase its halal and Indonesian food offerings, because that is important to Indonesian travellers.

Filipinos, in contrast, seem to like pizzas, burgers and other amusement park-type food sold in the park, so adding Filipino dishes wouldn't have much of an impact. Adding Filipino entertainment, however — such as a show by a popular Filipino performer living in Hong Kong — or offering tours in Tagalog would establish the cultural connection.

For the local market, it's important to focus on the factors that are most relevant to potential park-goers. Convenience and price are two of the biggest keys, particularly with the opening of the new train line. Recognising this, Ocean Park began offering promotions tied in to train travel. Local markets generally react well to short-term price promotions. You can't do it forever, though. The limited shelf life is part of what makes promotions work, as people know they've got to get out and do it while the promotion is still available.

6. Control

During difficult times, it's important to maintain perspective and avoid worrying or spending excess energy on things outside your control. Instead, effective leaders and businesses keep their focus and identify ways to adapt to achieve their goals.

In this case, Ocean Park can't control Chinese market sentiment towards Hong Kong, but it can control things like food, entertainment and price that will bring out target consumers. For each market, be it a new or existing one, ask "What can I control? What can I control that's culturally relevant, backed by measurement information and supports my objectives?"

Ocean Park is taking a number of actions in this regard:

- To address the revenue shortfall, it raised ticket prices.
- At the same time, to boost local patronage, it offered tens of thousands of steeply discounted tickets online, as part of a promotion coinciding with the park's 40th anniversary. Tickets were priced at HK$40 (about US$5) instead of HK$438 (US$56).
- During Halloween, it leveraged the PokemonGo craze with an augmented reality app, then during Christmas spent more than US$1.25 million on a highly-publicised show featuring performers from 'Australia's Got Talent'.
- A five-week dining festival with live music, extended nighttime hours, and special evening tickets that included one-way free on the train, was launched to attract more local visitors.
- The park is also collaborating with the Hong Kong Tourism Board on a Southeast Asia marketing campaign that aims to show that a visit to Hong Kong is about a lot more than just shopping and food. It's also boosting efforts to attract visitors from East Asian markets like South Korea and Taiwan.

7. Lead

During difficult times, a company needs 'present' leadership more than ever. Leaders need to regularly visit the shop floor and mingle with staff; their presence and availability is critical to the success and activation of programmes. They need to lead by example, encourage employees to think like owners, 'begin with the end in mind', catch people doing things right and be sure to thank them. They should continue to display the ten 'innate leadership traits' — Curiosity, Responsibility, Humor, Passion,

Conviction, Persistence, Initiative, Urgency, Creativity and Confidence — and encourage their development in others.

If leaders are not present and do not earn the confidence of their staff, their teams will lose focus and motivation, and when sales drop, morale will plummet.

In the case of Ocean Park, no matter what you do in the Control feature — whether it's food, entertainment, discounted tickets or some combination of the above — you need a leadership presence in the park to ensure that guests are getting the very best experience. Simultaneously, the leadership team must provide staff with a feeling for what's on the horizon — a sense that 'we are going to get through this and when we do, we'll be better than ever, with two new hotels, a water park, and an award-winning theme park that is rooted in the community'.

8. Disrupt

How do you cut through the noise to activate new markets or boost existing ones? There's no better time to 'be disruptive by nature' than during a market downturn. Aim to create communications that capture the imagination. Design differential products and services that will generate a buzz. Start by monitoring consumer and business trends for ideas, and remember to always under-promise and over-deliver, not the other way around.

9. Genuine

Good times or bad, it is always important to be both Genuine and Generous. Not only is it the right thing to do, it speaks volumes about your company's commitment to the community.

Despite the downturn, Ocean Park has remained true to its vision, mission and values. The park has not diminished its product offering, employment opportunities, nor its educational, conservation and community initiatives.

During the 2015–17 fiscal years:

- Over 900,000 Hong Kong residents enjoyed complimentary or generously discounted admission to the park. These free/discounted tickets were worth more than US$43 million.
- One hundred thousand students participated in courses at the Ocean Park Academy.
- The company donated more than US$3 million to the Ocean Park Conservation Foundation, which supports dozens of projects across eleven countries, involving 40 animal species.

These programmes are an integral part of Ocean Park's daily operations and strategy. Contributions to the Conservation Foundation are funded by ticket sales and some merchandise and food sales within the park. Social inclusion initiatives — like free tickets for people with disabilities and discounted or free admission for their families — are long-standing programmes. Education and conservation research are an essential part of what Ocean Park stands for. It would actually be more difficult to halt these policies than to continue, and not just because of a media or government backlash, though the company would certainly encounter these as well.

Of course, CSR is not only how you spend your money. It's how you make it. During this period, Ocean Park has not retrenched a single employee, nor instituted pay cuts for full-time staff. Disney, on the other hand, laid off one hundred workers. To be fair, the two companies face different pressures in this regard. As a publicly-owned entity, Ocean Park is expected to generate or maintain jobs, not cut them. Disney, though, faces stock market investors who demand cost-cutting measures when revenue is down. Regardless, Disney took a hit in the eyes of the community for retrenching workers, while the action did little to help its bottom line[68].

---

68 HKDL's earnings before interest, tax, depreciation and amortisation (EBITDA) was 11% lower than a year earlier and less than its operating cash flow. Ocean Park's EBITDA, on the other hand, was around 23% for the 2015–16 fiscal year (down from about 35% most years).

Disney's Path to the Future

Before I get to the last principle, let me say a few words first about Hong Kong Disneyland.

Despite the company's public losses, they're not going anywhere. Disney has made a commitment to the future, planning a seven-year expansion that is expected to cost US$1.4 billion. New attractions are going to build on the Iron Man Experience that opened in early 2017, and will bring more Marvel superheroes to life. Another themed area is going to be based on the 2013 hit animated film, Frozen.

Disney has recognized that they have to make continuous capital investments to improve their product, and that doing so will attract new markets.

These investments are good for the company and for Hong Kong. I expect they're also good for Ocean Park, as a percentage of tourists visiting Hong Kong Disneyland will visit Ocean Park too. Like the early days, when it was first announced that Disney would be coming to town, Disney's investments force Ocean Park to up its own game, to work even harder to ensure that every guest has a positively first-class, memorable experience.

Disney's return to the red in 2015, 2016 and 2017 — as well as its decision to lay off workers — has sparked an outcry in parts of the legislature and the public. Critics exclaim that Disney gave the city a bad deal, and that good times or bad, it profits while the city does not. The same thing happened in 2008, amidst Disney losses at the time, leading the government to require greater transparency from the company. For the first time, Disney was required to reveal annual attendance figures and a profit-loss statement. It will be interesting to see if the current outcry leads to any other requirements placed on the company, or any changes to the terms of the deal.

From Aspirations to Expectations

"Everything will be alright in the end . . . and, if it is not alright, then it is not yet the end," Dev Patel's character Sonny told his guests in The Best Exotic Marigold Hotel.

Life is cyclical, and so too is business. Of course, I'm not only talking about economic cycles, but rather the journey from Aspirations to Expectations and back again.

For the moment, Ocean Park has re-entered the aspirations space — which is fine. If we do not aspire in life, we do not grow and we do not achieve even greater things.

As long as Ocean Park's team strives for excellence and remains true to the company's values, I have no doubt that within a few years, they will emerge on a higher plateau and have sufficient reason to expect success again.

When I first moved to Hong Kong, Ocean Park's success was far from certain. If Disney was King Kong[69], then Ocean Park was Ann Darrow, the woman he kidnapped, fell in love with, and in our version of the story, even imitated. I'm inspired by what my team and I were able to accomplish. I hope our story inspires you too.

Just remember, there really is magic beyond Disney that can be harnessed! And you don't need to be a giant to succeed — or to have a giant's resources. So let me ask you, do *you* desire success?

---

69 Admittedly, this is an unlikely analogy. King Kong is a Universal Studios property, not a Disney one, and a gorilla is an awfully big jump for a mouse.

ACKNOWLEDGEMENTS

As I reflect on the stories and principles that have provided the basis for this book, not to mention my own personal growth, I am immediately reminded of the relationships that have made this possible: my ties to family, friends and mentors.

The demands of the theme park industry require that you work when everyone else does not. I've missed holidays, vacations, weekends and even special moments, or have had to reschedule them to fit my crazy calendar. Travel and international assignments that require relocating far from home have also been an integral part of my journey. Throughout, my family has supported, empowered, and motivated me with their love and understanding. I am truly blessed with a wonderful family.

My wife, Diana, has been a stalwart support through every move, relocation, opportunity and success.

My children, Katie and Drew, my parents, Bob and Nancy, and my in-laws, "T" and Barbara, have also been steadfast in their support.

This book is the culmination of lessons learned, practices honed, and philosophies tested over time within dynamic work and market conditions. These principles can be applied in any professional or personal setting. I would be remiss if I did not acknowledge the key people along my career path who took an active interest in my development:

Bill Filben hired me as a sweeper at Knott's Berry Farm — my first official job!

Larry McDaniel saw my potential and took a radical step — promoting me to Sweeper Supervisor, even though I was still a young college student.

Joe Meck shared my passion for sports, saw my potential for leadership, and offered me opportunities to move into other areas of the business, including Admission Operations, Guest Relations, Ticket Selling, Operations Management, Ride Operations and the Design and Development of future facilities.

Ken Kiser's leadership guided me to examine business metrics and 'quantify the qualifiable' elements of the guest experience.

Terry Van Gorder had a vision for what a theme park represents to society. He encouraged his teams to add a cerebral element to a park's visceral components and find the right balance to celebrate life and humanity. He viewed business from a global perspective and professed a philosophy of management that still guides my thinking today. I thank him for his leadership, guidance and mentorship.

Tom LeBouf keeps things in perspective, 'controls the controllable' and has a fantastic sense of humor.

Karl Holz inspired me with his dynamic leadership style, which was inclusive, practical, pragmatic and based on doing things right, while doing the right thing.

Dick Kenzel and Jack Falfas provided me the opportunity to seek new roles and opened the door to a career outside Knott's Berry Farm, which in turn opened my eyes to the world of possibilities that would characterise my career trajectory.

Kieran Burke and Gary Story's open-minded approach to acquiring talent, places people in roles that stretch their capabilities while building their character and potential to do more.

Allan Zeman, my chairman and partner for more than a dozen years, seeks solutions when others around him have given up. His optimism is grounded by a knack for turning negatives into positives. He is an extraordinary entrepreneur, a visionary and catalyst to the Ocean Park success story.

The Walt Disney Company chose Hong Kong as the destination for their entry into China and provided the impetus Ocean Park needed to rise and transform itself into a world-class destination.

The Government of Hong Kong has provided a vision for the city's growth, established tourism as an economic pillar, and supported the redevelopment and positioning of Ocean Park. In particular, I would like to express my gratitude to Hong Kong's Chief Executives — Tung Chee-hwa, Donald Tsang, CY Leung and Carrie Lam — as well as the legislators, government departments and officials who have stood with Ocean Park over the years.

Ocean Park's board members have served selflessly and volunteered their time to oversee the company and help the management team achieve their objectives and transform the park.

Be it in industry associations, other organizations, or in and outside of Ocean Park, I have had the honour of working and partnering with some amazing people. While there are too many to list here, I would particularly like to recognise my management team at Ocean Park: Matthias Li, Alan Chan, Celine Cheung, Alex Chu, Suzanne Gendron, Brian Ho, Todd Hougland, Randy Kalish, Walter Kerr, Vivian Lee, Joseph Leung, Paul Pei and George Tso. They are dedicated, passionate, creative leaders who were open to new ideas and shared an aspiration for success.

I could not have asked for a better assistant than Wendy Ngan, who preceded me at Ocean Park and worked with me for thirteen years. She is dedicated, committed to excellence, and has helped guide me many a time. I would also like to thank Wendy for her painstaking effort to transcribe and organise the hours and hours of audio notes for this book.

Some incredible leaders have taught and influenced me over the years. As a young boy, I met John Wooden and attended his basketball camps in southern California. I was inspired by Wooden's *Pyramid of Success*, which I have applied to my career path at every stage. In the late '80s, I had the great fortune to learn directly from Stephen Covey, when he visited Knott's Berry Farm to promote his book *The 7 Habits of Highly Effective People*. To this day, I still refer to and apply the seven habits. I was also part of a small group that participated in a seminar with Warren Bennis, the University of Southern California's Leadership 'Guru'. Bennis was studying family-run organizations in the third generation, which applied to Knott's Berry Farm, where I was working at the time. Bennis' ideas shaped my views on leadership; throughout my career, I have applied and propagated the innate qualities of leaders that he identified.

I would like to ultimately thank Michael Switow, the co-author of this book, for his patience, critical thought, fact checking and his sensitivity to the opportunity to take a colorful career in a theme park environment and assist in turning it into a practical story of assessment, process, anticipation, communication and execution that can apply across management and leadership disciplines in any industry.

THE AUTHORS

TOM MEHRMANN began his career in the theme park industry in 1977 cleaning the grounds at Knotts Berry Farm, an attraction located seven miles from Disneyland. A quarter century later, he built on the lessons learned there — as well as at other parks in the US and Europe — to ensure that Ocean Park Hong Kong did not wither in the shadow of another Disney resort. As the chief executive of Ocean Park Hong Kong from 2004–2016, Tom oversaw the attraction's transformation into a leading world-class family-travel destination that welcomes more than seven million visitors annually. A graduate of California State University Fullerton, Tom is currently the president and general manager of Universal Studios Beijing and is tasked with launching Universal Studios' first resort in China.

MICHAEL SWITOW is the founder of WOW Asia, which provides insights about the Asian attractions industry and conversations with the leaders that drive them. His in-depth and colourful features explore the launch and growth of major Asian brands, as well as the efforts of international players like KidZania, Lionsgate and Nickelodeon to penetrate new markets. Michael moved to Asia in 1996 to cover Hong Kong's return to China. He earned a Master's in Public Affairs, concentrating in Economics and International Relations, from Princeton University's Woodrow Wilson School. His reporting has been featured by the Associated Press, NPR's Morning Edition, PRI's The World, IAAPA's Funworld Magazine and Singapore's Money FM, among others.